LLOYD TILGHMAN

Confederate General in the Western Theatre

by

Bryan S. Bush, M.A.

A C C L A I M   P R E S S

Morley, Missouri

Acclaim Press

ACCLAIM PRESS, INC.
Your Next Great Book
P.O. Box 238
Morley, MO 63767
(573) 262-2121
www.acclaimpress.com

Design by:

Steward&Wise
GRAPHIC DESIGN

Book Design: Wil Sikes
Cover Design: Emily K. Sikes

Copyright © MMVI
Bryan S. Bush

Library of Congress Cataloging-in-Publication Data

Bush, Bryan S., 1966-
  Lloyd Tilghman : Confederate general in the Western theatre / by Bryan S.
Bush.
      p. cm.
  Includes bibliographical references and index.
  ISBN 0-9773198-4-9 (hardcover : alk. paper)
  1. Tilghman, Lloyd, 1816-1863. 2. Generals--Confederate States of
America--Biography. 3. Confederate States of America. Army--Biography. 4.
United States--History--Civil War, 1861-1865--Campaigns. 5.
Kentucky--History--Civil War, 1861-1865--Campaigns. 6.
Tennessee--History--Civil War, 1861-1865--Campaigns. 7.
Mississippi--History--Civil War, 1861-1865--Campaigns. I. Title.

E467.1.T55B87 2006
973.7'3092--dc22
[B]
                              2006016958

First Printing: 2006 A.D.
Printed in the United States of America

10 9 8 7 6 5 4 3 2 1

TABLE OF CONTENTS

"As a man, a soldier, and a General, he had few if any superiors."

-Conf. Col. A. E. Reynolds.

You are invited to visit the...

Lloyd Tilghman House & Civil War Museum

631 Kentucky Avenue
Paducah, KY 42001
(270) 575-5477
www.lloydtilghmanhouse.org

Open Mid-April through Mid-October
Friday & Saturday 12:00 pm–4:00 pm
(10:00 am–4:00 pm when riverboats are docked)
Group tours by appointment

Directions: *I-24 to exit 4, go five miles east on the I-24 loop (US 60) to downtown Paducah. Turn right on Kentucky Ave., go three blocks to the Tilghman House on the right at 7th and Kentucky Avenue.*

DEDICATION

This book is dedicated to the Bardstown Civil War Museum, for without their valuable assistance and support this work would not have been possible.

Rear Admiral George W, Sumner, U.S.N. - The Honorable J.W. Jewett of Kentucky appointed George Sumner to the U.S. Naval Academy on September 20, 1858. He graduated on July 1862. His first duty station was on the gunboat U.S.S. Colorado *off the coast of Florida to patrol for blockade runners. He was assigned to the* U.S.S. Massasoit *in August 1864 and served on the ship until the end of the war. He continued to serve in the navy and participated in the Spanish-American War in 1898 and retired from service on December 31, 1903 with the rank of Rear Admiral. He died in 1924. (The CWBWT Museum, photo by Bryan Bush)*

SPECIAL THANKS

Special thanks must be given to certain individuals, without whose help this book would have not been possible.

*The staff at Civil War Battles of the Western Theater Museum and the War Memorial Museum located on 310 East Broadway in Bardstown, Kentucky. I would like to thank them for their generous help in allowing me to photograph their incredible collection, especially Joe Masterson, Steve Munson, and Jack Harrison. For information on contacting the museum you can call 1-800-638-4877.

*Special thanks must go to Craig Brown.

*Special thanks must go to the Lloyd Tilghman House and Phil Phillips.

*Special thanks must go to Doug Sikes at Acclaim Press for believing in Confederate General Lloyd Tilghman and the importance he played in the Civil War.

*Special thanks must go to Elvin Smith, Jr.

-The Author

INTRODUCTION

L loyd Tilghman was brave, heroic, patriotic, loyal, and totally devoted to the cause in which he believed. He also has been described as a strict disciplinary military officer, which led many of his subordinate officers in the Confederate army to clash with him. This stemmed from his learning at West Point and his time in the Mexican War. Many of the officers in the Civil War were volunteers and didn't know military rules and regulations. Discipline was frequently lax in the ranks. Tilghman would not stand for disrespect for military protocol and he clashed with those officers who did not adhere to rules and regulations.

Tilghman was born on January 26, 1816 near Claiborne, Maryland and came from a family steeped in military tradition. His ancestors also played an important role in the early history of our country. His grandfather was part of the Continental Congress and served in the Senate. Because of Tilghman's family background, he was admitted to West Point. While at West Point, Tilghman would be brevetted Second Lieutenant of the First Dragoons and on September 1836 officially became a Second Lieutenant of the First Dragoons. At West Point, Tilghman would learn the skills to be an engineer. A career that was very highly sought after in the American market. The ever expanding railroads needed skilled engineers. Tilghman graduated from West Point on October 1, 1836, but resigned his commission in the military and decided that he would try his luck in the civilian sector.

From 1837 to 1845 Tilghman worked as an engineer on several different railroads. But in 1845 he decided to join the Army. The Mexican War had broken out and he felt it was his personal duty to fight for his country. Tilghman arrived at Corpus Christi in September 1845 and became a sutler supplying the army. Once the army found out that Tilghman was a Lieutenant in the Dragoons, he immediately became the aide de camp for General David Twiggs, who commanded the 2nd Dragoons.

During the Mexican War, Tilghman helped make reconnaissances of enemy positions, fought in the battle of Monterrey, and placed in command of a partisan corps of twenty men who fought with the enemy at La Mesa, La Puerta, and Sueesties, By 1847 Tilghman was at Matamoros and helped build the defenses of the defenses and fortifications around the city. Later that year he became a Captain and commanded a light artillery battery of six guns to serve with the Maryland and District of Columbia Volunteer Light Artillery. Tilghman was stationed with his battery at Jalapa. In 1848 he made several expeditions to Montigo, and at Mantoosco he relieved Captain Wheat, who was surrounded by six hundred men, and Wheat only had twenty men. Tilghman's one hundred men came to his rescue. The Mexican War ended on February 2, 1848. Tilghman learned valuable lessons during the Mexican War. He honed his skills as an engineer. He also became the leader of men.

After the war, Tilghman returned to his civilian life. He became a Chief Engineer for many railroads. In 1852 he moved to Kentucky to help build the Paducah branch of the Mobile and Ohio railroad. Tilghman bought a beautiful ten room antebellum mansion in Paducah and settled into civilian life. He and his wife Augusta Murray Boyd Tilghman had several children. He was making good money and was at the top of his profession. Tilghman officially became a resident of the state in 1852.

In December of 1860 Tilghman decided to join the Kentucky State Guard. The Kentucky State Guard became one of the best militia organizations in the United States. Tilghman became a Major in the Paducah Southwest Battalion. But all this would end when shots were fired at Fort Sumter in April of 1861. The country was now at war. Tilghman was commander of the western division of the Kentucky State Guard, which included the Paducah and Columbus area in Kentucky. Tensions in the state quickly came to a boil. Tilghman had to make his decision: would he stay loyal to the Union or join the Confederacy? The decision could not have been an easy one, but on July 5, 1861, Tilghman and the Third Kentucky Infantry, Company D, joined the Confederacy. His commander of the Kentucky State Guard, Simon Buckner, and Tilghman saw that the government was not following the Constitutionality of State Rights. They saw the Union forces invading their state against the will of the people to remain neutral. That one event would change Tilghman's life forever. His trail would lead to a series of events that would influence the outcome of the Civil War.

After Tilghman resigned from the Kentucky State Guard, he became commander of the 3rd Kentucky Infantry, C. S.. He had the almost impossible task to arm his men with weapons, clothes and accouterments. He was promoted to Brigadier General on October 18, 1861 at Camp Boone, Tennessee. On November 17th, 1861 he was sent to take control of Forts Henry and Donelson and their defenses. With Tilghman's military experience and engineering skills, it seemed that he was the perfect man for the task. But the forts were not equipped and were in horrible shape. He also had one thousand unarmed men, but Tilghman was loyal to the Confederacy and made the best of the situation. He worked diligently in building earthworks, rifle pits, and securing the approaches to the forts. By January 1862 He felt that work on the forts had progressed. But still Tilghman had two thousand men who were unarmed and he knew that the Union troops would soon arrive and try to take the forts.

Fate worked against Tilghman. Fort Henry was built on low ground and the fort was quickly filling with water from the river. The lower part of the fort was under water. The mines placed in the river to prevent the Union gunboats from approaching the forts were also underwater. Tilghman knew that an enemy with any common sense could control the entire fort, since most of the fort and the fort's defenses were underwater, but again Tilghman would carry out his orders and defend the fort.

On February 6, 1862 at 10:15 A.M. the attack began. Union Admiral Foote's gunboats and Union General Ulysses S. Grant's infantry approached Fort Henry. At 12:35 A.M. fate intercepted during the battle. Tilghman's twenty four-pounder burst, then he lost his ten inch Columbiad when it was accidently spiked. Several of the thirty two-pounders were lost. Tilghman knew it was time to fall back to Fort Donelson, but after seeing his courageous men working the batteries at Fort Henry, he decided to stay to the end. The rest of the Confederate army fell back to Fort Donelson while his one hundred men endured the fire that was falling into Fort Henry from the gunboats. The gunboats soon got to within six hundred yards of the fort. At 1:10 P.M. Tilghman's men were exhausted and only four cannons were left at the fort. At 1:30 P.M. Tilghman himself took charge of one of the thirty two pounders. Tilghman looked around and saw most of the crews were killed or wounded and that the gunboats were breaching the fort. He decided to stop the useless loss of life and surrender. Tilghman surrendered after a battle of two hours and a half. His plan of saving the Confederate army worked. He had bought enough time for the rest of the Confederate army to fall back to Fort Donelson.

Tilghman was commended by Flag Officer Foote after the Battle of Fort Henry. He said Tilghman was gallant in his defense of the fort. Colonel Heiman said Tilghman was heroic. His decision to send his army to Fort Donelson was correct, but his one major flaw in command was his decision to stay at Fort Henry. As overall commander, Tilghman had the responsibility to take command at Fort Donelson and leave his artillery crew. By staying at Fort Henry and working an artillery piece, Tilghman delegated himself not as a commanding general, but as a regular soldier. Tilghman left a void in the command structure, which contributed to the fall of Fort Donelson.

The fall of Forts Henry and Donelson would have detrimental effects on the Confederacy in the Western Theater. The Tennessee and the Cumberland Rivers were now open to invasion from Union forces. The Confederate earthworks and cannons protecting the Mississippi River from Union invasion at Columbus, Kentucky, were abandoned. Confederate General Albert Sidney Johnston, who was the commander of the Confederate forces, abandoned his defense line in Kentucky, and his headquarters in Bowling Green, Kentucky. He pulled all the way back to Corinth, Mississippi, giving up the valuable city of Nashville, Tennessee, which led to the Battle of Shiloh, in April of 1862. The next city to fall was New Madrid, Missouri on the Mississippi River. After the fall of New Madrid came the surrender of Fort Pillow, the last remaining stronghold between Island Number 10 and Memphis, Tennessee. The fort was abandoned on June 4th, 1862. Memphis surrendered on June 6th. The Mississippi River was slowly being controlled by Union forces.

After the Battle of Fort Henry, Tilghman became a prisoner of war, and was sent to Fort Warren. On August 27, 1862 he was exchanged for Union General John Reynolds. Ten thousand men were also exchanged. Those men were then under the command of Tilghman. Tilghman had to now equip, clothe, and arm them. He also had to form them into artillery, cavalry, and infantry units.

By October 1862 Union General Ulysses Grant began his move toward Vicksburg, Mississippi. Tilghman in December 1862 faced Grant's men once again at the Battle of Coffeeville, Mississippi. During the battle Tilghman pushed back the Yankees for almost three miles and overran the Union position. That battle in some small measure was Tilghman's payback for his surrender at Fort Henry.

The battle of Coffeeville, Mississippi did not stop the relentless pursuit of Grant's forces. Grant came up with several different plans to attempt to take Vicksburg. He built canals. He tried to maneuver his men and gunboats through the swamps, each being a failure. But Grant finally landed his men at Bruinsburg, located below Vicksburg. Confederate General Pemberton had to abandon Grand Gulf and fell back to Vicksburg. Grant gave up his supply base at Grand Gulf and decided to surround Vicksburg.

The last battle for Tilghman occurred at Champion's Hill. General Tilghman was ordered to hold the Yankees back, while the Confederates fell back from a brutal battle. During the battle, Tilghman delegated himself as a common soldier, ignored his role as a commanding general and courageously decided to personally man a cannon; he was killed by an artillery shell fragment. Tilghman's forces fell back to Jackson, Mississippi, and would not participate in the siege of Vicksburg. On July 4, 1863 Vicksburg, Mississippi fell to Grant's forces after a prolonged siege. The end of the Confederacy was then even closer. The surrender of Vicksburg split the Confederacy in two. The Key to the Confederate Heartland was in Lincoln's pocket.

Tilghman was brave, courageous, and loyal to the cause he believed and gave the ultimate sacrifice to his country. History has ignored the sacrifice that Tilghman gave to the government he believed in. For such a brave gentlemen, little has been written on General Tilghman. After the war, the Confederate Veteran magazine published a series of articles in which his men spoke of Tilghman, hoping that a biography would be published, which never came to fruition. In 1998, the author wrote a small biography in The Civil War Battles of the Western Theater. Three years later in 2001, James Raab wrote a dual biography on Generals Lloyd Tilghman and Francis Shoup. Tilghman was involved in one of the most pivotal battles of the Western Theater: the Battle of Fort Henry, yet little is known of this elusive general. As the years passed and the veterans of the war passed away, history began to overlook the sacrifice that Tilghman gave to the Confederacy that he believed in and the importance of Tilghman's role at Fort Henry and Donelson. Tilghman has been blamed for the loss of Forts Henry and Donelson, when in reality the loss of the fort was inept leadership of Confederate Generals Albert Sidney Johnston and Leonidas Polk, who ignored the importance of the river forts. Instead, they focused on Bowling Green, Kentucky and Columbus, Kentucky. There is no doubt that Tilghman had intelligence and fought well as a general. He would never achieve the rank of Major General, partially because of his loss at Fort Henry. The first purpose of my book is to suggest that Tilghman understood military tactics and strategy, but, like many other Confederate generals, he would risk his life unnecessarily to prove his courage and honor. By manning a cannon at Fort Henry and finally manning a cannon at Champion's Hill, Tilghman decided that at times the role of brigadier general did not matter; what was more important to him was displaying acts of desperate courage and bravery. Bravery, pride, and culture molded Tilghman into the man he was, and in the end he was not able to escape from it.

The second purpose of the book is to show how Tilghman's choice in deciding to stay with his artillerists and defend Fort Henry, more than stay to his original plan and take his role as commanding general at Fort Donelson left a gap in the command structure. General Albert Sidney Johnston was forced to choose a command general at Fort Donelson. John Floyd and Gideon Pillow were probably not the best choices to command the fort. Both generals entered into a power play for control of the fort, but when the escape from Fort Donelson did not happen as they wished, they left command to General Simon Buckner. Both Pillow and Floyd decided to abandon the fort and make their escape. Men, material, and the strategic importance of the forts were lost. If Tilghman had stayed at Fort Donelson and taken command of the fort, he might have had better control of the situation and might have been able to utilize the reinforcements sent to him in the areas where they were needed most. His men, who had known him longer than Buckner, Pillow, and

Floyd, would have stayed by his side. Tilghman probably would not have fled the fort as General Pillow and Floyd, but would have stayed to the end, since he was responsible for Fort Donelson. The result of the loss of Fort Henry and Fort Donelson led to massive changes in the Western Theater. General Albert Sidney Johnston had no choice but to abandon Kentucky and parts of Tennessee after the battles of Mill Springs, Kentucky and the loss of the forts. The resulting situation led to the battle of Shiloh and to the loss of the river forts, such as Fort Pillow, Island No. 10 and the fall of Memphis, along the Mississippi. Vicksburg, Mississippi remained. Once Vicksburg was lost, the Union forces had control of the most important river in the Confederacy, which tore the Confederacy in half.

CHAPTER ONE

The Military Career Takes Shape

Lloyd Tilghman was born on January 26, 1816, near Claiborne, Maryland, and was the only son of James and Ann Caroline Shoemaker; grandson of Lloyd and Henrietta M. Tilghman; great grandson of the Matthew and Anne (Lloyd) Tilghman and of James and Anna (Francis) Tilghman.

His great-grandfather James was born December 6, 1716 in Queen Anne County, Maryland. He was the son of Richard and Anna Maria (Lloyd) Tilghman. He was educated by private tutors, attended local schools and eventually studied law. He graduated law school, was admitted to the bar and practiced in Annapolis, Maryland between 1737 and 1760 and then moved to Philadelphia, Pennsylvania. He served as secretary of the land office of Pennsylvania and as common councilman of Philadelphia, and a member of the provincial council in 1767 to 1775. He was married to Anna, daughter of Tench and Anne (Willing) Francis of Philadelphia, Pennsylvania. He later practiced law in Charleston, Maryland and died on August 24, 1793.

One of James and Anna Tilghman's sons, Tench Tilghman, was born in Talbot County, Maryland, on December 25, 1744, graduated from the College of Philadelphia in 1761 and became a Captain in the Pennsylvania militia in 1776. He was married to Anna Maria, daughter of his uncle Matthew Tilghman. He was aide-de-camp to General Washington and received a promotion to Lieutenant Colonel in the Continental Army. He was present at the Battle of Yorktown and was entrusted by his chief to carry the dispatch to the Continental Congress announcing the surrender of Cornwallis. Congress recognized this service by presenting him with a vote of thanks, a sword and a horse and accouterments. In speaking of his services, Washington said, "Colonel Tilghman has been in every action in which the main army was concerned, and has been a faithful assistant to me for nearly five years, a great part of which time he refused to receive pay." After the war, he engaged in business in Baltimore, and established

15

there a branch of the house of Robert Morris of Philadelphia. He died in Baltimore, Maryland on April 18, 1786. [1]

Lloyd Tilghman's great-grandfather, Matthew Tilghman, was born in the "Hermitage," Queen Anne County, Maryland, on February 17, 1718; a son of Richard and Anna Maria (Lloyd) Tilghman; a grandson of Dr. Richard Tilghman who came from London to Maryland in 1660, and established the "Hermitage" in Queen Anne county, and of Colonel Philemon Lloyd. He was married to his cousin Anne Lloyd in 1741, and was justice of the peace for Talbot County; delegate to the general assembly of Maryland (1751-1777); speaker of the house of delegates (1773-75); and president of the Revolutionary convention that directed the affairs of the colony (1774-77). He was a member of the committee appointed in 1768 to draw up the protest against the stamp act. In 1774 he became chairman of the committee on correspondence, and in 1775 he was chairman of the committee of safety. He was a delegate to the Continental Congress (1774-77) and in June 1776, was sent as a delegate to the convention at Annapolis to frame a state constitution and presided over that convention. He resigned his seat in congress in 1777 to accept the position of state senator. Matthew Tilghman was reelected to the Senate in 1781 but resigned before the expiration of his term. He died in Queen Anne County, May 4, 1790. [2]

Because of Lloyd Tilghman's family lineage and the prestige of his family's military background, Tilghman was allowed to enter the United States Military Academy at West Point, on July 1, 1831, at the age of fifteen.

The United States Military Academy at West Point has a long and proud military tradition. In 1783 President George Washington called for a military academy, but at the time there were only one hundred officers in the United States Army. West Point was America's largest fort at the time. On September 10, 1790, West Point and the surrounding area was bought by the United States government for $11,085 dollars. On May 7, 1794, Congress provided for an increase in the Corps of Artillerists and Engineers and the rank of cadet was created. Cadets were junior officers assigned to West Point. They had the right to command, to be members of the court martial boards, and to employ servants. They were supposed to attend classes taught by older officers and learn the military art [3].

In February 1796 Lieutenant Colonel Stephen Rochefontaine took command at West Point with orders from the War Department to initiate a course of instruction. On July 16, 1798 an act increased the size of the Corps and four teachers were appointed to "Arts and Sciences for the instruction of the cadets and young officers in the Corps of Artillerists and Engineers. The War Department gathered students at West Point to organize a school, but no teachers could be found. [4]

Alexander Hamilton proposed a complete system of military education with a "fundamental school" at West Point, a school for engineers and artillerists, another for cavalry and infantry, and a forth for a navy. All cadets would spend two years at fundamental school, then two at specialized institutions. [5]

In September 1801 Lieutenant Colonel Tousard was going to West Point to take command of the fort. At the academy, Colonel Tousard had one teacher and twelve cadets. On September 21, 1801, the first class was held at West Point. Mathematics was the only subject being taught at the school. It was the first time that the cadets appeared as a military unit.

Thomas Jefferson was looking for a permanent Superintendent for West Point. In May 1801 Jonathan Williams was hired, and Tousard would remain as commander of the garrison. Williams split the school into two organizations: the Corps of Artillerists and Engineers, each with it's own special tasks. On March 16, 1802, Congress authorized the President to organize a Corps of Engineers, which "shall be stationed at West Point and shall constitute a military academy." The commander of the Corps and Chief Engineer would also become Superintendent of the academy. Classes began in April 1802. [6]

On April 29, 1812 the Academy was reorganized. Each cadet received a regular degree from an academical staff. Formation of the Academic Board consisted of permanent professors who presided over the superintendent. The Board supervised the academic program, examined cadets and made recommendations for degrees and commissions. The number of Cadets attending West Point increased to two hundred and fifty. The age to apply for West Point was between 14 to 21. The cadet must be well versed in reading, writing, and arithmetic. Cadets were organized into companies, and for three months each year they were sent into an encampment where they were taught duties of a private, a non commissioned officer and officer. [7]

In 1815 Madison provided for a permanent superintendent. In March 1816 new rules required a general examination of all cadets twice a year in July and December. New cadets entered only in September. A four year course of study and the cadet grey uniform was instituted at the Academy. [8]

Tilghman entered West Point when it was in its golden years. West Point had undergone massive changes. Sylvanus Thayer was the reason for the changes just before Tilghman had entered West Point. In June 1817 Capt. Sylvanus Thayer took command as superintendent. He presided over the academy from 1817 till 1833. He shaped the military academy into what it is today. Thayer made cadets live off only $18.00 dollars a month; no money could be brought from home. Cadets must also pledge to serve at least one year in the army. In 1821 West Point disbanded the company of bombardiers and replaced by various companies of artillery. Thayer abolished the practice of annual vacations and installed summer encampment, where cadets lived in tents, drilled and practiced tactical movements. Only the 3rd year class would enjoy summer furlough. He formed two companies, each with its own officers and non commissioned officers selected from the upper two classes. A Captain of Infantry was to act as instructor of tactics. A Lieutenant of artillery was to superintend the artillery drills. A quartermaster and a subaltern was to act as personal aide. A professor of French was added to staff. He set up two formal examinations, one in January and one in June, and all cadets were tested. Only after the June exams could any cadet graduate. The most important addition was the merit roll. It ranked each cadet within his class, so that at the end of the four years, the school would say that the cadet ranking second in his class should be an engineer, while the cadet ranking 31st ought to be in the infantry. The merit roll eliminated all subjective feelings and took into account everything a cadet had done for four years, both in and out of the classroom. A system of demerits for each infraction of regulations lowered cadets' standing. Cadets were automatically dismissed for two hundred demerits in a year. Each cadet was graded every day and ranked every week. [9]

All cadets were treated alike. Active competition was encouraged among the cadets. The higher they stood, the better the corps they could get into. Each cadet received an assignment from the text each day, upon which he recited and was graded the next. [10]

Colonel Thayer hired a Commandant of Cadets. His duties were to impart tactical training to the cadets, take charge of their discipline, and assign demerits. West Point soon became a great scientific school. French and mathematics were the main courses. French, algebra, geometry, trigonometry, mensuration, drawing, analytical geometry, fluxions, topographical drawing, natural philosophy, engineering, mineralogy, rhetoric, and moral and political science were also taught at West Point. With the exception of Rensselaer Polytechnic Institute, West Point was the only school training Civil Engineers. After graduation from West Point, many former cadets became teachers. In 1833 twenty five West Point graduates were serving as civil engineers, and by 1836 there were thirty-nine; by 1838 it had grown to one hundred and twenty. West Point emphasized training engineers to meet the demand for skilled professionals who could ease the problems of westward expansion. West Point was one of the few schools providing civil engineers to build bridges, canals and railroads. [11]

In 1836, Tilghman graduated 46th in his class from West Point. While at West Point, Tilghman would be promoted to brevetted 2nd Lieutenant of the 1st Dragoons on July 1, 1836 and became a full Second Lieutenant of the 1st Dragoons in September of 1836. Some of Tilghman's classmates in the class of 1836 who would go on to become Civil War Generals and officers were Union General George Thomas, who would become known as the "Rock of Chickamauga"; Union General Thomas Sherman, who was brevetted Major General and wounded at Port Hudson, Louisiana; Confederate General Joseph Reid Anderson, who was the Superintendent for the cannon foundry in Richmond, Virginia; Union General Montgomery Meigs, who was the Construction Engineer for the Capitol Extension and architect for the pension office in Washington, D.C.; Union General Daniel Woodbury, who was in charge of the pontoon bridges during the battle of Fredericksburg; Colonel David Porter DeWitt of the New York Volunteers, Union General John Wolcott Phelps, who organized the first black troops for the Union army; Union General Henry Hayes Lockwood, who was a professor at the United States Naval Academy and Union General Robert Allen, who supplied Grant and Halleck's armies with supplies from 1861 to 1863. [12]

On October 1, 1836, three months after Tilghman's graduation from West Point, he resigned his commission. Tilghman was no different from most of the West Point Cadets at that time, and would also pursue a civil engineering career in railroads.

Tilghman's first position in civilian life as an engineer was on the Baltimore & Susquehanna Railroad, which he held until 1837. In 1837, he was assistant to Colonel Kearney, U.S. Topography. He was engaged as an engineer in the survey of the canal from Norfolk and Wilmington, and from April 1838 to March 1839 he was assistant engineer under Colonel Kearney on the Eastern Shore Railroad. In June of 1839, Tilghman resigned his position as assistant engineer under Colonel Kearney to later work as assistant engineer for the Baltimore & Ohio Railroad. During this time until 1840, Tilghman was engaged in locating the Baltimore and Ohio railroad at and near Harper's Ferry. In 1840 Tilghman resigned his position as assistant engineer of the Baltimore and Ohio Railroad, and between May of 1840 to August 1840 Tilghman was engaged in superintending public improvements in and around the city of Baltimore. [13]In 1843, Tilghman married Augusta Murray, daughter of Joseph C. and Isabella (Southgate) Boyd of Portland, Maine, who was the granddaughter of Mary, sister of Rufus King, U.S. Minister to England. [14]

From August 1840 to September 1845, Tilghman was engaged as a contractor with the U.S. Ordnance Department and Navy Department. In September 1845, Tilghman rejoined the army. America became involved in its first major conflict: the Mexican War. After many rebellions, in 1821 Mexico won its independence from Spain. The people of Mexico were divided both politically and geographically. Mexico was also left with a legacy of Spanish militarism and a state church. Santa Anna declared that Mexico was unready for democracy and took over the country as dictator. Anna knew nothing of statesmanship or techniques of warfare. He led an army into Texas to quell the rebellious whites in that state. He battled with the forces at the Alamo and later massacred three hundred and forty two Texas inhabitants in Goliad. In 1836, the Battle of San Jacinto was fought. The Texans under Sam Houston captured Santa Anna. Anna agreed to recognize Texas independence, with the boundary at the Rio Grande. [15]David Nevin, *War with Mexico*, (Time Life

Books, Inc.: New York, 1978); John Edwards Weems, *To Conquer a Peace: The War Between the U.S. and Mexico* (Doubleday and Co. Inc.: Garden City, New York, 1974).

President Andrew Jackson only formally recognized the Texas Republic and would not agree to annexation of Texas, because the anti-slavery Northerners did not want the annexation of Texas, because it would become a slave state. Southerners sympathized with Texas. Jackson did not want to divide the country over the issue of Texas. In 1844 U.S. President Tyler wanted to annex Texas and ordered military units to Louisiana, where American troops could help defend Texas against Mexico. Two months later the Senate voted the proposal down. President Polk was an expansionist president and, like many of his fellow Americans, he spoke of Manifest Destiny. Tyler invited Texas to enter the Union. On July 4th, 1845 Texas accepted, and in December Texas became a state. [16]

America was going through one of the most expansive and prosperous periods in the 1840's. The Northern states manufacturing companies were booming, and the Southern plantation farms grew even larger. Eli Whitney's cotton gin increased cotton production, which revived a dying slave economy. The Northwest Territory, a quarter of a million miles of land north of the Ohio River, east of the Mississippi, south of the Great Lakes, and west of Pennsylvania was ceded by Britain in 1783. In 1803 the French sold the Louisiana Purchase to America. In 1821 Spain sold Florida to the United States. But Polk wanted more land. He wanted upper California. He wanted to buy California, New Mexico, and Texas from the Mexicans. [17]

The Americans failed to see that Mexico was determined to resist U.S. encroachment on their land. The Mexicans had a pride that forbade them to sell their land to the United States. Mexico had never acknowledged Texas independence. They saw Texas as being in rebellion and still part of their country. If the United States planned to make Texas a part of the Union, it was a declaration of war.

Mexico also stopped paying reparation payments. In 1841 a neutral claims commission accepted by both nations had awarded two million dollars in damage to American citizens. Mexico agreed to pay the debt and had paid three of the twenty quarterly payments, when they stopped paying. Mexico had just run out of money. But the Americans were angered and saw the Mexicans as irresponsible. [18]

When the news that Texas had been accepted into the Union reached Mexico, the Mexican people became outraged. General Mariano Paredes y Arrillaga formed an army and began to march into Mexico in 1846 and made himself president. [19]

On July 22 the U.S. army had marched from New Orleans to Corpus Christi Bay. On July 23rd, 1845 the *Alabama* began its voyage to Texas. It landed on

St. Joseph's island. By July 28th the 3rd U.S. regiment had landed. The 4th U.S. Regiment arrived in mid-September. The American army consisted of Twigg's 2nd Regiment of Dragoons, five infantry regiments, four batteries, and few companies of Louisiana volunteers, and detachments of Texas Rangers. The U.S. forces came to only 3,900 men, and many of them were foreign born. They were about to face a Mexican army that was four times larger. [20]

Tilghman arrived at Corpus Christi in September and became a sutler, supplying goods to the American army. In June the Mexican Congress had authorized an increase in the military forces to prevent annexation, and in July the Mexican president had recommended to his Congress a declaration of war upon receipt of information that the U.S. was moving into Texas.

Although the American forces were small in number, they did have some advantages over the Mexican army. The Mexican army was mainly made up of Indians or citizens who had been forced into service. The Mexican military tactics and regulations remained the same as those used by Spaniards before their departure. Army discipline was low because of the many revolts. Pay was short and men lacked the basic needs such as uniforms and equipment. The infantry carried the smoothbore flintlock musket bought from England twenty years earlier. Artillery was comprised of heavy gun tubes mounted on even heavier carriages. [21]

The American forces had new weapons in their possession. The new six pounder bronze cannon that could fire 1,523 yards. The new six pounder also fired a six pound ball, three inches in diameter or exploding shell or canister shot. The tube was only four foot long and was mounted on a very light carriage. These batteries were known as flying artillery, because of their easy mobility around the battlefield. The infantrymen also carried flintlock muskets, but the new Springfield rifle, Model 1841, was given to sharpshooters. [22]

Once the army was made aware of Tilghman's background from West Point, he quickly became the aide-de-camp to General David E. Twiggs. Twiggs commanded the 2nd Dragoons and since Tilghman had been a Second Lieutenant in the Dragoons before the war, it only made sense for Tilghman to serve as Twigg's aide.

On February 3rd, 1846 Taylor planned to make Point Isabel, a mainland location, accessible through the pass known as Brazos Santiago that lay between those two offshore islands. He built a fort some miles south on the north bank of the Rio Grande opposite the town of Matamoros. [23]

General Mariano Arista arrived at the town of Matamoros. He replaced Mejia as the commandant. Arista arrived with 2,000 troops, comprised of the Tampico Veterans, 2nd Light Infantry, 4th and 10th Infantry and 1,600 mounted lancers under cavalry General Anastasio Torrejon. Arista demanded that Taylor withdraw toward the Nueces. Taylor ordered a blockade of the mouth of the Rio Grande, which was being used by the Mexicans for transporting supplies to Matamoros after leaving Point Isabel. Taylor was concerned about his supply base at Point Isabel and moved his main army to Point Isabel. He left five hundred men of the 7th Infantry, under Major Jacob Brown in charge of Fort Texas. [24]

In April 1846 Tilghman made a reconnaissance of the Mexican position at Burita on the Rio Grande for Colonel Monroe, commanding at Point Isabel. He was in command of a small party of men, and made a map of the country between Point Isabel and Burita for Major Saunders, U.S. Engineer. [25]

On May 13th, 1846, President Polk signed the declaration of war. Congress voted for fifty thousand volunteer troops to be raised for the war and ten million dollars to be allotted for the war. Polk had already used his powers as commander-in-chief and President to deploy troops, so Congress was merely just recognizing that a state of war then existed with Mexico. [26]

Torrejon and 1,600 men had crossed over the river above the fort. Torrejon had crossed Taylor's vital supply road that linked Fort Texas with Point Isabel. He then continued to a location below the fort. They deployed on the banks to cover five thousand Mexican infantry commanded by Arista, who were heading north. Arista hoped to get between Fort Texas and Point Isabel before Taylor could move, but a shortage of boats prevented him from carrying out his mission. [27]

Taylor arrived at Point Isabel on May 2, and Arista realized that Taylor had rushed past him. Arista positioned his men in a grove of trees called Palto Alto, or Tall Timber, to await Taylor's return. General Ampudia was ordered to assault Fort Texas with cannon. [28]

Taylor reinforced Fort Polk at Point Isabel and loaded two hundred wagons with supplies for Fort Texas. On May 3 the Mexicans began to fire their cannons on Fort Texas. The American eighteen pounders fired back into Matamoros. Two Mexican twelve pounders were knocked out, but other cannons smashed the fort's walls while mortars fired shells into the fort. One sergeant was killed. The artillery duel continued until May 5. Another Mexican cannon was also knocked out. [29]

Five days later, on May 7, Mexican cavalry and infantry formed assault positions outside the fort, and at dawn the cannon began to fire. Taylor moved his men toward Fort Texas, leaving two hundred undrilled recruits from Louisiana and five hundred sailors and marines from Commodore Conner's Home Squadron to protect Fort Polk. The Mexican cannons had fired 2,700 rounds into Fort Texas for five days. Polk marched out of Point Isabel with 2,228 men. [30]

On May 8, Arista formed his line of battle with infantry, artillery, and cavalry. His army faced the plain. On Arista's right, on top of a wooded elevation, he placed his light infantry regiment. To the far left he placed an artillery piece, a battalion of sappers, then his main force of infantry and artillery. Four hundred yards away to the left was General Torrejon's cavalry supported by two field pieces. There were between 4000 to 5000 Mexicans awaiting Taylor's two eighteen pounders. The Mexicans had twelve cannons; two were eight pounders on massive carriages. The Mexican battle line was one mile long. [31]

Taylor was two miles away from the Mexican line when the Mexicans came into view. Tilghman was selected by Captain Blake to make by Captain Blake the reconnaissance of the Mexican position. Blake and Tilghman approached the Mexican line and was able to count the rank and file of their various regiments with the naked eye. Blake and Tilghman returned to Taylor with the information they had gained. [32]

Taylor ordered his line of battle. He placed three artillery batteries between the infantry regiments. On his right he placed the 5th Infantry. Next to it was Major Ringgold's battery of flying artillery, then on the farther left, the 3rd Infantry, the two eighteen pounders and the 4th Infantry, another battery of field artillery, commanded by Capt. Duncan and the Eighth Infantry. A rear guard of the dragoons stayed with the wagons. [33]

Amazingly, the Mexicans did not attack; they waited for the Americans to form their line of battle and even allowed the Americans to fill their canteens with water from a nearby pond. The Mexicans started the battle with the commencing of artillery fire. At 2:30 P.M. Taylor ordered his men forward. Tilghman would experience his first real battle. The American troops marched across the open, rolling, treeless prairie. The Mexicans fired their artillery but they hit the ground before they reached the American position, so most of the Union troops stepped aside and let the cannon balls roll by them. But Duncan's and Ringgold's six pounders had the range of Arista's position and eight six pounders began to fire shot and shell into his infantrymen's ranks. The American infantry stayed out of musket range, and were ten to twenty yards behind the artillery. The American artillery were firing at the Mexican infantry while the Mexican artillery were firing at the American cannons. The bursting shells created havoc with Arista's men. Arista did not have bursting shells, and his powder was weak. [34]

After an hour of the artillery duel, Arista ordered General Torrejon to mount an attack with lancers and infantry, with two cannons. Torrejon was trying to get around Taylor's right flank to get at the supply wagons. The 5th Infantry saw what Torrejon was up to and moved out to intercept him. The 5th Infantry formed a square and eight hundred lancers came charging at the Americans. The lancers fired a hundred feet from the 5th Infantry and continued their charge. The fire of the United States second front blew the Mexican lancers out of their saddles. Off to the 5th Infantry's right came Sam Walker's twenty men, who also fired a deadly round into the lancers. Torrejon's cavalry fled in horror. [35]

Torrejon managed to rally his troops and ordered his two cannon to fire on the 5th Infantry. Sam French and Lieutenant Randolf Ridgely brought two six pounders from Ringgold's battery C into action. They fired grape and canister into the Mexican artillery before the Mexicans had a chance to fire their guns. Torrejon ordered his guns off the field. French and Ridgely fired into the Mexican cavalry, and the Mexicans ran. Taylor sent the dragoons to chase and push the Mexican left flank back. [36]

The Mexican artillery soon found the range of the two eighteen pounders and the 4th Infantry. The U.S. eighteen pounders continued to deliver a continuous fire on the Mexicans as Ringgold's battery moved his guns around the field. Ringgold was struck by a Mexican six pound ball. It tore out both sides of his thighs. By that time twenty artillery pieces were engaged. [37]

After an hour a fire broke out on the grassy plain, and the battle stopped as heavy smoke obscured the battlefield. Under the cover of smoke, Taylor advanced his right while Arista withdrew his left and advanced his own right. After another hour the smoke began to clear and Duncan saw the Mexican line opposite his line had advanced. The Mexicans charged, but Duncan drove them back. [38]

Taylor ordered Captain Charles May's dragoons against the Mexican left. May charged but the Mexican artillery opened fire and drove May's men back. Cannons continued to fire until darkness settled over the battlefield. The Mexicans made one last charge, and then the fighting stopped. Taylor lost five men killed and forty three men wounded. As many as five hundred Mexicans lay dead or wounded. [39]

The next day the Mexicans fell back to a new position at Resaca de la Palma. The resaca was part of the old bed of the Rio Grande. It formed an arc facing the road from Point Isabel to Matamoros. Arista hid his men behind the brush-covered banks of the old bed. The road crossed the ravine and was the only way through acres of dense chaparral. The Mexicans could lay down a heavy fire on the Americans moving along the road not only from the front but also from the sides. One cannon was directly on the Matamoros road; the other was on the Mexican side of the resaca. Tilghman was about to experience his second battle in just two days. [40]

Taylor sent his wounded to Point Isabel with a small escort, and continued toward Fort Texas, which was only ten miles away. The 5th Infantry and Ringgold's battery marched in front, and behind them was the 4th Infantry. The Mexicans were reinforced by troops from Matamoros. Taylor approached Arista's position and immediately ordered Ridgely's battery to knock the Mexican cannon. The 5th Infantry was ordered to the left of the road and Lieutenant Ulysses Grant's company, and the 4th Infantry began their movements to the right of the road. Units became confused and mixed as they made their way through the thick chaperrel.

Off to Grant's left, General Taylor ordered his battery aside to allow the dragoons under Captain Charles May to charge the Mexican cannon. May charged the Mexican cannon and rode right past the Mexicans manning their gun. The Mexican artillery crew was pushed back to the ravine, but the Mexican infantry fired at May's dragoons, and nineteen men were killed or wounded. May rode back to his lines, but he did manage to capture General Romolo Diaz de la Vega, who had been the acting commander of all Mexican troops on the field. [41]

The infantry had canister and grape fired at them while they were slowly making their way to the Mexican position. On the right of the road, Grant and his company came upon a Mexican infantry line and charged the position, capturing several Mexicans. On the left of the road, Captain E. K. Smith, commander of the 5th Infantry, could see the Mexican position and decided to charge them. Smith with his 4th Infantry and the 5th Infantry, charged the Mexican infantry and hand-to-hand combat broke out. Bayonets on both sides gleamed in the sun and were quickly stained with blood. The Mexican line began to break and finally Taylor ordered his 1,700 men to a final charge. The Mexican center broke as the Mexicans fled. [42]

By 5 P.M. Arista's line along the resaca had broken, and his men fled toward the Rio Grande. Only two boats were available for the men to cross the river. Many of the Mexican soldiers drowned. American casualties amounted to one hundred twenty two dead and wounded. The Mexicans lost 1,500 men, including eight cannon and 1,500 muskets, along with loaded wagons. [43]

Taylor arrived to Fort Texas and found that Major Brown had been hit by an exploding shell and had died. The fort was renamed to Fort Brown. Taylor halted his men at Fort Brown. [44] On May 18, Taylor planned to take Matamoros. The Americans crossed the river and found the Mexicans heading toward Linares, sixty miles away, leaving four hundred of their wounded comrades behind. Taylor did not follow. Taylor began to make Matamoros his staging ground for his next move, which was a push deeper into Mexico. [45]

During the summer of 1846, the war was going well for the United States. Britain had signed the Oregon Treaty, relieving any sign of war with Britain over the territory. This helped America focus her total attention to the Mexican War. California was occupied , and New Mexico was conquered. Political matters in Mexico were also in an upheaval. Paredes decided to take control of the army, and when he left Mexico City on July 31, a massive revolt broke out. The people cried out for Santa Anna to return to power. On August 6, Parades resigned as president. On August 16, Anna arrived at Vera Cruz. America had talked to Anna while he was in exile in Cuba and thought that they could negotiate with him. But unfortunately most Americans were unaware of the great successes that America had made during the war. [46]

By midsummer, Taylor had amassed fourteen thousand soldiers on the Texas-Mexico border. His next move was to take Monterrey. On July 6, General William Jenkins Worth, who commanded the 7th Infantry, boarded steamers and headed for Camargo, one hundred miles away. At Camargo, disease killed as many as one thousand men. Taylor left most of his heavy artillery at Camargo and took only his ten inch mortar, two twenty-four pound howitzers, and his light artillery. [47]

On August 19, Taylor moved out. Taylor's force was 6,000 men, which was made up of Worth's 2nd Division, Major General William Butler's division, and Twigg's 1st Division. He also had a detachment of dragoons, infantry, and artillery, and two regiments of mounted Texas Rangers, one led by Sam Walker, the other led by Jack Hays. Several thousand volunteers were left at Camargo. [48] On September 19, the Americans reached just outside the entrance to the city. The Americans camped at Walnut Springs.

Monterrey was defended by seven thousand Regular Mexican Infantry and three thousand irregulars and forty cannon. The Mexican General in charge at Monterrey was Pedro Ampudia. He was commander of the Army of the North. To the south, the city was protected by mountains and the Santa Catarina River. To the west, guarding the road to Saltillo and the interior of Mexico, were two steep hills, Independencia and Federacion; both were fortified and garrisoned. The frontal terrain was made up of orchards and tall crops of corn, cotton, sugar cane, and grain blocking visibility. The Mexicans also threw up obstacles. The town was also made up of a series of forts and gun emplacements. To the north was the Citadel, which was a large unfinished church with twelve cannon, and four hundred men. A large moat and earthworks surrounded it. The Americans called it the Black Fort. To the east was a La Teneria. It was a stone building housing a tannery that had been converted to a fort, with four cannon and two hundred men. To the northeast part of town near the Santa Catarina River was El Rincon del Diablo or Devil's Corner. It was a three gun redoubt, with one hundred and fifty men. A smaller work was placed at Purisima Bridge, which was the main crossing of the ravine that cut through the northern suburbs. North of the bridge was a twelve pound cannon, and east of it were two more guns.

The interior of the city was also defended. Stone houses had been built with openings through which weapons could be fired. Parapets were placed on the roofs. The streets were also lined with cannons and barricaded with infantry taking positions behind them. [49]

Taylor decided to divide his army, sending the large part of his army to the southwest around the Citadel. On September 20, General Worth and his two thousand men began their movement toward the hills. Hays Texas Rangers were in the lead. The Mexicans saw the movement and sent reinforcements to Independencia Hill. [50]

On September 21, Taylor's cannons fired at the Black Fort with little effect. General Twigg's division of regulars, commanded by Lieutenant Colonel John Garland and Butler's Divisions of volunteers, moved northeast against Monterrey. Garland led the charge and headed between the Black Fort and La Teneria. The advance went too far right and came into range of the Citadel's guns. Garland's troops then came under a hail of fire from the Citadel's guns, La Teneria's guns, and the Black Fort's guns. The men broke and ran toward the houses. The Mexican troops on top of the houses began to fire down into the American ranks. Three companies of the 4th Infantry charged La Teneria and one third of them were cut down. The 4th Infantry fled in retreat toward the east away from the Black Fort. The order to retreat was given. Captain Electus Backus managed to gather up one hundred men from various other companies and headed for a ravine that cut through northern Monterrey and toward some stone buildings on the other side of the ditch. His men climbed to the rooftops. They were able to fire into La Teneria and a redan and other fortifications on the opposite side. Mexican officers and men fled for El Rincon del Diablo. La Teneria surrendered along with four cannon. [51]

General Butler and the Ohio troops then attacked Diablo. The canal slowed them down and a hidden battery fired at the oncoming Americans. Butler was wounded during the attack. The Ohio troops fell back to La Teneria. Darkness ended the carnage. Taylor had lost almost four hundred officers and men during the attack. [52]

The next day General Worth attacked Independencia Hill. The men climbed from rock to rock. The American troops finally reached the top. After considerable fighting between both sides, the Americans finally jumped over the Mexican parapets and the Mexicans retreated down the slope. Worth had captured a twelve-pound howitzer and began to fire on the Bishop's Palace. The American troops started to feel their way around the ridge. The Mexican troops came out of the fort, and when they came between the American on both sides of the ridge, the Americans caught the Mexicans in a cross fire. The Americans charged the Palace. The Mexicans in the Palace fled toward Monterrey. The Mexican flag in the Palace came down, and the American flag went up over Bishops' Palace. [53]

On September 15, Santa Anna had entered Mexico City and had overthrown Mexican President Parades. [54] On September 23, Taylor and Worth attacked Monterrey. General Ampudia had retreated into the center of the city and concentrated his forces around the plaza and cathedral. Taylor headed toward the plaza from the north and east, while Worth came from the west. The Americans came under the fire of Mexican troops stationed on rooftops, and the streets were lined with barricades and cannon to stop the American advanced. Worth's men decided not to go into the streets to meet the hail of fire, but entered the buildings lining the streets and burst through the walls of each building, heading for the plaza, thus avoiding the open streets. Taylor drove Mexicans toward the plaza. Toward the west, Worth continued to advance and began to shell the plaza with mortars. [55] The next morning Ampudia surrendered the city. Ampudia's soldiers were allowed to leave with arms and one battery of six guns.

In October 1846 Tilghman was placed in command of a partisan corps of twenty men at Matamoros. Colonel Clarke was the commander at Matamoros. Tilghman and his men were assigned a mission to rescue a wounded Texan, who was left by his companions near La Prissta after a severe fight with a guerrilla Corps. Tilghman and the twenty men succeeded in finding the body, but only after several hard skirmishes with the guerrillas, who were under the command of Inan Antonio Bayesne. At La Mesa, La Puerta, and Sueesties, Tilghman's men were successful against Bayesne. At different times Tilghman and his group of men faced odds of five to one. After burning the villages at La Mesa, La Puerta, and Sueesties, Tilghman and his men returned to Matamoros without the loss of a single man. [56]

Anna left Mexico City in the autumn of 1846 and left Farias in Mexico City. He headed for San Lois Potosi, and ordered that Ampudia's men be placed under his control. Anna had managed to raise a twenty-thousand-man army, and in January of 1847, he set out to destroy Taylor's army. [57]

By January of 1847 Tilghman was still at Matamoros, and on January 27, 1847, Tilghman was requested by Col. Drake, commander of Matamoros, to fortify the defenseless position against attack. Tilghman laid out the fortifications and made the town secure by the construction of five batteries, which were placed to defend the entrance to the town and made the main plaza the strong-hold in case the outer works were carried. [58]

Also in January of 1847 Taylor was ordered to Saltillo and was to leave Worth's troops at Saltillo as a garrison force. General Wool arrived and added to Taylor's force, making his force 6,000 men strong. Taylor headed for the capital city of Victoria and Tampico. He arrived in Victoria on January 4th. After ten days, Taylor ordered a withdrawal and sent 4,700 men to General Winfield Scott at Tampico. In November 1846 plans were changed and the new target was Vera Cruz. Winfield Scott had taken command of the army. [59]

Anna knew the number and position of Taylor's men, and on January 27, Anna moved out with twenty cannon and 20,000 cavalry and infantry toward Saltillo. General Minon's cavalry was to attack Taylor's east flank and to stand by for a final assault. Taylor had moved to Agua Nueva. On February 21, 1847 the Mexicans headed toward Agua Nueva. Taylor had sent out Ben McCulloch to La Encarnacion for a reconnaissance mission. McCulloch reported to Taylor the size of the Mexican army. Taylor decided to abandon Agua Nueva and withdrew to Buena Vista. Taylor left Wool in charge of the troops while he rode to Saltillo to look for defensive positions. He decided to place his troops in a valley known as La Angostura, or the Narrows. Near the Saltillo-San Luis Potosi road, Wool placed his artillery and infantry. Eight cannons were lined up in the Narrows, facing south. Anna soon came upon the defensive works and immediately asked for Taylor's surrender. Taylor had 4,759 men compared to Anna's sixteen thousand men. Almost five thousand men of Anna's force had succumbed to the heat or had deserted. [60]

The 4th Artillery, under Captain John Washington, was directly in the road. Supporting his guns were three regiments of the 1st Illinois, 2nd Illinois, with a group of Texas volunteers attached, and the 2nd Kentucky. To the extreme left of the American line, near the base of the mountain were two cavalry regiments, made of Kentucky and Arkansas troops. Held in reserve were the 2nd Indiana, and the 3rd Indiana, and two artillery batteries of the 3rd Artillery, the Mississippi Rifles under Jeff Davis and a squad of dragoons of the 1st and 2nd Dragoons. [61]

On September 22, the Mexicans attacked the American line. Anna ordered Ampudia's infantry to move toward the American left and ascended the ridge of the mountain. The plan was to outflank Taylor and strike from the rear. The Americans saw the movement and the Kentucky cavalry, under Col. Humphrey Marshall, dismounted, and moved to meet the Mexican threat. Three cannons from Washington's artillery, supported by the 2nd Indiana, also moved up the mountain. The cannons fired, and Ampudia's men moved farther up the mountain. Darkness ended the fighting. [62]

The next morning Ampudia was reinforced by the Mexican divisions of infantry and cavalry under Fransico Pacheco and Manuel Lombardini, with the support of artillery. The Mexicans attacked the 2nd Indiana. Lieutenant John Paul Jones O'Brien with his three small field pieces tried to hold off 7,000 Mexican soldiers. Dismounted Arkansas cavalrymen climbed the mountain to reinforce the Kentucky cavalrymen under Marshall. Wool saw what was happening on the left of his line and ordered the 2nd Kentucky and cannon to the left. The 2nd Indiana broke under the pressure of Lombardini's and Pacheco's attack and ran, along with four companies of the Arkansas cavalrymen. A regimental order was given to retreat, but countermanded by Colonel Bowles, but it was too late to save the regiments and the men fell back. O'Brien rallied the men who were left and abandoned one field piece and rode away. The Kentucky cavalrymen mounted and rode toward Buena Vista. Taylor's left flank was collapsing. The Americans formed a line parallel to the valley. Taylor arrived at 9 A.M. and sent Jefferson Davis Mississippi Rifles forward. Davis stopped the Mexican assault and pushed the Mexicans back. The 2nd Indiana had broken and fled but the 3rd Indiana came to the aid of Davis Rifles. The Mississippi Rifles went down a ravine and up another side, fighting with bayonets, and the Mexican assault began to slow. The Mexican cavalry swept down the left side of the American line to strike the

LLOYD TILGHMAN

Arkansas cavalry. The Mexican charge was stopped and the lancer fell back to the main line. The 3rd Indiana and the Arkansas cavalry formed into a wide angle forming a V with the open facing the Mexicans. The lancers rode to a slow walk and then halted less than eighty yards from the Americans. At that moment the Americans opened fire from the V. The Mexican cavalry broke and ran. [63]

The Mexicans along the base of the mountain withdrew, and hand to hand combat broke out. A counterattack was ordered by Taylor and both sides agreed to a temporary truce. Anna made a final assault at the center of Taylor's line. Colonel John Hardin of the 1st Illinois fell dead, and Colonel William McKee of the 2nd Kentucky fell dead. Lieutenant Colonel Henry Clay also fell dead. O'Brien took the attack until all his gunners were gone and all his horses lay dead. His remaining two guns fell into the hands of oncoming Mexican troops. The Mississippi and Indiana troops, along with another cannon, fired into the Mexican ranks at musket range. Taylor turned to Captain Braxton Bragg of flying artillery and said "What are you using, Captain, grape or canister?" "Canister, General." "Single or double?" asked Taylor. "Single" said Bragg. "Well double shot your guns and give'em hell, Bragg." The musket fire and artillery broke the Mexican line of battle and they were soon in full retreat. Dusk stopped the fighting. [64]

Neither side won, but Taylor held his ground. He had lost 746 men. Anna lost 2,000 men. Anna decided that night to retreat to Agua Nueva, then to San Luis Potosi. He took the cannons recently captured from O'Brien. [65]

The next morning Taylor found that the Mexicans had left. Anna later arrived in Mexico City and assumed the presidency. He had claimed that the Battle of Buena Vista was a Mexican victory. He collected two million dollars from the Catholic Church and began to form a new army. Farias left in exile. Taylor left for America and Sam French also left for home. [66]

While Taylor was taking Victoria, General Winfield Scott was planning his attack on Mexico City. Scott chose Lobos Island in the Gulf of Mexico as the launching point for an invasion of Mexico and assault on the capital city. Scott would assemble the largest American amphibious landing up to that point. Sixty ships would be used for the invasion. Eventually one hundred ships would be used to transport Scott's 12,603 men and equipment. Commodore Conner squadron would transport the troops on fourteen naval vessels and five military steamers to Anton Lizardo, fourteen miles below Vera Cruz. The ships were then to proceed to Sacrificios for the point of landing. On March 9, the movement began. At 3:30 P.M. Worth's men went into the surfboats. They were 40 feet long, 12 feet wide and 4 feet deep. At 5:30 P.M. the ship Massachusetts fired and the men pushed for the beach. By 10 P.M. ten thousand men had reached the shore. Scott's plan was to encircle the fort and the forces of Vera Cruz, forcing them to surrender, without directly attacking the fort. The brigades of Worth, Quitman and Shields began to encircle Vera Cruz. [67]

Vera Cruz was made up of nine forts that protected the approaches to the city. Facing the sea was Fort San Juan de Ulua. A high wall enclosed the land side of the city. Outside the walls deep holes had been dug, fitted with shrapnel sticks pointing upward, then covered. Inside the walls the Mexicans had two hundred guns and around 3,360 men. [68]

In three days, Scott had managed to encircle Vera Cruz from the shore north to the shore south and completely shut off the water supply to the city. Two cannons were put ashore and Captain Robert E. Lee and other engineers had the job of placing the cannons. Lee helped to place the cannons and buried the gun's platforms. Six naval guns were hauled three miles across sand dunes and a lagoon two feet deep, quite a task considering each gun weighed about three tons each. Lee planted the guns only seven hundred yards from the Mexicans, who were totally unaware of the locations. [69]

On March 22, Scott demanded the Mexican's surrender. Of course they refused, so Scott unleashed his artillery barrage. Scott's mortars fired, but did little damage to the walls. The U.S. Naval ships approached the stations near the fortress and sent rounds into the city. The Mexicans fired back. Shells began to rain down on the city. Scott decided to bring heavier naval guns onto shore. Three thirty-two pounders, and three Naval eight inch cannons were placed seven hundred yards from the city walls and hidden from the Mexican view. [70]

The naval gun began to fire at the city on March 24, and the thirty-two pounders opened a fifty foot hole in the city walls. Every artillery piece the Mexicans owned began to fire on the naval guns. The Naval battery ceased fire at 4 P.M. because of lack of ammunition, not because they were knocked out by the Mexican guns. The Naval battery had fired 1,300 shells at Vera Cruz. [71]

On March 26, General Juan de Landero admitted defeat and the firing ceased. Two days later, the city surrendered, including Fort San Juan de Ulua. Scott had lost thirteen killed and fifty-five wounded. [72]

On April 8, Scott moved to his next objective, Jalapa, which was seventy four miles from the National Road to Mexico City. General Twiggs led the troops out of Vera Cruz and headed toward Jalapa. The men headed into the mountains. Jalapa was four thousand feet above sea level. Patterson's troops left the next day and Worth's troops would leave last. Scott remained in Vera Cruz. [73]

Anna also headed for Jalapa and set his headquarters at Cerro Gordo. His battle line extended across the National Road for two miles. Its right was on steep bluffs overlooking El Rio del Plan. Anna placed his artillery on three ridges. On April 11, Twiggs arrived at the bridge that spanned the Rio del Plan. Patterson arrived on the scene and, since he outranked Twiggs, he assumed command of the army and advised waiting for Scott. On April 14 Scott arrived and camped near the bridge across the Rio del Plan. Scott sent out reconnaissance teams to search for a way around the ridges. His men returned and informed him that to the right of the road a passage was possible-the same road that Anna thought was impassable because it was heavily wooded. Scott came up with a plan to assault the Mexicans at two areas. He would swing around the Mexican's left flank. On April 17 Captain Robert E. Lee guided Twiggs and his men along a trail and were given orders to attack on the 18th. A diversionary assault would be made on the Mexican front. Twiggs, along with Worth's troops, started to climb La Atalaya with their artillery. The Mexicans had seen their movement and began shooting at them. The American infantry took the hill after a small skirmish. The Mexicans were pushed toward Telegrafo. Darkness ended the fight. [74]

During the night, Lee guided the infantry force to the location of the Jalapa road at Anna's rear. Three more cannons were dragged up Atalaya. By 7:00 A.M. the Americans at Atalaya began their artillery barrage. The Mexicans on Telegrafo began to fire back. In the Mexican front Gideon Pillow made his assault. Gideon Pillow was exposed to fire from all three Mexican batteries. Pillow was wounded during the assault. The main attack was made against Telegrafo hill and the Americans pushed the Mexicans off the hill top and down the hill. The Mexican cannon that was captured on Telegrafo was used against the fleeing Mexicans. They ran toward the Jalapa road, but the Americans charged to block the road. Anna soon realized that he was outflanked. The Mexican soldiers who had just routed Pillow's men watched the action on Telegrafo hill and realized that their escape route had just been blocked. They surrendered. Anna lost half his army by 10:00 A.M. Scott during the attack had lost only four hundred men and sixty-three were killed. [75]

Anna managed to rally three thousand men and made it back to Mexico City. On April 22nd Worth occupied Jalapa and the fortress Perote, which was abandoned by the Mexicans leaving fifty four cannons in the possession of American hands. Jalapa would become the American headquarters for a month. Three thousand soldiers had only signed up for one year enlistments, and those enlistments were up. None of them wanted to sign up again. This left the army with only around four thousand troops. [76]

By July 1847 Anna had managed to collect twenty five thousand soldiers in Mexico City. Mexico City would not be easy to take. Lakes and extensive marshlands surrounded the city. A series of fortifications and strongholds guarded each road into the city. Causeways across these water barriers were the only access to the city, which was protected at every entry point by fortified gates. North and east of the city was Lake Texcoco. Entrance from the north must come by way of Guadalupe Hidalgo. Southeast of the city lay more marsh and two more lakes; Chalco and Xochimilco. Perote, and Puebla entered Mexico City from the east, over a causeway erected along the southern shore of Lake Texcoco. Just south of that road, a large hill named El Penon rose above the marsh to a height of three hundred feet, but Anna had placed three hundred cannon and thousands of troops. Another road led into Mexico City from the south. At Mexicaocingo, Anna placed more artillery and troops. Mexico City also had a population of two hundred thousand people. [77]

During the same month Tilghman became a Captain and was placed in command of a light artillery battery of six guns to serve with the Maryland and District of Columbia Volunteer Light Artillery, under the command of Colonel George W. Hughes. The battery was on the line from Vera Cruz to Mexico City. Tilghman was stationed at Jalapa with his battery. [78]

Worth was in Puebla and Scott was in Jalapa. Four thousand reinforcements arrived. Two thousand five hundred recruits arrived at Vera Cruz. By August Scott had 13,000 troops. On August 7, Twiggs' column camped at Ayotla, just north of Lake Chalco and on the National Road leading toward El Penon and Mexico City. Worth halted at Chalco. Scott set up his headquarters at Ayotla. The Mexicans saw the approach of the Americans and the alarm was sounded. [79]

By August 15, Scott marched his troops southwest, skirting Lake Chalco. Worth's division led the column followed by Pillow and Quitman. Twigg's division would remain at Atoyla as a screen for one day then move southwest on August 16. On August 18 Scott assembled his men around San Agustin, nine miles south of Mexico City, which blocked the road north for two miles above San Agustin. The town of San Agustin could only be entered through a narrow cause-way. To the right of the causeway was a marsh. To the left of the causeway was a lava field. Lee told Scott that the army could advance through the pedregal. Three thousand Americans moved off to the right. They took the town of San Geronimo. This force would be able to attack Mexican General Gabriel Valencia's Army of the North from the flank or rear to cut off retreat, when the rest of Scott's army stormed the hill from the front. Anna sent between 5,000 to 12,000 Mexican soldiers to support Valencia. The reinforcements occupied a height overlooking the town of San Geronimo. The Americans were caught between two large Mexican armies. Anna was to the north and Valencia was to the south. [80]

Anna withdrew to the northeast in the direction of Churubusco. He ordered Valencia to do the same, but Valencia refused to move. Anna never thought to attack the Americans west of the pedregal. [81]

The Americans realized that the Mexicans could be attacked by surprise. A diversionary assault would be made on the front while the true force would attack from the rear. On August 20, at 1 P.M. Twiggs organized the diversionary attack. At 5 A.M. the battle began. Valencia soon discovered that Americans were preparing to assault the rear of the hill. Panic set in and the Mexican gunners ran from their pieces. After seventeen minutes the battle was over. One thousand five hundred Mexicans had been killed, wounded or captured. The Americans captured twenty-two cannons, including two American guns captured at Buena Vista. The American suffered only sixty casualties. [82]

Anna ordered his men to withdraw from San Antonio and fall back to the bridge across the Rio Churubusco and the stronghold of San Mateo. San Mateo was defended by seven cannon and 1,800 men. A fortified bridge was three hundred yards away across the Churubusco River toward Mexico City. The bridge was defended by three cannon and several thousand troops. [83]

Worth's men would try and take the bridge to the south, while the rest of Scott's men would ford the river west of the town and storm the bridge from the north. For more than three hours the battle raged around Churubusco. Twigg's men were attacking the convent of San Mateo, with no success. Worth's division came under fire from San Mateo and the bridge. Worth left the road away from San Mateo and into a cornfield on the right, and was met with heavy fire from the Mexicans in ditches and corn rows. The Americans started back toward the road. They entered a cross fire. The Americans charged at 3 P.M.. Worth's troops reformed and began to push the Mexicans back. Some Americans worked their way around to the Mexican right and were able to outflank the Mexicans. The Americans advanced toward the bridge. Twigg's artillery had to fall back after losing twenty-four men and thirteen horses. [84]

On the far right, the Americans crossed the river and headed for the bridge. The 5th and Eighth American Infantry charged up the road into the Mexican cannon at the bridge. The Mexican cannon fired point blank into the Americans, but the Americans pushed on against overwhelming odds and jumped over the parapets with bayonets fixed, and after a brief fight they pushed the Mexicans away from the bridge toward Mexico City. [85]

The Americans seized the Mexican cannon and aimed it at San Mateo's walls. Holes were opened in the walls and the American infantry climbed over into San Mateo. The fighting ended on August 20th, 1847. Four thousand Mexicans lay dead or wounded on the battlefield. Three thousand more were captured. The Americans lost one thousand men killed, wounded, or missing. Worth's division camped at Tacubaya. Scott's headquarters was at Archbishop's Palace. Pillow was camped at Mixcoac and Quitman's force was camped at San Agustin. Scott had only eight thousand men left. [86]

On August 24, a truce went into effect. On September 6 the peace talks broke down and the forces at Tacubaya prepared for battle. Mexico City was protected by Chapultepec Hill, which was a military school with a fortified castle with cannon. Molino del Rey was several stone buildings that made up a foundry. Casa Mata was located a quarter mile west of Molino del Rey, which was a stone building used as a powder magazine. Scott thought that Molino del Rey was making cannon in the foundry. [87]

On September 7, Scott ordered Worth and 2,600 men and nine cannon to attack Molina del Rey. Little did the Americans know that General Antonio Leon and Joaquin Rangel brigades, under General Fransico Perez were waiting for the Americans. Seven artillery pieces under General Simeon Ramirez's brigade also were at Molino del Rey. Four thousand cavalry under General Juan Alvarez were a mile west of Casa Mata. Lieutenant Colonel George Wright's five hundred men were to take the battery. Within five minutes Major Wright's men were torn to pieces and they fell back. Fewer than half of Wright's men were left. Captain Kirby Smith's battalion and one of Cadwalader's reserve regiments were ordered to attack the foundry. To the left and right of Smith other infantry went forward to assault Casa Mata and strike the Mexican left, while Smith drove the Mexicans back. Simon Drum's two six-pounders opened fire on the Mexican battery and Kirby Smith took the Mexican cannon. Smith was hit in the face and died three days later and Mexican General Leon was killed. On the left Worth ordered attack on Casa Mata. When the Americans came to within one hundred yards of Casa Mata Perez opened fire. The Mexican cavalry then came at the American left flank. Duncan's artillery began to fire on the Mexican cavalry. Lieutenant Colonel Edwin Sumner and his two hundred and seventy dragoons charged at the Mexican cavalry. In ten seconds he lost forty-four men. At Casa Mata the Americans fell back. The Mexican infantry left their positions and chased after the Americans, but Cadwalader's reserves and Duncan's artillery stopped the Mexicans at Casa Mata. Perez abandoned his position and Molino del Rey were captured and cut off from Chapultepec. By 7:00 A.M. the fighting was over. The Mexicans lost three thousand men and Casa Mata and Molino del Rey was captured. The Americans lost seven hundred and eighty seven men killed and wounded. It turned out that Molino del Rey was not making any cannons. The Americans withdrew from Molino del Rey and Casa Mata. The Mexicans still held Chapultepec. [88]

The way into Mexico City entered from the west at a fortified gate at San Cosme, southwest at Belen. Both roads passed Chapultepec Hill before the approach to the city. The hill rose two hundred feet in the air. A series of sturdy buildings had been built. One thousand soldiers and cadets led by General Nicolas Bravo was at Chalpultepec with mine fields and thirteen cannon. Scott ordered Twiggs division to Piedad, south of the capital, while other units would assault upon Chapultepec Hill. An artillery assault would start the battle. Cannons were placed south and southwest of the hill, and at Molino del Rey and Casa Mata, cannons were placed to aim at Chapultepec. [89]

The Americans fired endlessly for fourteen hours at the castle with little effect. The guns were re-aimed, which allowed the shells to rip through the walls and roofs. The Mexican artillery fired back, but was ineffective at stopping the American artillery barrage. [90]

At 8 A.M., on September 13, after one hour of cannon fire, the infantry would assault Chapultepec. Pillow's division from the west was assisted by two hundred and fifty men from Worth's division. Quitman division was southeast, aided by two hundred and fifty men from Twigg's division. The remainder of Worth's division were held in reserve to support Pillow and part of Twigg's division would serve the same purpose for Quitman. [91]

Americans carried the lower works of Chapultepec, and the Mexicans were unable to explode the mines. The men halted at the ditches at the base of the retaining wall that supported the buildings standing at the rocky summit hill. They had no ladders. The ladders finally arrived and the men secured a foothold on the crest of Chapultepec. The Mexican cadets refused to abandon the castle. The battle for Chapultepec lasted about one and a half hours. Scott lost five hundred men and everyone at the Mexican garrison died. [92]

Worth's division headed up the Veronica causeway. Quitman's division took another causeway entering from the southwest through Belen Gate. Quitman captured Belen Gate before noon. A counterattack drove them back. By 4 P.M., Worth's men reached San Cosme Gate. Mexican artillery and small arms fire covered the causeway. Worth headed for the adobe buildings and tore holes through the walls. Ulysses Grant climbed a church steeple with a mountain howitzer and carried it to the belfry, only three hundred yards from San Cosme. Grant and his men dug holes through the adobe walls and managed to gain the rear of San Cosnme Gate, which ended the defense of Mexican City perimeter. By Sept. 13, 6 P.M. the Americans captured San Cosme and Belen. [93]

Anna fell back to Guadalupe Hidalgo. On September 14 a delegation of citizens surrendered the city. Anna led his men against Americans at Puebla but failed. On October 16 Anna was relieved of command by Pena y Pena.

On January 6, 1848 negotiations began. On February 2, 1848, the Treaty of Guadalupe Hidalgo was signed and ratified on March 10, 1848. The treaty gave the United States more than half of Mexico's territory. The American boundary would run from the Gulf of Mexico up to the Rio Grande to the New Mexico border. From there it would continue west to reach the Pacific, three miles south of San Diego. The United States would pay Mexico fifteen million dollars in cash and pay three million dollars in reparations. [94]

In April of 1848 Tilghman made an expedition against the town of Montigo, capturing a large body of deserters, and later he made another expedition against the town of Mantoosco relieving Captain Wheat, who was surrounded by six hundred men, and he had only twenty men. Tilghman's force consisted of one hundred mounted men. [95]

On May 30, 1848 Mexico ratified the Treaty. On June 12th the last of the American troops left Mexico. Tilghman's artillery battery was finally disbanded on July 13th, 1848 at Pittsburgh, Pennsylvania. [96]

The Mexican War had cost the Americans over thirteen thousand lives. Over 1,700 Americans died in action; another 11,155 were dead from disease and exposure. A high mortality rate remained in the American army years after the war, which was blamed on the effects of disease contracted during service in Mexico. The war had divided the nation. The Whig party held that the United States shouldn't acquire any territory as a result of the war. The radical wing insisted that slavery be forbidden in any territory acquired. The Democratic Party was divided into those who supported the expansion and those strongly against slavery being admitted into the newly won land. Lincoln spoke out against the war and lost his nomination for the Whig party. He would later turn to the Republican Party. The issue of slavery would not go away. [97]

America had increased its territory. New land could be expanded. The plantation owners expanded, and the North's industrial complex also expanded. America became a wealthy nation.

Many of the tactics used in the Mexican War were later used in the Civil War. The Americans for the first time mounted a large scale invasion of a foreign land. The United States blockaded the Mexican's coastal areas, which is what the Union army attempted to do to the South during the Civil War. [98]

The Mexican War also proved to the world that America was a new military power. The new nation had proven itself in war. America had a well taught, armed force. How ironic that less than thirteen years later many of the men that fought side by side in battle would be on opposing sides. Captain Robert E. Lee, Pierre G. T. Beauregard, Benjamin McCulloch, and Gideon Pillow, would join the Confederacy, while Ulysses S. Grant, and George Thomas would stay with the Union. Thirteen years later Grant would be opposing Tilghman.

Tilghman would learn valuable lessons from the Mexican War. He had improved his skills as a artillerist. He had honed his skills as a leader and continued to improve his skills as a engineer.

After the Mexican War, Tilghman returned to civilian life and picked up where he had left off. He continued his career as a civil engineer for the railroad until the Civil War. In January 1849 Tilghman was appointed principal assistant engineer for the Panama survey, but resigned in October 1849. On January 1, 1850, he was offered the appointment of Chief Engineer of the East Tennessee and Virginia railroad extending from Knoxville, Tennessee to the Virginia line at Bristol. In December 1852 Tilghman became chief engineer of the Tennessee Central Railroad extending from Nashville to Fulton on the Mississippi. From April 1 to July 1, 1853, Tilghman became chief engineer of the LaGrange and Bolivar Railroad extending from LaGrange to Bolivar in Tennessee. From June 1, 1853 to July 1 1854, he became engineer in charge for the location and construction of the Paducah branch and Kentucky portion of the Mobile and Ohio Railroad. From September 1853 to August 1854, he was the chief engineer for the location and construction of the Hickman and Obion Railroad extending from Hickman, Kentucky to a junction with the Mobile and Ohio and Nashville and North Western Railroad in Obion County, Tennessee. Under Tilghman's direction, the first seven miles of track were laid from Paducah to Florence, Kentucky. Tilghman extended the rails to Mayfield, Kentucky, twenty six miles south of Paducah. From November 1853 to April 1854, Tilghman became the chief engineer of the Nashville and North Western Railroad, west of the Tennessee River, extending from Nashville, Tennessee to Madrad Sun on the Mississippi. He was also the engineer selected to report on the engineering facts connecting with the passage of Reel Foot Lake by the Iams Company. Between 1853 till 1859 Tilghman was chief engineer for the location and construction of the Mississippi, Machita, and Red River railroad extending from near Gaines Landing in Arkansas to the Texas line in Bowie County, Texas. Between 1854-1858 he was chief engineer for the location and construction of the Little Rock and Napoleon railroad extending from Little Rock, Arkansas to Napoleon on the Mississippi River in Arkansas. In 1857, Tilghman extended the New Orleans and Ohio Railroad into Rives, Tennessee. Where the NO&O rails crossed the Tennessee border, he built a depot. Between 1858 till 1861, Tilghman was chief engineer of the Mobile and Ohio Railroad. He officially became a resident of Paducah, Kentucky, adopting the state as his own in 1852. [99]

Tilghman had done very well in the engineering business. He stated that in January 1856, when he was forty years old, that he was well paid and his income from salaries alone was $13,000 dollars per annuus. He added that he was making "rather better than most men can say at my age." Tilghman also had the "satisfaction of knowing that since I held the position of Chief Engineer I have never solicited a single appointment." Little did Tilghman know that many of his railroads would be used in the Civil War to carry supplies and troops. [100]

CHAPTER TWO
Kentucky Men Cast Their Lots

While Tilghman was still working for the Mobile and Ohio Railroad in Paducah, Kentucky, he decided to join the Kentucky State Guard militia on December 3rd, 1860 and was given the rank of Major, commanding the Paducah Southwest Battalion. Tilghman may have missed his days as a Captain in the Mexican War. He may have missed the camaraderie with the men and the military life. The commander of the Kentucky State Guard, Simon Bolivar Buckner, had a lot in common with Tilghman. Buckner graduated from West Point in 1844 and was a former assistant professor of ethics for the school; he was a veteran of the Mexican War in which he was wounded and promoted for gallantry. Buckner had also resigned from the Regular Army in 1855 and had settled in Louisville, Kentucky. The Kentucky State Guard was formed when Kentucky's legislature passed an ordinance to re-organize the State's militia in March of 1860. It was drawn up by Simon Buckner. All of the able-bodied men in the state between the ages of eighteen and forty-five were made part of the Enrolled Militia. Out of this group were to be taken those who should be trained and fully equipped, designated active or Volunteer Militia, or State Guard. The law was signed by Governor Beriah Magoffin on March 5th, 1860, and Simon Bolivar Buckner was made Inspector General of the Kentucky State Guard with the rank of Major General. Buckner was in command of his own local militia called the Citizen's Guard and used it as the nucleus for the new State Guard. Buckner started with almost nothing but quickly built up a real army, with trained and equipped men. Most of the money used to buy equipment came from donations from Louisville and Jefferson County, Kentucky. In the summer of 1860 Buckner held a summer encampment at the fairgrounds in Louisville, Kentucky. John Hunt Morgan and the Lexington Rifles joined the Kentucky State Guard and were present at the encampment. The encampment drew national attention, when Harper's Weekly carried one of the photographs taken there for its paper. The encampment was a major success for Buckner, and money began to filter into his organization. Many of Kentucky's prominent families began to join the State Guard. Thomas Crittenden, son of Senator John Crittenden, and Ben Hardin Helm, Abraham Lincoln's brother-in-law joined the Guard. By the beginning of 1861 Buckner had sixty-one companies made up of four thousand men. He also collected twelve thousand muskets, and rifles were in the hands of the State Guard. Buckner, along with his officers, such as Tilghman, molded the Kentucky State Guard into a well-drilled, uniformed, armed organization. The Kentucky State Guard boasted a military effectiveness unequaled by any organized militia society in the whole country except perhaps the Regular Army. Buckner made sure he surrounded himself with men who had military training and that those men held the same views as himself. Buckner was pro-Southern in sentiment, and was a state's rights Democrat. But Buckner supported his state first even in a crisis. [101]

In November of 1860 the Presidential elections were held, and the people of Kentucky were divided as to which party to elect. Breckinridge received 145,862 votes and Lane received 52,836, Steven Douglas and Johnson received 25, 644, while the Constitutional Union ticket of Bell and Everett received 66,016 and Lincoln and Hamlin received only 1,366 votes. The people of Kentucky did not agree with the Republican ticket, which stood for the abolition of slavery. The people of Kentucky did not approve of secession. [102] The reason for Kentucky's unwillingness to secede was the people's intense love for the Union. Kentucky also had an insistence of their rights and powers that they claimed as their own. The preservation of states rights was in every way as important as the preservation of the rights of the Union, and must be insisted upon with equal force. Kentucky felt that both could exist in harmony. Even though slavery was dying out in the state in 1860, Kentucky still held its constitutional right to have slaves. There were 36,645 slave holders in Kentucky. [103] Another reason Kentucky did not want to secede was that Kentucky identified herself as neither North or South but American. Kentucky feared that if the state went for the South, thousands of Union troops would flow into the state's borders. There were twelve points on the Ohio River opposite Kentucky where railroads came down from the North; only two points could connect with the South. [104]

On December 20, 1860 South Carolina became the first state to secede from the Union. Kentucky quickly adopted its stance on secession. On January 21, 1861 the Kentucky legislature introduced a series of resolutions. The first declared that "the General Assembly had heard with profound regret of the resolutions of the States of New York, Ohio, Maine, and Massachusetts, tendering to the President men and money to be used in coercing sovereign States of the South into the Federal government." The second resolution stated that the Governor of Kentucky should inform these States that if they sent armed troops to the South for the purpose of forcing the States of the South into the Federal government, " the people of Kentucky, uniting with their brethren of the South, will as one man resist the invasion of the soil of the South at all hazards and to the last extremity." Both resolutions were passed. The following passage was later added, which stated that "we deplore the existence of a Union to be held together by the sword, with laws to be enforced by standing armies." [105]

On April 4, 1861 a new state arsenal at Frankfort, Kentucky was provided for by the legislature and $19,400 was allotted to buy machinery and labor to repair state arms. The state was gearing for war.

On April 12, 1861, the Civil War began with Confederate General P. G. T. Beauregard firing upon Fort Sumter, in the Charleston, South Carolina harbor. Fort Sumter, commanded by Union General Robert Anderson, surrendered to the Confederates. Kentucky declared its neutrality. Three days later Lincoln called for seventy-five thousand troops and the Secretary of War informed the Governor of Kentucky Beriah Magoffin that four regiments of militia should be raised for the Union. Magoffin wrote back to Secretary of War Simon Cameron that "Kentucky will furnish no troops for the wicked purpose of subduing her sister Southern states." [106] Kentucky Senator John J. Crittenden, who had just retired from the Senate, and was a member of the Union State Central Committee, urged for neutrality and to deny the Union troops from Kentucky. He gave a lecture in Lexington, Kentucky in which he said: "..if the President should at any time hereafter assume the aspect of war for the overrunning and subjugation of the seceding States through the full assertion therein of the national jurisdiction by a standing military force, we do not hesitate to say that Kentucky should promptly unsheath her sword in behalf of what will then have become a common cause. Such an event...could have but one meaning, a meaning which a people jealous of their liberty would be keen to detect, and which a people worthy of liberty would be prompt and fearless to resist. When Kentucky detects this meaning in the action of the government, she ought, without counting the cost, to take up arms at once against the government. Until she does detect this meaning, she ought to hold herself independent of both sides, and to compel both sides to respect the inviolability." [107] It was clear that Kentucky wanted neutrality. After a large meeting in Louisville, Union leader John Crittenden and Democratic leader Senator John C. Breckinridge clasped hands with the assurance from both that Kentucky would forever be neutral.

But neutrality was slowly falling apart. Throughout the state, individuals and groups left to join the Confederacy in Virginia or Tennessee. On April 20, 1861 two companies from Louisville, under the command of Captains Ben Anderson and Fred Van Osten left for New Orleans and were later joined by Captain Jack Thompson's company and became the Third Kentucky battalion. On April 25, Captain Joe Desha and one hundred men from Harrison County, along with three companies from Louisville under Captains John Pope, J. B. Harvey and M. Lapielle, left the state to join the Confederate army. They were joined in Nashville by two companies from southwest Kentucky under Captains Edward Crossland and Brownson. Others joined the Union army in Indiana or Ohio. [108]

In April 1861 Kentucky took out loans to pay for arms. The money was to be used "for arming the State for self defense and protection, to prevent aggression or invasion from either the North or South, and to protect the present status of Kentucky in the Union." [109]

On April 24, 1861 a Chicago militia seized Cairo, Illinois. Cairo was just across from Kentucky, and Union soldiers could cross by boat from Illinois to Kentucky.

Governor Magoffin also refused the Confederate call for troops from Kentucky, but many Kentuckians joined the Confederacy anyway. On May 15 a Confederate regiment was formed at Harper's Ferry, Virginia, under Col. Blanton Duncan. Buckner maintained the that Kentucky State Guard was to remain neutral in this conflict and protect Kentucky from both factions, but since many of the State Guard were pro-Southern in sentiment, large numbers of the Guard resigned and joined the Confederacy. The Kentucky legislature ordered the organization of the enrolled militia into companies, to be called Home Guards, for home and local defense. [110]

In May 1861, a supply of five thousand muskets with bayonets and a quantity of ammunition was sent by the U.S. War Department to Cincinnati for distribution to "faithful and reliable Union men in Kentucky." Each man was to pay one dollar for each weapon. Garrett Davis of Kentucky sent these arms for the Home Guard with one thousand five hundred arms going to Fleming and Mason county, two hundred to Boyd, two hundred to Greenup, one hundred to Montgomery, one hundred to Bath, one hundred to Clark, one hundred to Madison, two hundred to Fayette, two hundred to Scott, three hundred to Bourbon, and five hundred to the city of Covington. The arms were delivered on May 18th, and two days later Governor Magoffin issued an armed neutrality proclamation, and warned both Confederate and Union to stop the acts of war on Kentucky soil. The Confederacy immediately recalled its recruiting agents from the state. [111]

On May 6, 1861 the state legislature provided for the arming of the state under supervision of five commissioners, who were Governor Magoffin, Dr. J. B. Peyton, General Peter Dudley, George Wood, and Samuel Gill. An appropriation of $75,000 was made for the purchase of arms and accouterments to be distributed to the State Guard and the Home Guards. Power mills were erected and the state was given control over state arsenals and arms. The State guard was to be trained in camps and that neither the militia nor the state arms were to be used against the Union or Confederate states, unless they were protecting the state from unlawful invasion. The arms and ammunition were only to be used for the defense of the state. Magoffin appointed Scott Brown as Adjutant General and M. D. West quartermaster general of the State Militia. [112]

Neutrality was quickly eroding, and both sides were accusing the other of breaking the neutrality. An interview was held between Colonel Lloyd Tilghman and Colonel Benjamin Prentiss at Camp Defiance, in Cairo, Illinois on May 6, 1861. At the time Tilghman was in command of the western division of the Kentucky Militia, including Paducah and Columbus, Kentucky, and Colonel Prentiss was in command of the 10th Illinois Infantry. The reason for the interview was that Colonel Prentiss, who was at Cairo, Illinois, was accusing Tilghman of harassing the Union troops in Paducah, Kentucky and Cairo. The interview was published in the *Chicago Tribune* and the *New York Evening Post* on May 11, 1861. The interview is as follows:

Colonel Tilghman- "I have visited you, sir, for the purpose of a little official intercourse with reference to the late questions which have excited the people of Kentucky, and to cultivate, as far as in my power, peaceful relations. Some portions of the public press have erroneously used the name of Kentucky, the name of her organized militia under my command, and my own name, in referring to the hostile movement of troops against you from Tennessee." [113] (Colonel Tilghman referred to an article in the *Louisville Journal*, which stated that hostile movements from Tennessee could go through Kentucky only by the aid of troops under Colonel Tilghman's command. He characterized the statement in severe terms, and said that Kentucky was still in the Union, and had no stronger wish than to remain so.)

Colonel Prentiss- "I can hardly express, gentlemen, how gratifying it is to me to find these the sentiments of all the leading men I have met from your side of the river. I assure you that, so far as I understand the sentiments of my State, my command and myself, those friendly feelings are cordially reciprocated. We must, however, when we understand that certain points in either Kentucky, Tennessee, or Missouri are menacing us, prepare to defend them." [114]

Colonel Tilghman- "Let me say, in defense to Tennessee, that, so far as her authorities and official acts are concerned, she was, three days ago, in the Union. I have just come from there, where, in an official capacity, I defined to them, firmly and effectually, the policy of my State. She has a mercurial population, like every state, that is hard to control. But I feel fully authorized to say in deference to Governor Harris, [of Tennessee] with whom I had an interview, and in deference to the State of Tennessee, that there are no hostile menaces toward you." [115]

Colonel Prentiss- "I want you to understand me that, in designating certain points as hostile and menacing, I am far from including the whole State. As to Memphis, I am reliably informed that bodies are arming and drilling with a proposed destination to some place North; and I will say to you frankly, that we are prepared for the attack and await it. But I am inclined to think they are the mob, without official encouragement." [116]

Colonel Tilghman- "Yes, sir, I feel authorized to express that view of it. The press ought to be restrained in its ready circulation of errors. There is not a word of truth in the statement of there being 12,000 men at Paducah for invasion; or, as to the concentration of troops in any part of Kentucky under my control. As to the recent arrival of arms at Columbus, they were the property of the State. This, as her right, Illinois cannot raise any objection to. Kentucky has her own rights to defend, and no State can do it more powerfully. She is a warm and generous friend, but a hearty enemy. We do not wish war. We are now electing our representatives to Congress, with the intention of holding out the olive branch. But the commerce of Kentucky is large, and our people do not understand how much of it is to be interrupted in transit. They feel that they cannot ship a barrel of flour without being subjected to this system of espionage, which is entirely inadmissible." [117]

Colonel Prentiss- "I am instructed to seize no property unless I have information that such property consists of munitions of war, destined to the enemies of the United States Government." [118]

Colonel Tilghman- "Then you would not consider munitions of war shipped to Kentucky under her authority, as contraband?" [119]

Colonel Prentiss- "That would depend upon the point whether Columbus is arming and menacing us."

Colonel Tilghman- "They have not been and are not, allow me to say."

Colonel Prentiss- "Then I have been misinformed. Generally, there would be no detention of munitions of war destined to the authorities of Kentucky."

Colonel Tilghman- "The position I wish to assume is, that Kentucky is the peer of Illinois, and would not consent to anything of the kind, under any pretense. Kentucky probably would never consent to the blockade of the Ohio."

Colonel Prentiss- "But if, as you say, Kentucky is a loyal State, she would have to allow the blockading of the Ohio. I assure you Illinois would allow it, if it required by the General Government. Kentucky has not done her full duty to the government. She has not furnished her quota upon the demand of the President, in defense of the national flag; and this shows we are right in apprehending States; and whereas, the State of Virginia has certain disaffected and disloyal communities which rule to some extent the sentiment of the State." [120]

Colonel Tilghman- "I frankly acknowledge that you have the advantage of me there. But after my intercourse with you, and reassuring you of the groundlessness of your fears in my official capacity, it would be very inconsistent with your previous intimations for you to credit counter rumors. My dear sir, there are not organized fifty men in Western Kentucky outside my command." [121]

Colonel Prentiss- "As soon as our forces are completely organized here, I intend to visit the other side."

Colonel Tilghman- "We shall receive you with every kindness. The position of Illinois and Kentucky relatively is very delicate, and on that account allow me to say that I hope you will continue in command here. Affairs must be managed on both sides with calmness, I think there is hardly a man in a hundred in the State of Kentucky but would fight for the old Constitution as interpreted by the Supreme Court. I am highly gratified at this interview, and I hope to see yourself and staff over there some day." [122]

The interview was referring to a whole series of events that were occurring on the riverways. Kentucky had not stopped river highway traffic and free trade both to the North and South. In the spring and summer of 1861 immense amounts of materials were being moved to the Confederacy through and from Kentucky. The Louisville and Nashville Railroad made ninety five percent of its revenue from freights received at Nashville and only five percent from that originating from Nashville. On April 12th, 1861 the citizens of Cincinnati, Ohio seized one hundred casks of bacon for Charleston and Nashville, and thirty boxes of guns destined for Tennessee and Arkansas were seized including a large order of black powder. The city of Louisville in retaliation seized a steamer from St. Louis, which they thought was carrying arms for Pittsburgh. The citizens also stormed the arsenal and took two six-pounders and placed them in a bend of the river to aim on a ship. They stopped when Buckner told them the guns were for Kentucky State Guards. On April 27, the citizens of Ohio demanded cessation of trade with the South. Governor Dennison of Ohio passed legislation to seize all contraband to a seceded state. Indiana also placed restrictions on trade in Kentucky. [123]

Cairo, Illinois was an important point into the heart of the South. It dominated the great river routes. Governor Yates of Illinois put a blockade on the rivers. Governor Harris of Tennessee felt the effects of the blockade when a steamer of one hundred tons of lead from St. Louis was seized. This interference was one of the reasons that drove Tennessee into the arms of the Confederacy. [124]

Kentucky also protested the blockade of the river routes. Colonel Prentiss told Buckner on May 3 that all arms and ammunition destined for Columbus, Kentucky would be stopped unless the items were loyal and inspected. Colonel Tilghman had protested the blockade before the interview and said that the people of Kentucky "feel that they cannot ship a barrel of flour without being subjected to this system of espionage, which is entirely inadmissable." [125] The blockade was lightened but not for very much longer.

On May 16 the committee on Federal relations in the House of Representatives reported the following resolutions:

"Considering the deplorable condition of the country and for which the State of Kentucky is in no way responsible and looking for to the best means of preserving the internal peace and securing the lives, liberty and property of the citizens of state; therefore, Resolved, by the House of representatives, that this State and the citizens thereof should take no part in the civil war now being waged, except as mediators and friends to the belligerent parties; and that Kentucky should, during the contest, occupy the position of strict neutrality." [126]

"Resolved, that the act of governor in refusing to furnish troops or military force upon the call of the executive authority of the United States under existing circumstance is approved." [127] The preamble and the resolutions passed. Governor Magoffin again stated his stance that Kentucky must remain neutral. He warned all States both Union and Confederate that he forbade "any movement upon the soil of Kentucky, or the occupation of any port, post or place whatever within the lawful boundary and jurisdiction of this State, by any of the forces under the orders of the States aforesaid for any purpose whatever, until authorized by invitation or permission of the legislature and executive authorities of this State previously granted." [128]

On May 20, 1861, Tilghman became a Colonel of the 4th Regiment of Infantry, Kentucky State Guard, at Paducah, Kentucky.

Early in June Inspector General Simon Buckner, who was head of the Kentucky State Guard, went to Cincinnati to meet with Union General George B. McClellan, who commanded the department that included Ohio and western Virginia. They agreed that the Union would not invade Kentucky unless the Confederacy invaded first, although McClellan would later deny this statement. In that instance Buckner would preserve the State's neutrality without Union aid; if that was not possible he was to call on Union troops. Buckner also met with Governor of Tennessee Isham Harris, and the same agreement was made. [129]

While Buckner was meeting with Governor Harris to discuss Kentucky's neutrality, Gideon Pillow, who was in command of the navigation of the Mississippi, was heading to Columbus, Kentucky and was going to occupy the city. The Mayor of Columbus, B. W. Sharp, gave permission for Pillow to enter his town and take it. Sharp told Pillow that the town was already being occupied by Union forces from Cairo, Illinois, and those soldiers were unwelcome. Buckner informed Pillow of Kentucky's neutrality. Pillow decided to suspend his invasion of Columbus, saying that he would respect Kentucky's neutrality. But Pillow's promise would not be kept for long.

Buckner told Lloyd Tilghman, who was commanding the 4th Kentucky Regiment of the State Guard, in Paducah, to call into service six companies of the State Guard, four of infantry, one of artillery, and one of cavalry. He was instructed to send those companies to Columbus, Kentucky, and that

Captain Lyon's artillery company be included. Tilghman was put in charge of the entire command. Its goal was to carry out the neutrality of the State of Kentucky. He was to restrain Kentucky citizens from acts of "lawless aggression", and Tilghman's forces would be under the control of the judicial officers of the district. He was also to give protection to all citizens who requested it, and who may be threatened. On June 24, 1861 Colonel Tilghman arrived in Columbus, Kentucky with the Kentucky State Guard. [130]

In June 1861, the state held their elections. The people of Kentucky elected men in Congress and the Legislature who were pro-Union. During this same month, Tennessee seceded. That would totally change the way Kentucky would hold its neutrality position. Kentucky had enjoyed its neutrality up to this point because both sides saw the state as an important buffer state. For the Confederacy, the state guarded seven hundred miles of the Ohio River front and made the State a safe frontier in rear of which the armies of the South could organize free from molestation. For the North, the State made the Tennessee line instead of the Ohio line the limit of the Southern advance and gave time for organization and for the ultimate occupation of Kentucky when the necessity should arise or the conditions prove favorable. When Tennessee officially seceded, the line had changed. Both sides became suspicious of Kentucky's real motives and purposes. Northern cities denounced Kentucky's neutrality as nothing more than a device of the secessionists for holding Tennessee border safe from invasion. The Southerners saw Kentucky's neutrality as "hypocritically and treacherously to deceive the Confederate States and allow the despot, Lincoln, to cover Kentucky soil with his mercenaries and from that cover to invade Tennessee." [131]

During the months of June and July, members of the Kentucky militia and State Guard left the state to enlist in either the Confederacy or the Union army. The men heading for the Union enlisted at Camp Clay, across the Ohio River from Newport, or at Camp Joe Holt, in Indiana. In Louisville the "Union Club" was formed which was a secret organization that raised over one thousand men and armed them with arms secretly purchased from Washington through the agency of Lieutenant William Nelson and Joshua Speed. Early in July Camp Boone was established for the Kentucky Confederate enlistments. Camp Boone was located in Montgomery, Tennessee, just over the Kentucky border. [132]

In July Camp Dick Robinson was established in Garrard County, by Brigadier General William Nelson, in direct violation of Kentucky's neutrality. This camp was to expedite Union recruiting in eastern Tennessee. Both Nelson and Garrett Davis worked for Adjutant General L. Thomas in recruiting Union troops. On July 1, 1861 Thomas wrote to Nelson to muster into service five regiments of infantry and one of cavalry in East Tennessee and one regiment of infantry in West Tennessee. The ordnance bureau would send ten thousand arms, six pieces of field artillery, two smooth bore and two rifle bore cannon and two mountain howitzers and ample supplies of ammunition to be carried through Kentucky into East Tennessee for the distribution among the Home Guards. He was also to muster into service three regiments of infantry from southwest Kentucky. On July 14, 1861 Nelson reported back to Nelson that he had appointed Speed Fry to be Colonel of the First regiment of infantry; Theophilus Garrard was made Colonel of the Second; Thomas Bramlette was made Colonel of the Third; and Frank Wolford was Lieutenant Colonel of the cavalry regiment. Thirty companies of infantry and five of cavalry would soon be raised. This was in direct violation of Kentucky's neutrality. [133]

Tilghman tried to remain neutral, but on July 5, 1861, he and his 4th Kentucky Infantry Regiment joined the Confederacy. Tilghman was made Colonel of the Third Kentucky Mounted Infantry, and A.P. Thompson was made Lieutenant Colonel. Colonel Ben Hardin Helm, Lincoln's brother-in-law, took over the Kentucky State Guard troops at Columbus, Kentucky. On July 23, 1861 Buckner also resigned from the State Guard and joined the Confederacy. Both Tilghman and Buckner tried to keep Kentucky neutral. General Buckner, Tilghman, and the rest of the Kentucky State Guard were assured by McClellan and President Lincoln that Kentucky's neutrality would be respected. When Buckner, Tilghman and the rest of the officers discovered that arms were being shipped to Kentucky and recruits were being raised within the State while the Kentucky State Guard could do nothing to enforce the neutrality, they followed their conscience and joined the Confederacy. That must have been a hard decision for Tilghman. He had fought for the Union in the Mexican War and knew that many of the men who had fought with him in Mexico would now be facing him in battle. But how could he support a government that lied when they said they were preserving Kentucky's neutrality and were going against the doctrine of states rights. The Kentucky Guard disbanded and its arms and ammunition were turned over to the Union Home Guard. On July 21, 1861 all Kentucky troops that were raised for the Confederacy were accepted by the Confederate Congress.

On August 19 Governor Magoffin asked Lincoln for the removal of Camp Dick Robinson, but the request was denied. Lincoln stated: "I do not believe it is the popular wish of Kentucky that this force shall be removed beyond their limits, and with this impression I must decline to so remove it." [134] Magoffin wrote to Confederate President Jefferson Davis telling him that a "military force has been enlisted and quartered by the United States authorities within this State." [135] He also wrote Davis that he had also written Lincoln and asked for the troops to be removed from Kentucky. He was worried about the build-up of Confederate troops along the Southern frontier. He wanted an assurance that the Confederate States would respect Kentucky's neutrality. Davis wrote Magoffin back on August 28, 1861 saying that the Confederacy "neither intends nor desires to disturb the neutrality of Kentucky. The assemblage of troops in Tennessee to which you refer had no other object than to repel the lawless invasion of that State by the forces of the United States, should their government attempt to approach it through Kentucky without respect for its position of neutrality." [136] He went on to say: "But neutrality to be entitled to respect must be strictly maintained between both parties; or it the door be opened on the one side to aggression of one of the belligerent parties upon the other, it ought not to be shut to the assailed when they seek to enter it for purposes of self defense." [137]

On August 16, the U.S. War Department established the Military Department of Kentucky, and native Kentuckians were put in command. Union General Robert Anderson, who had lost his command at Fort Sumter in April of 1861, was given command of the Department of the Cumberland, which consisted of Kentucky and Tennessee.

By early September the Union army made its move toward the occupation of Kentucky. Major General Robert Anderson moved his headquarters from Cincinnati to Louisville. William "Bull' Nelson was commissioned a Brigadier General. The troops raised at Camp Dick Robinson was placed under the command of Brigadier General George Thomas. The Union forces began a shift of troops from Cairo to Columbus, Kentucky. On September 2, 1861 Union troops occupied Belmont, Missouri across the river from Columbus. General Fremont put General Ulysses S. Grant in command of the forces in southeastern Missouri and made it known that he wanted to take Columbus, Kentucky, because it was a strategic location on the Mississippi river. Columbus was located on the Mississippi below the bluffs called "Iron Banks". The "Iron Banks" could command the river and the surrounding countryside for miles. Ships would have to slow down to get past the bend in the river which the "Iron Banks" commanded, and cannons could easily stop the traffic along that particular part of the Mississippi. [138]

On September 3, Confederate General Leonidas Polk ordered Confederate General Gideon Pillow to fortify Columbus, Kentucky, which violated Kentucky's neutrality and provided the North the justification to invade Kentucky. Polk justified his action by saying that the Union army had already broken Kentucky's neutrality. In a telegram sent to President Davis, Polk gave his reasons for invasion. Polk stated that he was invited in a letter by George Taylor of Columbus to enter Columbus. In the letter Taylor pointed out to Polk the reason why the citizens of Columbus needed the Confederate army. Taylor pointed out that the Yankees were the first to organize at Cairo, and it was understood that its objective and destination was down the Mississippi, to overrun Tennessee, and take possession of Memphis and finally march into New Orleans. Taylor also pointed out the incident of Captain M. H. Wright, who had organized a company of Rangers from Columbus for the purpose of drill, to learn camp life, and learn hunting. A squad of this company traveled ten miles up the river on the Kentucky side. Citizens reported their movement to the commander at Cairo, and the commander decided he would either capture them or kill them. Two hundred men landed at night and marched toward the encampment. The Rangers had already returned to Columbus the evening before and returned to their homes. Taylor saw this as a flagrant violation of Kentucky's neutrality. Taylor also related the story of an incident that occurred at Columbus. A Confederate flag was flying from a pole on the river bank. The steamer *City of Alton* from Cairo, came down to Columbus filled with troops and had several cannon on board. She ran into shore where the secession flag was flying and Colonel Prentiss demanded by whose authority was that flag placed there. He was told the secession flag had been erected by citizens of Columbus. He then ordered the flag to be taken down. He was told the Confederate flag would not be taken down by any citizen. He then said if the secession was not taken down immediately he would shoot the flag down. He was told to shoot the flag down. Three men came on shore and standing under the protection of the cannon and guns bearing in point blank range of the people on the shore and buildings, one of the men tore down the flag, and took it on board the boat, and was carried away. On August 23, 1861 the steamer W. B. Terry was seized by Captain Stembel, commander of the gunboat *U.S.S. Lexington*. At the time of capture the steamer *W. B. Terry* was in Paducah, Kentucky. Stembel justified his actions by saying that the *W.B. Terry* was running supplies for the Confederacy. The crew of the *Terry* and several other citizens seized the steamer *Samuel Orr*, from Evansville, Indiana as retribution for the illegal seizure of the *Terry*. [139]

On September 4, Governor Harris learned of Pillow's invasion into Kentucky and the seizure of Columbus. Harris was trying hard to get Kentucky into the Confederacy. He had just sent three Tennessee citizens to Frankfort, Kentucky as commissioners, in hopes to get the Kentucky government to side with the Confederacy. Harris immediately telegraphed Polk and Jefferson Davis to withdraw the troops.

The next day President Jefferson Davis told Secretary of War Leroy Walker to telegraph Polk to withdraw the troops from Kentucky and explain his actions. Davis sent a telegram to Harris telling him that the action was unauthorized. Polk sent a telegram back that he was not going to withdraw his troops. On September 4, Polk sent a telegram to Davis saying that he was keeping his troops in Kentucky. On September 5 Davis telegraphed Polk: "Your telegram received. The necessity must justify the action." It is of some interest to note that this statement can have several interpretations. It can mean the necessity does justify the action or the necessity had better justify the action. [140]

Later in the month of 1861, Polk recopied correspondence forwarded by Polk to the Confederate War Department The telegrams sent from Secretary of War Walker to Polk were falsely dated by Polk September 4; that from Davis to Polk also was falsely dated the 4th and altered to make President Davis' approval seem more emphatic and disguise the fact that such approval was given only after Polk's telegram of the 4th. Polk was clearly acting on his own and kept the President in the dark about his actions. [141]

The seizure of Columbus was a huge Confederate blunder. The invasion of Kentucky by the Confederates enraged Kentucky's legislature, as well as

Robert Dafford's mural of the Battle of Paducah, which occured on March 25, 1864. The mural can be seen on the flood wall in Paducah, Ky.

Governor Magoffin. The seizure of Columbus also alienated many citizens in Kentucky. The Confederates were viewed as the aggressors, offsetting whatever advantage Columbus may have had in providing the defense of the river-ways. On September 7, the House of Representatives of the Kentucky Legislature ordered the U.S. flag to be hoisted on the State Capitol, Frankfort, Kentucky. [142] The Confederate blunder at Columbus pointed out on the major flaws with President Jefferson Davis. Davis failed to keep tabs on the actions and intentions of Polk and Pillow. Davis's friendship with Polk had clouded his judgment. Davis could have salvaged the situation by ordering Polk to leave the state immediately and condemn the action, but instead, he allowed Polk to stay in the state. Davis continued to have faith in his old friend and kept Polk in his position. [143]

On that same day Brigadier General U. S. Grant, along with five thousand men from Fort Holt, which was located on the Kentucky shore opposite Cairo, Illinois, entered the city of Paducah. Grant said that when he entered the city Tilghman had left with his "Rebel Army". Grant took over the city without firing a gun. Grant goes on to say that "Before I landed, the secession flags had disappeared, and I ordered our flags to replace them. I found at the railroad depot a large number of complete rations and about two tons of leather, marked for the Confederate Army. Took possession of these...took possession of the telegraph office..I took possession of the railroad...I left two gunboats and one of the steamboats at Paducah, placed the post under command of General E. A. Paine...Last night I ordered the Eighth Missouri Volunteers..to reinforce General Paine at Paducah tonight." [144]

On 4th and Broadway in Paducah, a large Confederate flag was flying to welcome the supposed Confederate army that was on its way, but Grant's gunboats put a stop to all that. After the Union army entered the city of Paducah, it would not be long before the Union troops began to fortify the town. Construction began on Fort Anderson, named after Union General Robert Anderson, and was manned by five thousand Union troops. During his Mississippi River Campaign in 1863, Paducah would become an important city for Grant later in the war. The situation must have been difficult for the inhabitants of the town. Most of them supported the Confederacy cause, and the town was under the control of the Union army. Tilghman could no longer return to his house in Paducah for the rest of the war.

As the war progressed, the Union army dealt harshly toward those who supported the Confederacy or who supported the Confederate soldiers. Life also became difficult for the Jewish people of Paducah. On November 9, 1862, Grant wrote to Major General Stephen Hurlbut to "refuse all permits to come south of Jackson for the present, the Isrealites especially should be kept out." [145] On December 17, 1862 Grant wrote to the Assistant Secretary of War, C. P. Wolcott about his hatred for the Jewish people. He wrote:

I have long since believed that in spite of all the vigilance that can be infused into post commanders, the specie regulations of the Treasury Department have been violated, and that mostly by Jews and other unprincipled traders. So well satisfied that I have been of this that I instructed the commanding officer at Columbus to refuse all permits to Jews to come South, and I have frequently had them expelled from the department, but they come in with their carpet sacks in spite of all that can be done to prevent it. The Jews seem to be a privileged class that can travel everywhere. They will land at any wood-yard on the river and make their way through the country. If not permitted to buy cotton themselves, they will act as agents for someone else, who will be a military post with a Treasury permit to receive cotton and pay for it in Treasury notes which the Jew will buy up at an agreed rate, paying gold. There is but one way that I know of to reach this case; that is, for Government to buy all the cotton at a fixed rate and send it to Cairo, Saint Louis, or some other point to be sold. Than all trader (they are a curse to the army) might be expelled." [146]

On that same day Grant issued Proclamation Eleven, in which he ordered: "The Jews as a class violating every regulation of trade established by the

Treasury Department and departmental orders were hereby expelled from the department within twenty four hours of the receipt of this order." [147] Paducah and the surrounding area had a large Jewish population. The city was immediately made an example of. The Jewish people of Paducah were made to leave their homes and businesses without warrant or charge, and their homes and businesses were looted by Union soldiers. The Jewish people of Paducah were forced to head south. What prompted this hatred for the Jewish people is not clear, but it seems that Grant thought that they and the cotton speculators were one and the same. It was not long before a stop was put to Grant's policy of expelling the Jewish people from his department, including Paducah.

On January 21, 1863 General In Chief of all Union forces wrote to Grant: "It may be proper to give you some explanation of the revocation of your order expelling all Jews from your department. The President had no objection to your expelling traitors and Jew peddlers, which, I suppose, was the object of your order; but, as it in terms proscribed an entire religious class, some of whom are fighting in our ranks, the President deemed it necessary to revoke it." [148]

But the harassment of the poor city of Paducah would not stop there. On July 5, 1864, President Lincoln suspended the writ of habeas corpus and declared martial law in Kentucky. Union General Stephen Burbridge was made military governor of Kentucky. On July 19 Brigadier General Eleazer Paine took command over the city of Paducah, even though General Paine had committed atrocities against the civilians. On August 1, Paine levied a fine of 100,000 dollars upon each resident for the benefit of the Union soldiers living in Western Kentucky. On August 10, he banished a large number of residents to Canada for disloyalty. The group consisted mostly of women, children, and old people. When they were arrested their property was seized. While Paine was in command of Paducah, he allowed and committed a variety abuses including murder, robbery, rape, and vandalism of property. He also extorted fees and permits that changed daily against any citizen. Paine was guilty of using the elderly, the crippled, and the infirm to do hard manual labor unless they were able to pay the fees each day. [149] Luckily for the people of Paducah, General Paine was replaced on September 8, 1864.

After Grant entered the city of Paducah on September 6, Tilghman was located twenty four miles outside of the city with two thousand Confederates. Paine feared that Tilghman, along with General Pillow, would march on Paducah, and asked for reenforcements. Union General C. F. Smith arrived with reinforcements in Paducah and began to build defensive works, and moved on the garrison at Smithland, which was located on the mouth of the Cumberland. [150]

On September 11, the legislature demanded that the Confederate troops must leave Kentucky. The Union troops were allowed to stay. The Governor saw his State quickly swaying to the Union cause and breaking his precious naive neutrality.

On September 15, Confederate General Albert Sidney Johnston arrived in Nashville, Tennessee. He had resigned his commission in the old army and the command of the department of the Pacific at San Francisco. He was assigned by the Confederacy to command Department No. 2 which embraced the States of Tennessee, Arkansas, and that part of the State of the Mississippi west of New Orleans, Jackson, and Great Northern and Central Railroad; also the military operations in Kentucky, Missouri and Kansas, and the Indian country immediately west of Missouri and Arkansas. Johnston appointed Buckner as Brigadier General. He was assigned to command the forces at Camp Trousdale and Camp Boone. [151]

On September 16, 1861, Tilghman was sent to the State line and was to secure the telegraph operator, and prevent the evening train from escaping to Louisville. He was to connect the two tracks from Louisville to Camp Boone, which was the training ground for the Kentucky Confederate troops. [152]

Three days later, on September 18, the Kentucky legislature passed resolutions which constituted a declaration of war on the Confederacy. The resolutions passed over the veto of Governor Magoffin. On that same day on September 18, General Buckner led his four thousand five hundred troops to occupy Bowling Green. He also sent five hundred men to Munfordville, Kentucky, instructing them to build fortifications around the city. Buckner told the citizens of Bowling Green that his force was to help the government of Kentucky in carrying out their neutrality and that the city was to be used only as a defensive position. Buckner pointed out that the Union government had already broken Kentucky's neutrality by setting up recruitment stations and camps, and President Lincoln's support of these Union troops meant that he ignored Kentucky's neutrality. He pointed out that the Confederate troops support the Constitution and that the President does not since he had declared martial law, and suspended the writ of habeas corpus, making Lincoln a tyrant in Buckner's eyes.

In Columbus, Kentucky, Confederate General Leonidas Polk began to build trenches, some becoming fifteen feet deep. He also placed one hundred and forty cannons from the bluff top to the river's edge, built sandbag strong points and planted land mines and torpedoes or water mines. He also laid a tremendous heavy chain across the river to stop the ships trying to sail down the Mississippi. General Albert S. Johnston arrived on September 18 to inspect the progress of the fortifications at Columbus.

By September 23, Tilghman had reached Columbus, Kentucky. He was ordered to Columbus by Buckner. Tilghman was under the impression that there would be arms waiting for his men, but when he arrived in Columbus, there were none. Tilghman wrote to General Albert Sidney Johnston on September 23, 1861, that "not a single gun can be procured, of any sort, under any circumstances. The brigade numbers near 3,000 men, about one sixth badly armed. The brigade is in advance...and the want of arms has a most demoralizing effect on the men. A failure to arm us promptly will act ruinously on our friends in Kentucky." [153] Tilghman had heard that there were 8,500 Enfield rifles arriving in Savannah, Georgia. He asked General Johnston if these weapons could be sent to his men. Tilghman sent some of his men, and Major Boyd to Nashville, Tennessee, and ordered 2,500 arms from Savannah. Colonel Trabue who was in Nashville informed Tilghman that he was to take his men to Camp Trousdale and call upon the quartermaster, commissary, and ordnance officer for supplies. [154]

Johnston covered a wide area with his troops in Kentucky. His left rested at Columbus, Bowling Green as his center, and the Cumberland Gap on the right, which was seized by Confederate General Zollicoffer. Johnston faced many problems in holding this line. He had no direct communication by rail between the center and either wing and no possibility of rapidly concentrating his forces. Polk had only ten thousand men and was being confronted by Union General Ulysses S. Grant at Paducah and Cairo, and the east side of the Mississippi, along with a large force under General John Fremont. At Bowling Green, General Buckner had fewer than five thousand men and worried about the large force of Union troops assembling in Louisville, under General Don Carlos Buell. General Felix Zollicoffer, with five thousand men, faced Union General George Thomas's large force. [155]

By the end of September the Kentucky legislature ordered the Governor to call for forty thousand troops for service. He was also allotted 1,500 sharpshooters and five hundred cavalrymen and scouts. Governor Magoffin vetoed the act, but the bill was passed over his veto. All these troops would be used for the Union Army. The Kentucky legislature wanted the Confederates out of their state, and Kentucky was quickly becoming an armed showdown. Skirmishes were already breaking out between Buckner's forces and the Home Guard. Skirmishes broke out at Barbourville, Grayson, Lucas Bend, Buffalo Hill, and Smithland. The bridge over the Rolling Fork River and locks at Green River were destroyed by Buckner. [156]

On October 1, the Kentucky legislature made it a felony for a Kentuckian to join the Confederate Army, which was planning to invade the state. Recruiting and enlistment in the Confederacy was classified as high misdemeanors. [157]

On October 4, Buckner informed Polk at Columbus that fourteen thousand Union troops were attempting to cross the Green River and were planning to attack the Confederate defensive line. Reinforcements arrived with General William Hardee. Hardee informed Johnston, who was still at Columbus, that the Union troops were heading for Elizabethtown, and asked for Johnston to return to Bowling Green. Johnston immediately reorganized the army in Kentucky into two divisions under Buckner and Hardee. Hardee's division was sent to Munfordville, which was eighteen miles from Bowling Green. Johnston hoped that Hardee's activity along his defensive line would give the Union army an exaggerated idea of how large his army really was and be seen as a threat of attack. [158] The plan worked. But Johnston was forming tunnel vision in his mission in Kentucky. He only focused on Columbus and Bowling Green, while ignoring the Tennessee and Cumberland Rivers. Johnston had sent for Major Jeremy Gilmer to help him build a second defensive line at Nashville. If the Union army seized the Tennessee and Cumberland Rivers both Bowling Green and Columbus would be outflanked, but Johnston failed to realize this flaw in his line.

During the spring and summer, Union Commander John Rodgers and Commander Roger Stembel, Lieutenant S. L. Phelps, and Mr. James Eads built, manned and equipped three wooden gun boats, and named them the Tyler, the Lexington, and the Conestoga. Most were equipped with thirty-two pounders. These three gunboats quickly took control of the rivers above Columbus. On October 12, 1861, the St. Louis was launched at Carondelet, near St. Louis, and became the first of seven iron clad gunboats ordered by the Government. Pook's Turtles was the nickname given to seven iron clad Union gunboats designed by Samuel M. Pook to operate on the Mississippi River and its tributaries. On August 7, 1861, the War Department contracted with James Eads to construct the vessels and have them ready for their crews in sixty-five days. Eads employed Thomas Merritt as engine designer. Within two weeks, more than four thousand people in seven states were employed in the construction of the boats, cutting trees for lumber, building twenty-one steam engines and thirty-five boilers, and rolling the iron armor. Four were built at Carondelet, near St. Louis, Missouri, and three in Mound City, Illinois. The gunboats, which cost $89,000 each, were called "city class" because they were named after cities on western rivers. Besides the *St. Louis*, there were the *Carondelet, Cincinnati, Louisville, Mound City, Cairo*, and *Pittsburgh*. Each round-nosed, flat-bottomed vessel weighed 512 tons, was 175 feet long and 51.5 feet wide and drew only six feet of water. Plated with 2.5 inch thick iron, the gunboats had flat sides, with front and rear casemates sloping at a 25 degree angle, and carried thirteen heavy guns each, both rifled and smoothbore. Propelled by a stern paddle wheel that was completely covered by the rear casemate, the coal powered Pook Turtles proved to be underpowered and cumbersome, but also very deadly. The Turtles were manned by sailors of the regular navy, volunteers, detailed army personnel and contracted civilians. Later the *Benton* and *Essex* would be added to the Union ironclad fleet. Flag Officer Andrew Foote arrived in St. Louis on September 6th and assumed command of the Western flotilla. These seven gunboats and three wooden gunboats would soon play a major role in the Union army's upcoming campaign to take the river ways. [159]

On October 16, the Confederate Secretary of War, Judah Benjamin wrote to General Johnston, whose headquarters was in Bowling Green, that the supplies in Nashville were for the troops in Virginia. Benjamin told Johnston that he should no longer rely upon Nashville for his supplies, and that he should buy his arms in Kentucky. He also told Johnston to stop calling on Mississippi and other states in the Confederacy for men. General Polk, who was in command of Columbus, was instructed to call upon Arkansas and Tennessee only. He also chastised Johnston for taking brigades from Mississippi. Benjamin informed Johnston that this was against the Laws of Secession. He was to take only regiments. Benjamin also attacked Johnston for forming Buckner and Hardee into two divisions. He reminded Johnston that the President alone had the power to form regiments into brigades and divisions. Benjamin also was brought to the attention of General Johnston as to who should command as brigadier general over Columbus, Kentucky. Johnston recommended Major A. P. Stewart. Benjamin recommended Lloyd Tilghman. Benjamin said that Tilghman's "rank and experience greatly outweigh those of Major Stewart, and whom we could not pass by without injustice." [160] Tilghman's "record shows longer and better service, and who is, besides, as a Kentuckian, especially appropriate to the command of Columbus. He has therefore been appointed Brigadier General." Benjamin also apologized for the delay in arms, and said that he would order four thirty-two pounders for Bowling Green as soon as possible. Johnston's pleas for help were going unheaded. President Jefferson Davis had full confidence in his old friend Johnston, but even Johnston could have not been able to work miracles in procuring men and supplies. Davis did not realize the extent of the need in the Western Theater. Davis' proximity to the Virginia front of war caused him to lose perspective on the war as a whole. [161]

Also on October 16, a Union conference was held in Louisville. In attendance were U.S. Secretary of War Simon Cameron, Adjutant General L. Thomas, General William T. Sherman, General Wood, and James Guthrie, the mayor of Louisville. Sherman had replaced General Robert Anderson. Sherman told Cameron that the arms sent to Kentucky had been given to the Home Guard, and could not be recovered. Recruitment for Union soldiers was poor and the young men of Kentucky were mostly pro-Southern, while the aged and "conservative" would not enlist to fight their own relatives who had joined the Confederate side. Guthrie pointed out to Sherman that Kentucky's defense would have to be left to the Union free states of the Northwest, not to its own citizens. Garrett Davis wrote to Sherman asking for troops. Sherman quickly became frustrated with the conditions in Kentucky and wrote to Garrett Davis: "I am forced into the command of this department against my will, and it would take three hundred thousand men to fill half the calls for troops." Although Johnston had only a small army to confront the Union army, it was plain to see that the Union army had problems of its own. [162]

Colonel Tilghman arrived at Camp Boone, near Clarksville, Tennessee, where he was promoted to Brigadier General on October 18, 1861. A.P. Thompson was promoted to Colonel of the Third Kentucky Regiment on the same day. Tilghman was then sent to Hopkinsville, Kentucky where he trained three thousand men, although getting arms for these men was a massive undertaking. Tilghman was so desperate for arms that he spent his own money. On October 11, he bought a light battery for $1,200 dollars, and a stand of first class small arms, which cost him four hundred and ninety two dollars. He asked Johnston to refund the amount that he had spent on the arms. [163]

Hopkinsville and Clarksville were on the western rivers and were very important areas because of their iron industry. The limonite or brown hematite ore was shipped to Clarksville, Nashville, or to Ohio. The Clarksville Iron Works made small arms, and the foundry of Whitfield, Bradley and Company made cannons and shells. Seventeen furnaces in Kentucky produced 42,500 tons of iron per year. According to J. P. Lesley, Secretary of American Iron Association, there were thirty-nine furnaces, thirteen forges, and three rolling mills in an area northwest from Nashville in the lower Cumberland Valley. Unfortunately the true nature of the importance of these iron producing areas were lost on not only Johnston but also the national and state leaders. The area was used for training of Confederate troops, but the full potential of producing iron to make weapons and black powder, which was desperately needed by Johnston, was not utilized and the towns went unprotected. [164]

On October 21, 1861 General Zollicoffer attacked the Federals at Camp Wild Cat in the Rockcastle Hills where he lost eleven killed and forty two wounded. He fell back but the Union troops also fell back to Lancaster, abandoning property and spreading dismay throughout central Kentucky. [165].

On October 22, 1861, Albert Sidney Johnston responded to Judah Benjamin's letter written on October 16, 1861. Johnston said that he would comply with Benjamin's orders and not order any more supplies from Nashville. Johnston told Benjamin that procuring supplies from Kentucky was a very difficult task. The farmers in Kentucky would only take gold or Kentucky paper currency for their goods, and that they would not accept the money that Johnston had which was Tennessee and Confederate currency. Johnston thought that he should go ahead and furnish a supply depot for his troops in Nashville, and set up a fund just for that purpose. Johnston agreed that Tilghman should command the fort at Columbus. He also told Benjamin that he was only requesting troops from Tennessee, Mississippi, and Arkansas. He also denied accepting a brigade. Johnston noticed that the Kentuckians were passive if not apathetic. He noticed that there were thousands of friends to the South in Kentucky, but there was no need for action among them. Johnston also said that the Kentucky legislature was against the South and the political relations had soured when Johnston and his troops entered Kentucky, and that there was no longer any obligation for the State of Kentucky to remain neutral. The Kentucky legislature had passed a law for the expulsion of the Confederates in the State. Johnston's pleas for help from Richmond were falling on deaf ears. Johnston had 23,000 poorly armed troops and had a defensive line that stretched for 150,000 square miles. Nashville was Johnston's only hope for supplies. Nashville made cannons, swords, percussion caps, uniforms, muskets, revolvers, powder. Warehouses were bursting at the seams with supplies, but the supplies were being transported away from Johnston's troops and shipped to Virginia. Nashville was the only supply for black powder for Johnston's men. Johnston was fighting an uphill battle. The Kentuckians did not support his troops, his supplies were cut off from Nashville, and when he did try to buy supplies, the people of Kentucky would only accept gold or Kentucky money. [166]

While Johnston was having problems supplying and forming troops in Kentucky, Grant had formed his command under McClernand, Oglesby, W. H. L. Wallace, John Cook, and Plummer. His regiments consisted of the 7th, 8th 10th, 11th, and 22nd Illinois Infantry, the 2nd Illinois cavalry, the 7th and 10th Iowa, 11th Missouri, as well as Schwartz's, Taylor's and MacAllister's batteries.

On October 23, 1861, Tilghman arrived at Hopkinsville, Kentucky. He found it in horrible condition. The Confederate troops were without proper clothes and in short supply. On October 27, 1861, he wrote a letter to General Albert Sidney Johnston that stated "a vast deal of suffering exists, owing to the condition of the men. I have made arrangements for 200 women to work on clothing, and hope for a better contribution of blankets and clothing from the society at this place." [167] He also mentions that "I am sorry to hear about the inefficient condition of things at Fort Donelson." [168] He also made a plea for "artillery, wagons, mules, harness, forage, and horses for artillery commands." [169]

Fort Donelson was one mile from Dover, Tennessee. The hill rose seventy five to one hundred feet above the river. It was surrounded by deep gullies. Several roads linked the fort with the town of Dover and led to other middle Tennessee towns on the river and the railroad. Brigadier General Daniel Donelson chose a site for another fort twelve miles west of the Dover fort and on the east bank of the Tennessee River. On June 9th Major Bushrod Johnson arrived at Dover and selected Donelson's original site at Kirkman's Old Landing. He selected Fort Henry. Colonel Adolphus Heiman's 10th Tennessee began work on Henry and Heiman. Johnston had ordered Lieutenant Joseph Dixon, an engineer at Columbus, to visit both forts. Johnston would never visit the forts personally.

59

While Tilghman was still in command at Hopkinsville, he wrote a letter to Colonel W. W. Mackall, Assistant Adjutant General at Bowling Green, on October 29, 1861. Tilghman reported that conditions had gotten worse at Hopkinsville. Tilghman said that the camp was one big hospital. "Over one half the entire command are on the sick list with very types of different diseases....The measles have made their appearance, and the battalion will average 20 new cases per day...The morning brigade report...shows only 716 for duty out of a total of 2,237." [170]

Equipment and supplies were no better for his men. Tilghman reported only 376 men, one third of whom are armed, and with no equipment. Cavalry was non existent, with only Meriwether's company of untutored recruits. Captain Huey's company of cavalry was completely unarmed. As for artillery, there was not even an organized squad for a single gun. There were only five pieces of artillery; two six-pounders, two nine-pounders, one twelve-pounder, all of which were unfit for service because of the terrible manner in which they were mounted. The carriages were poorly constructed. As for clothing, the conditions had not improved. Tilghman wrote to Johnston "I have no force with which to operate in any direction, and our people are greatly suffering terribly within the lines assigned to me for my operations. The defenses of the Cumberland cannot, I believe be perfected, unmolested, unless my position is strengthened for this purpose." [171] Tilghman was also worried that the Union forces knew that he was unmanned, and he asked for reenforcements as soon as possible. He mentioned that the enemy had already made a movement at Henderson, Kentucky. Tilghman was afraid that the 50,000 hogs in Hopkinsville could be taken and requested five hundred cavalry to protect them. He also asked for trained graduates of artillery. He also requested artillery and infantry supports as soon as possible. [172]

On October 30, 1861, Powhatan Ellis, Jr., Assistant Adjutant General for Tilghman, wrote to Colonel Mackall that a Union force was assembling on the Green River, and that they planned to move on Madisonville. Tilghman could not write the letter himself because he was too ill. [173]

On October 31, Major General Leonidas Polk wrote to Colonel Mackall informing him that a commander of "large experience and military efficiency (be) put in charge of the defenses of the Tennessee and the Cumberland Rivers." Polk said that if these two rivers were taken by the Yankees, the result would be disastrous for the Confederates in Kentucky. Polk recommended that Tilghman should be put in charge of the defenses. Even though Polk was in command of Columbus, he knew the dangers that were present if the Tennessee and Cumberland Rivers were seized. The route to Nashville, Tennessee's state capital, and Middle Tennessee would be open for invasion and that this would lead to a direct invasion of northern Mississippi and Alabama. [174]

On that same day, Tilghman reported that Union forces in Ashbysburg were strengthening and that the Union forces were north of his current position.

During the last week of October the Union gunboat *Conestoga* was reported moving upstream on the Cumberland River. Colonel Nathan Bedford Forrest who was camped at Fort Donelson, was ordered to move to the Cumberland and watch for the boat's arrival. General Tilghman had been made commander of the defenses of the Cumberland and Tennessee rivers, and he ordered Forrest to report with his command to Hopkinsville, Kentucky. While in Hopkinsville, Forrest was to patrol the south bank of the Ohio between the Cumberland and Tennessee Rivers. Forrest's regiments proceeded as far as Princeton where Major D. C. Kelly was detached with a squadron to intercept a steam transport boat that was due to pass on the Ohio River the next day. Major Kelly captured this boat and obtained large quantities of coffee, sugar, blankets, and other army stores for the Confederates. Meanwhile the *Conestoga* was headed for Canton where the Confederates had a store of army clothing. Colonel Forrest with his entire regiment marched to Canton. The *Conestoga* came into view just as they arrived on the scene. Forrest had a four-pounder cannon and placed it into position in a thicket that occupied a commanding point above the river. The *Conestoga* anchored at the Canton landing, but after a half hour it pulled back a few hundred yards, and prepared to make an attack, and opened fire of grapeshot and canister. Forrest's men fired into the open ports at close range, with accuracy that forced the Union gunboat to close her gun ports and fall back. As the *Conestoga* pulled out of sight, Forrest returned to Hopkinsville. [175]

On November 1, Tilghman was ordered by Johnston to fall back to Clarksville, Tennessee. Tilghman arrived with a battery under Maury, and Col. Nathan Bedford Forrest's cavalry would be waiting for him. Johnston ordered Tilghman to build defensive works as soon as possible. Col. Gregg's Texas regiment was to cover Tilghman's movement into Clarksville, Tennessee. Tilghman's mission was ordered to protect the valuable railway in Clarksville, Tennessee. [176]

The next day on November 2, 1861, Tilghman wrote to General Simon Buckner, commanding the Kentucky Division, that Union forces were moving through Hopkinsville and that they had obstructed the Ingram's Shoals. Union Lieutenant Phelps and the gunboat *Conestoga* led a raiding party against a Confederate camp near Eddyville, Kentucky. Tilghman reported that he managed only to assemble four hundred men and two pieces of artillery to prepare for an attack from the approaching Union forces. But Tilghman did not have to engage the Union forces, the Union force had turned off from Princeton and were moving north. Tilghman said that his army was "one of the poorest clad, shod, and armed body of men I ever saw, but full of enthusiasm." The surgeon had found the army so unfit for service that he begged that the infantry should not go. [177]

On November 3, 1861, Major J. F. Gilmer, Chief Engineer of the Western Department, wrote to General A. S. Johnston, who was now in Nashville, Tennessee, outlining the changes and improvements that needed to be made on the Cumberland River. He recommended that the "Red River, which empties into the Cumberland just below Clarksville, to be strengthened. The fords, one near Hopkinsville Bridge, one just above the mouth of West Fork, one below the Russellville Bridge, and one a few miles above the last named bridge, should be destroyed, by felling trees.

Once the fords had been obstructed, the two turnpikes bridges and the railroad bridge over the Red River should be guarded by two encampments, one just south of the Hopkinsville Bridge, the other between the railroad bridge and the Russellville Bridge. Field pieces should be placed so as to sweep these bridges, or at least the approaches to them. He recommended that wooden platforms be built for the cannons, and that breastworks should be constructed. The high ground just north of Red River and to the left of the Hopkinsville turnpike should be occupied by Confederate troops.

For the defenses of the Cumberland River below Clarksville, they should be at least extended as far down as Fort Donelson. Their efforts for resisting gunboats should be concentrated there. To obstruct the Cumberland River below Donelson, old barges and fiats should be sunk at Ingram's Shoals, a few miles above Eddyville, and at Line Island, three miles below Line Port. "[178] Tilghman was instructed by Gilmer to obstruct the fords at once and establish the camps for guarding the bridges.

On November 6, Tilghman received a Texas Battalion of infantry, under Colonel John Gregg. Tilghman was glad to receive the infantry supports, but still needed cavalry. Private Cyrus Love, of Captain Moody's Company, Colonel Gregg's Texas Infantry Regiment, wrote home on November 6, 1861 from Camp Alcorn at Hopkinsville, Kentucky that his regiment was ordered from Memphis to Clarksville. They traveled by steamboat down the Cumberland to Clarksville. The next day they arrived at Hopkinsville. He wrote: "this post is commanded by Gen. Tilman-I have seen him and his conduct together with his reputation here indicates that he is the right kind of a man." He goes on to say of Tilghman "there is a strong enough force here now to cause Gen. Tilman to feel confident that he will be able to whip any number of the enemy that can come against him. "[179] The Texas Battalion was in as sad shape as the rest of the units in Tilghman's command. Gregg pointed out to Mackall that the nine companies comprising the battalion were full of sick men. The battalion was also poorly armed. Captain Van Zandt's company had only thirteen double barrel shotguns and sixteen rifles in good working order. They also had nine double barrel shotguns and twenty-five rifles that were in need of repair. Captain

Granbury's company had no guns at all. Captain W. B. Hill's company had nineteen double barrel shotguns and eight rifles in good working conditions, but had twenty rifles and fourteen double barrel shotguns in disrepair. Captain Smith's company had sixty nine muskets in good condition but no equipment. Captain Jack Davis company had sixteen rifles, (three were broken), and sixteen double-barrel shotguns, (two which were broken). Captain R. S. Camp's company had only one musket, twenty-seven double barrel shotguns and eleven rifles, all in working order. They also had thirty-one double barrel shotguns and rifles, and twelve other types of guns. Captain William Moody's company had three muskets, thirteen double-barrel shotguns, and twenty six rifles, all in good order. It must have been a quartermaster's nightmare to try and equip all these different types of rifles, muskets, and shotguns. [180]

Tilghman told Mackall that conditions still had not improved at Clarksville. Tilghman had seven hundred and fifty sick men. Tilghman requested Lyon and Anderson to be sent to him to help with training of the recruits. He also requested Adams and Captain Woodward's cavalry. He was also short of cannons and still requested more. He wanted permission to draw upon the supply warehouses at Nashville and Memphis. He requested "clothing, money, and unless the depots can supply me with clothing I will have my own quartermaster to have them made. I need funds for quartermaster's department for purchase of wagons, mules, harness, forage, and horses for artillery commands...I need supplies from ordnance departments, such as sabers and pistols. [181]

On November 7, Tilghman sent a small cavalry force to Ashbysburg to stop the Yankees from attacking the Rebel forces in the surrounding areas. Tilghman mentioned that a gunboat had passed him on the way to Dover, and was firing on Fort Donelson.

By November 7, conditions at Fort Donelson were horrible. Senator G.A. Henry reported that Donelson demanded immediate attention. There were only eight hundred cavalry and only five hundred infantry. There were not even enough men to form a regiment. The guns at Donelson were unprotected, and would remain that way if someone did not take command and push the work to completion. Henry also pointed out that gunboats were making it past the sunk barges. The sunk barges were completely useless as a blockade.

On November 6, Grant with 3,114 men, made ready to attack Belmont, a key Confederate stronghold, defended by heavy guns and a huge garrison. Grant and his men left their camp at Cairo, Illinois and boarded transport boats for the trip to Missouri. Grant landed his men just north of the hamlet of Belmont, and found himself facing a Confederate force of 5,000 men, 2,330 manning the garrison and Gideon Pillow's 2,300 men. Polk learned of the Union force shortly after daybreak. Polk ordered Pillow's division to move to support Colonel Tappan, who was in command of the force at Belmont, with only four regiments. Colonel Russell, Colonel Wright, Colonel Pickett, and Colonel Freeman's regiments of Tennessee troops were sent. Colonel Tappan had the 13th Arkansas, Captain Beltzhoover's Watson Battery, and a squadron of Lieutenant Colonel Miller's battalion of cavalry. Grant's men attacked Belmont at 8:30 AM, November 7th, 1861. Polk expected an attack to come from the Columbus side of the river. General McCown had charge of the left flank, and moved a long range battery under Captain R. A. Stewart, of the Louisiana Point Coupee Battery. At the fort in Columbus, the heavy siege battery, under Capt. Hamilton opened a heavy fire upon the Yankees. The cannon fire was returned. After half an hour, the boats were driven up the river. But the Union boats again dropped down and renewed the cannonade. This artillery duel continued for an hour, and again the Union boats had to fall back. [182]

At 10:20 A.M. the Yankees advance guard began to fire upon the pickets, and within forty minutes the entire Union force had arrived to the scene. Pillow sent for help. Polk sent him Colonel Knox Walker's regiment and a section of artillery. Captain Beltzhoover's battery had ceased firing from the lack of ammunition, and the Yankees began to fire with a heavy battery. The battery never made it to the opposite shore, because there were no stage planks to unload the guns onto the shore. Capt. Polk's battery was landed, but was too late for the battle. [183]

Colonel Carroll and Colonel Mark regiments were sent forward. Colonel Marks was ordered by Polk to land his regiment higher up the river, with a flank movement. General Pillow ordered Colonel Russell with his brigade to support the flank movement. The Confederate troops were falling back at Belmont. Polk ordered further reinforcements. General Cheatham, with the First brigade, under Colonel Preston Smith was ordered down to the transports, which they boarded and headed for Belmont. The Yankees soon set the camp tents on the Belmont side on fire, and the Union batteries were advancing near the river bank and opening fire on the Confederate transport ships. The Confederate boats Prince, the Charm, the Hill, and the Kentucky were transporting 2,000 troops across. Polk ordered Captain Smith's Mississippi battery to the river bank, opposite the battle, and to open fire on the Yankees. Polk also ordered Major A. P. Stewart to open the guns at the fort to fire down on the Yankees. The fire was so heavy that Grant and his troops had to fall back to his transport ships. Grant then ran into Colonel Marks and then General Cheatham in his flanks. [184]

Polk arrived on the field and ordered Captain White's company of Lieutenant Colonel Logwood's battalion of cavalry, across the river, with two regiment of General McCown's division to follow. On landing General Pillow and Cheatham met Polk. Polk ordered them to push the Yankees to their boats. The route over which Polk passed was strewn with the dead and wounded from the battle between Col. Marks and General Cheatham and Grant. [185]

Left: *General Lloyd Tilghman in his Confederate General's uniform.*

Below: *Lithograph by Seth Wilmarth. Early steam engines, such as this 4-4-0, dominated the railroads during the time that Lloyd Tilghman was an engineer in Paducah, Ky. (Dec. 57 American Heritage Magazine)*

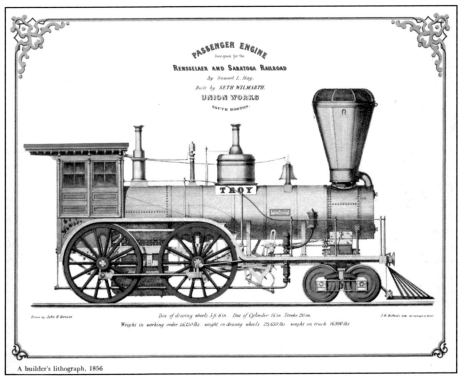

PASSENGER ENGINE
Designed for the
RENSSELAER AND SARATOGA RAILROAD
By Samuel L. Hay.
Built by SETH WILMARTH.
UNION WORKS
SOUTH BOSTON.

TROY

Dia. of driving wheels 5 ft. 6 in.   Dia. of Cylinder 16 in.   Stroke 20 in.
Weight in working order 46,150 lbs.   weight on driving wheels 29,650 lbs.   weight on truck 16,800 lbs.

A builder's lithograph, 1856

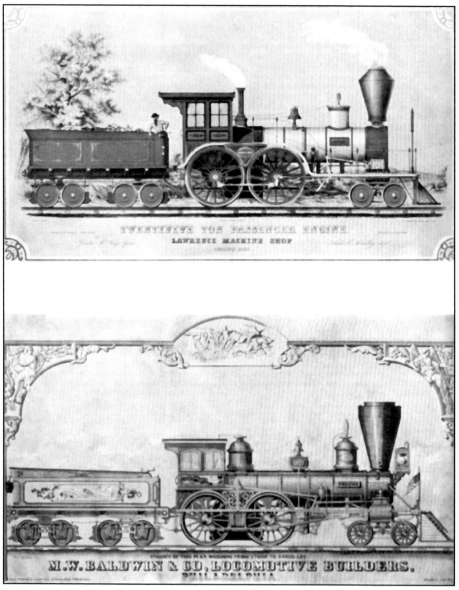

During the early history of steam engines, the 4-4-0 trains were brightly decorated. The <u>Lawrence</u> was constructed in 1853; the <u>Wyoming</u> was constructed by Richard Norris & Son of Philadelphia in 1857. (Dec. 57 American Heritage Magazine)

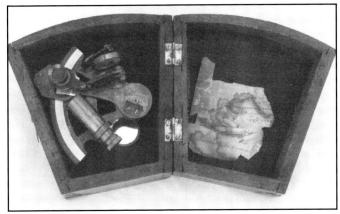

Top: Sextants used by the Navy during the Civil War. (The Civil War Battles of the Western Theater Museum, photo by Bryan Bush)
Middle: Octant, which was a navigational instrument used by the Navy. (The CWBWT Museum, photo by Bryan Bush)

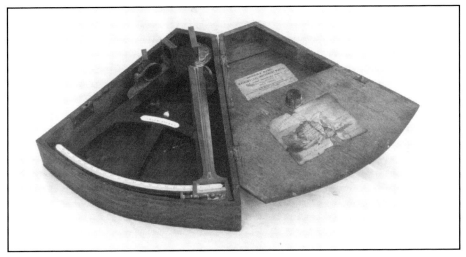

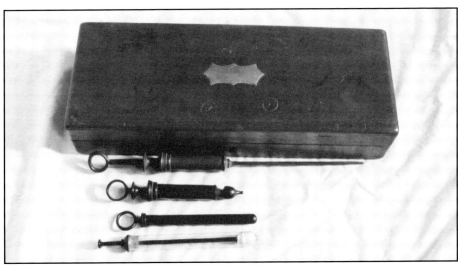

Top: *Painting of the U.S.S. Cairo (American Heritage Magazine)*

Bottom: *Wash drawing of the U.S.S. Benton by F. Muller (U.S. Naval Historical*

Bottom Left: *Medical kit containing syringes, used by Surgeon William R. Seamans. Seamans was a surgeon aboard the* U.S.S. Louisville, *a city class iron clad, which was a part of the Mississippi Squadron. The ship was built in 1862 and participated in the battle of Fort Donelson, the siege of Island No. 10, the battle of Memphis, the engagement with the* C.S.S. Arkansas, *bombardment of Drumgould's Bluff, Yazoo River, December 1862, capture of Fort Hindman, January 1863, expedition of Steele's Bayou, Miss., March 1863, ran past the batteries at Vicksburg, Miss., April 1863, bombardment of Grand Gulf, Miss., April 1863, Red River Campaign, March through May 1864, and patrolled the Mississippi until the end of the war. (The CWBWT*

U.S.S. Cairo

U.S.S. Cincinnatti (U.S. Naval Historical Center)

69

U.S.S. St. Louis (US NHC)

U.S.S. Lexington (US NHC)

U.S.S. Tyler (US NHC)

Confederate Gen. Lloyd Tilghman's model 1850 Foot Officers Sword with brass mounted leather scabbard (The CWBWT Museum, photo by Bryan Bush)

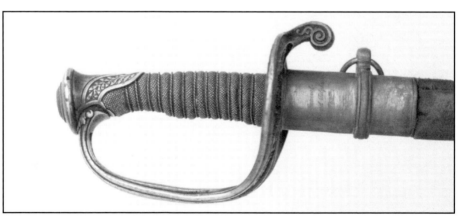

Confederate Gen. Lloyd Tilghman's model 1850 Foot Officers Sword. Inscribed on the scabbard is "General Lloyd Tilghman '62'". (The CWBWT Museum, photo by Bryan Bush)

Close up of the inscription on Confederate Gen. Lloyd Tilghman's sword

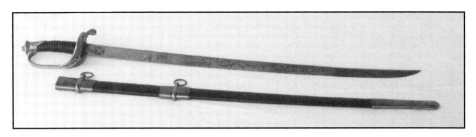

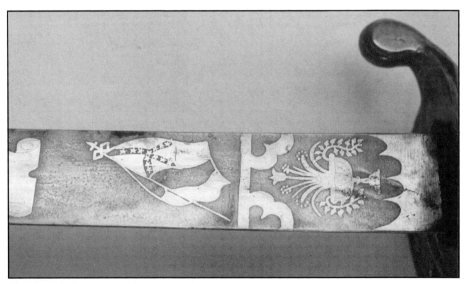

For description see caption on next page

LLOYD TILGHMAN

Col. Albert P. Thompson

**Previous page top, middle,
bottom and right:**

Confederate Officers Sword presented to General Lloyd Tilghman by Colonel Albert
P. Thompson and the men of the 3rd Kentucky Infantry, C.S.A. This sword was
manufactured by an as yet unidentified Confederate maker. It has leather wrapped
wood grips and brass pommel cap, knuckle bow and guard. The guard has a fancy,
pierced, floral design. The 30 inch curved and completely flat blade was hand forged
without a fuller and has an eight inch false edge. The iron tang is forge welded to the
steel blade. The blade is etched in stylized relief rhythms of a flowering floral unit and
detail has been added with hand chasing. Also etched and chased on the blade is a
soldier firing a musket, a cannon mounted on a fort/naval type carriage, a block letter
C.S.A. inside a panel, a Confederate battle flag in on a standard which is topped by a
raptor, wreath, and battle axes, the 2nd national flag, a scalloped panel containing an
urn which holds cotton plants, the Confederate motto "Deo Vindice" contained within
a half wreath of laurel leaves and an 18 line presentation that reads: "Presented to
my good friend and comrade, Colonel Lloyd Tilghman C.S.A. A citizen and soldier
of the first order, by A.P. Thompson C.S.A. and the men of the 3rd Kentucky Regt. of
Inf. 1863." The scabbard is back stitched leather over wood with brass mountings.
All brass on sword and scabbard has a high tin/zinc content and all metal parts are
marked with the Roman numeral X. (Courtesy of the late Lyle Sloan, photo by Elvin

74

Rear Admiral George W. Sumner, U.S.N. - The Honorable J.W. Jewett of Kentucky appointed George Sumner to the U.S. Naval Academy on September 20, 1858. He graduated on July 1862. His first duty station was on the gunboat U.S.S. Colorado *off the coast of Florida to patrol for blockade runners. He was assigned to the* U.S.S. Massasoit *in August 1864 and served on the ship until the end of the war. He continued to serve in the navy and participated in the Spanish-American War in 1898 and retired from service on December 31, 1903 with the rank of Rear Admiral. He died in 1924. (The CWBWT Museum, photo by Bryan Bush)*

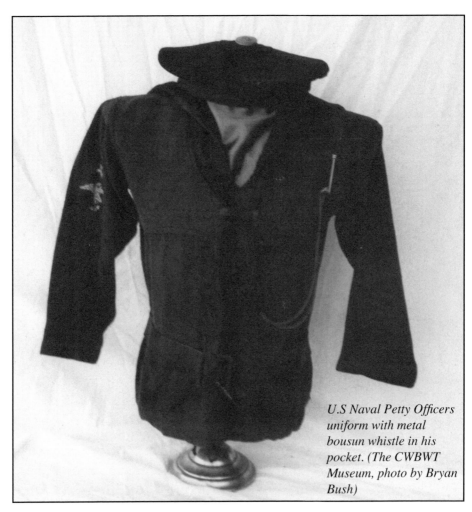

U.S Naval Petty Officers uniform with metal bousun whistle in his pocket. (The CWBWT Museum, photo by Bryan Bush)

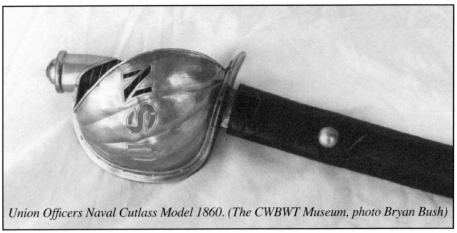

Union Officers Naval Cutlass Model 1860. (The CWBWT Museum, photo Bryan Bush)

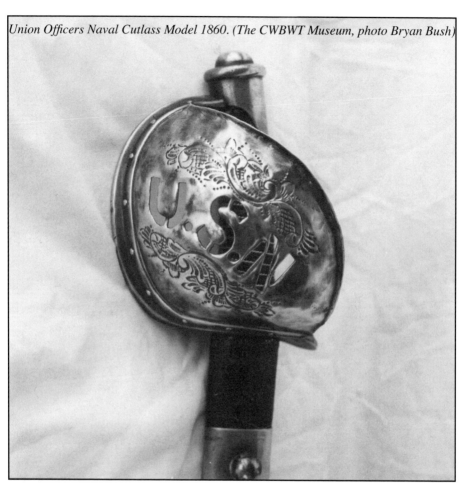

Union Officers Naval Cutlass Model 1860. (The CWBWT Museum, photo Bryan Bush)

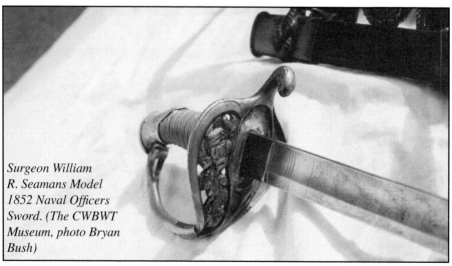

Surgeon William R. Seamans Model 1852 Naval Officers Sword. (The CWBWT Museum, photo Bryan Bush)

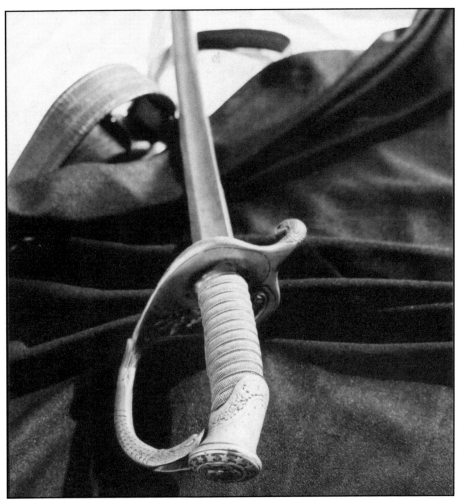

Close up of Surgeon William R. SeamansModel 1852 Naval Officers Sword

Confederate Artillery Sword belonging to Private Thomas Plemans, Co. B, 4th Kentucky C.S.A. "Graves Battery." Graves fought at the Battle of Fort Donelson. Private Thomas Plemans was captured after the surrender of Fort Donelson and was sent to a Union prison. He was later exchanged and rejoined the 4th Kentucky Infantry. (The CWBWT Museum, photo Bryan Bush)

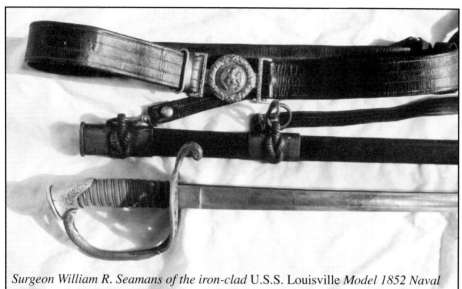

Surgeon William R. Seamans of the iron-clad U.S.S. Louisville *Model 1852 Naval Officers sword and sword belt. (The CWBWT Museum, Photo Bryan Bush)*

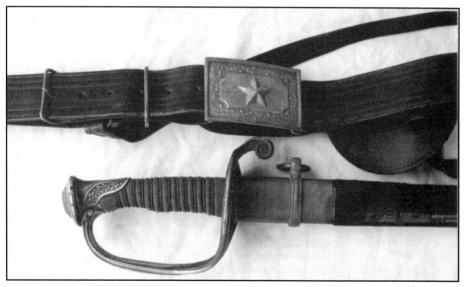

Confederate General Lloyd Tilghman's Model 1860 Foot Officers Sword and Officer's sword belt with a militia style belt buckle

Lieutenant William G. Shackford's Navy Uniform. Shackford served aboard the U.S.S. Maumee, N.A.B. Squadron. The U.S.S. Maumee was one of eight vessels in the Nipsic class gunboats. The Maumee was a wooden hulled, two mast, topsail schooner, which was also steam powered. The Maumee was 190 feet long and 29 feet acroos the beam. The Maumee was launched on July 2, 1863. The Maumee participated in the attack on Fort Fisher, off the Wilmington, North Carolina coast on December 24 through the 25, 1864 and the second attack on Fort Fisher on January 13 through 15, 1865. On February 20 through 21, 1865, the Maumee bombarded the C.S. Forts Strong and Lee on Cape Fear River. The Maumee was decommissioned at Philadelphia on June 17, 1865 and,was sold to Hong Kong, China

When Polk arrived at the point where Grant's transports were, he ordered the column, headed by the 154th Tennessee, under the cover of a corn field to deploy along the river bank within range of the boats. A heavy fire was opened upon the Yankees. Under this fire Grant had his lines cut and retreated from the shore. Grant was surrounded and had to fight his way back to his transports. Once the Union troops had boarded the transport ships, the Confederates were fired upon by the cannons from the gunboats, as they headed for Cairo, Illinois. Polk ordered his men to retire. The Confederates counted Belmont as their victory. Grant said that Belmont was a victory for the Union. In fact, neither side won or lost. There were 607 Union casualties and 641 casualties for the Confederates. The Battle of Belmont was General Ulysses Grant's first Civil War Battle, and would not be his last. He would learn a valuable lesson at Columbus, and now looked for a new area to attack. His attention would soon turn away from the Mississippi and draw to Johnston's most weak point in his defensive line: the Tennessee and Cumberland rivers. [186]

On November 9, Kentucky was admitted to the Confederacy by an act of the Confederate Congress. This action gave the Confederacy the legal right to draft Kentuckians into the army. The day before, the Kentucky Sovereignty Convention met at Russellville and adopted a declaration of independence and a ordinance of secession. The formation of a provisional government was established and Colonel George W. Johnson of Scott County was elected Governor. [187]

Private Cyrus Love, Captain Moody's Company, Colonel Gregg's Texas Infantry Regiment, wrote home on November 10th, 1861 that a messenger arrived at Camp Alcorn, Hopkinsville, Kentucky brining news of the attack at Columbus, Kentucky. Love wrote that the battle was "another glorious victory for us." He writes of Tilghman: "We are under the command of General Lloyd Tilghman who gave us an informal review yesterday-he then went from here to town where he found a messenger from Columbus bearing news of the fight-he immediately returned to camp to inform us-he seemed to me to be the right sort of a man and his talk indicates that he will give us a fight the first favorable opportunity. He say we are a fine Regiment-thinks or at least he said we could whip them ten to one-there are said to be 600 men from this country in the Federal army-there are also 600 or 700 secessionists-there are said to be about 5000 Ky.'s in the Federal army-the Secessionists of the country are the true men of Kentucky-liberal whole souled men." Conditions must have improved in the Gregg's regiment since November 6, 1861. He wrote that most of Gregg's Regiment "are almost entirely armed and equipped-we are now ready for any thing that can come against us and the Almighty being with us we will whip anything that does come." [188]

On November 11, Tilghman again suspected a Union attack on his position. He sent out the Third Mississippi and Kentucky Battalion, which formed on his right, resting on the right of the Greenville road, just south of the bridge. On the bridge was posted three artillery pieces. On his left formed the First Mississippi and a battalion of Texans, resting on the Madisonville road near Brenaugh Bridge, supported by three pieces of artillery. The center was held by the seven remaining companies of Texans on a crossroad connecting the right and left, with one piece of artillery. A small cavalry force participated with each body, and a small force left the town. A messenger from Madisonville informed Tilghman that the Yankees had struck camp and where heading back to Ashbysburg; the Greenville force had already gone north. [189] Tilghman decided to retire the Texas regiment, and maintain his position with the rest of his force.

Tilghman commented that the community was not supportive and was outright bitter toward his men in Hopkinsville. Tilghman had to arrest three citizens who were engaged in arranging with the Yankees to rise behind Tilghman's in case the Yankees had advanced upon Tilghman's position. Tilghman managed to find two full boxes of percussion muskets. He requested to General Johnston that five hundred more men be sent to him from Tennessee, and he would supply the arms to these men. Tilghman managed to form a battalion. He had nine companies. Tilghman also requested more horses, because Captain Wilcox had lost thirty of them when he was routed from Eddyville. [190]

Colonel Nathan Bedford Forrest arrived at Hopkinsville on the 11th, and Tilghman used his force to strengthen his position. Tilghman sent Major Kelly with three hundred of his cavalrymen, two hundred and fifty infantry, and one piece of artillery to try and capture a Union force of three hundred, who had crossed the Ross Ferry on the Cumberland. [191]

On November 14, Colonel Nathan Bedford Forrest wrote to Mackall requesting that he be sent to Tilghman's service since he found the country around Forts Henry and Donelson impracticable for cavalry. Forrest had already moved his command to Canton, on the north side of the Cumberland River, leaving two companies at Dover. He was of no use south of the Cumberland. [192]

On that same day, Assistant Adjutant General Mackall informed Tilghman that he was no longer in control of Hopkinsville, that was left to Brigadier General Charles Clark. Forrest was ordered to Hopkinsville. The five hundred men requested by Tilghman to be armed was sent to Clarksville, Tennessee and Tilghman was ordered to send the arms to Clarksville. Tilghman was assigned to Columbus, Kentucky and was to report to General Leonidas Polk. Tilghman was to take command of the fortifications in Columbus. But Tilghman would not get that opportunity. On November 17, 1861, Johnston ordered Tilghman to take control of Forts Henry and Donelson and their defenses, which would forever change Tilghman's life. [193]

On November 15, 1861 Union General William T. Sherman was relived of command and replaced with General Don Carlos Buell. Buell began to shorten his lines and concentrated his troops in the direction of Bowling Green. Union General George Thomas was moved to Somerset, Kentucky and occupied the points on the upper Green River on General Johnston's right flank. The Green River bridge at Munfordville was to be repaired in order for an advance to be made on Johnston's flank. Confederate Major General George Crittenden was sent to reinforce Zollicoffer. [194]

President Jefferson Davis in his message to the Confederate Congress on November 18 tried to justify his seizure of Kentucky. He said: "Finding that the Confederate States were about to be invaded through Kentucky, and that her people, after being deceived into a mistaken security, were unarmed and in danger of being subjugated by the Federal force, our armies were marched into that state to repel the enemy and prevent their occupation of certain strategic points which would have given them great advantages in the contest- a step which was justified not only by the necessities of self defense on the part of the Confederate States, but also by a desire to aid the people of Kentucky." The Confederates had made a major flaw in it's thinking. The people of Kentucky had seen the Confederate forces as the aggressors. If the Union forces had made the first move in invading the state sentiment may have shifted somewhat to the Confederate cause. But another problem that Kentucky had in trying to bring Kentucky into the fold of the Confederacy was that the state had no aggressive leadership. Senator John C. Breckinridge and Buckner were both outspoken supporters of states rights but they would not take a stand in actual secession. The Union force on the other hand were a minority in the state, but they were very organized and active. But it was too late to look back, Confederate General Albert Sidney Johnston had to defend his vast defense line with his poorly armed, poorly trained troops. Johnston's defensive line in the coming year would be put to the test with a series of battles in Kentucky. Decisions would have to be made as to where his men would be most useful, and these decisions would directly affect Colonel Tilghman.

Tilghman had undergone many changes in 1860 and 1861. He had gone from being a prosperous civilian working as an engineer on the Mobile and Ohio Railroad to becoming a Brigadier General in the Confederacy, commanding the Tennessee and Cumberland Rivers. His life was quickly changing. Tilghman would now face a man that he had fought with in the Mexican War: General Ulysses S. Grant.

CHAPTER THREE

The Battle of Forts Henry and Donelson

In the fall of 1861, Colonel Adolphus Heiman and the 10th Tennessee infantry began work on Forts Henry and Heiman. During that summer, the unfinished Fort Donelson was garrisoned by only forty unarmed men and was to be abandoned until October 1861. Conditions were horrible at both forts, and Tilghman knew about the conditions at Fort Henry and Donelson. General Tilghman, in reference to Fort Henry, referred to "its wretched military position" and "its unfortunate location...The history of military engineering records no parallel to this case." [195] Five barges of 1,200 tons of stone were dumped in early November to block the Cumberland, and torpedoes were laid in the river to stop the gunboats, but heavy rains during the fall filled Fort Henry and covered the torpedo defenses with thirty feet of water. When Tilghman took command at Forts Henry and Donelson, he faced overlapping authority, unclear command channels, and conflicting orders, along with the existing problems of the lack of ordnance, manpower and fortifications. It was a task no man would want, but Tilghman was ordered to take the mission.

Tilghman was ordered to complete the works and their armament and was to use the surrounding labor to help in the task. Johnston said that the Forts up to that point had been grossly managed. The officer in charge of the batteries was frequently absent and the commander of Fort Donelson was away from his post nightly. Governor Harris of Tennessee was requested by Johnston to send four additional armed companies to the Forts. Once these companies arrived they would be joined with the other six companies already there to form a regiment. Tilghman was to report to Confederate General Leonidas Polk monthly. Forts Henry and Donelson fell under Polk's jurisdiction. [196]

General Tilghman pointed out to Lieutenant General Leonidas Polk, district commander, that both forts where in horrible shape and were not ready for battle. Tilghman requested more heavy guns for both Forts, four for each Fort, and one to be long ranged, such as sixty-four pounders. Tilghman also had one thousand unarmed men. Tilghman wrote in a letter to Colonel W. W. Mackall on November 29, 1861 that he was discouraged, but would not give up. [197]

On November 29, Tilghman requested two twelve-pound howitzers, and horses. He also pointed out that the Confederates should occupy a position on the opposite side of the river from Fort Henry, and build a small field work, with several heavy guns. He also requested the occupation of an advanced point with a small force, aided by a field battery. He needed at least five hundred men for the task. Tilghman was informed that Alabama was sending five hundred blacks in order to build the new fortification across from Fort Henry. Tilghman figured it would take about $28,280 dollars to buy 202 horses and equipment he needed. [198]

By December 2, 1861, Tilghman had taken control over Forts Henry and Donelson. Already, his task was not going to be an easy one. He had heard about the problems at the two forts. He had heard about the mismanagement, and the forts being under manned. Tilghman wrote that "it is too plain that instant and powerful steps must be taken to strengthen not only the two forts in the way of work, but the armament must be increased materially in number of pieces of artillery as well as in weight of metal." [199] He wrote to President Jefferson Davis for his need of arms and the exposed position of the Cumberland and Tennessee Rivers and that it would be impossible to receive arms from Tennessee. He wrote: "I am deeply solicitous about our condition on the Tennessee and Cumberland and believe that no one point in the Southern Confederacy needs more aid of the Government than these points." [200] Confederate General Gideon Pillow wrote to Assistant Adjutant General Mackall on December 11 that the Union troops were preparing to move up the Tennessee river in force and that they would use their water power to capture Fort Henry and take the Tennessee bridge and separate Mackall's command and General Polk's and advance down the railroad to Memphis. Tilghman agreed with Pillow's assessment of the situation, since he knew that the Yankees were planning to invade the Cumberland and Tennessee Rivers.

By January 1862, Tilghman had some bright news. He still had two thousand men who were unarmed, and not enough men to man one half the lines within the fortifications, but he felt that progress in the main fortification was satisfactory. He mentioned that in only a few more days, the gap would be closed up in the works. The heavy batteries were progressing rapidly and efficiently. He was ready to place them into position as fast as they arrived.

His army was comfortably housed with well built, well situated buildings, quite a change from his days in Hopkinsville. He reviewed Fort Henry and noted that the entire command was in "admirable state of efficiency." A heavy rifled eighty-two pounder arrived at the fort. He had seven companies and three were arriving later in the week. He also had five hundred African Americans arriving to help with the construction of the forts. Tilghman immediately put Col. J. W. Head, commanding the post at Fort Henry to work on cutting timber and preparing rifle pits to protect the approaches to the forts. [201] By January 14, four gunboats, one transport, and one mortar boat had arrived. Four days later on January 17, eight boxes of guns arrived including knapsacks, haversacks, and canteens. All of the guns were mounted on the fort and plenty of ammunition was available. Ten days provisions and forage were sent to the camp. Captain Dixon and Colonel Head both reported that they were ready to meet any attack. [202]

On January 18, Tilghman reported from Fort Donelson that two thousand Union infantrymen and two hundred Union cavalry had landed at Eggner's Ferry and encamped six miles out on the road to Murray. They had fifteen wagons and their objective was Paris, Tennessee. Three Union gunboats had fired on them the day before on Fort Henry, but they were out of range, and they retired with all transports. Tilghman reported that he would destroy the Wood's Creek Bridge to try and stop the Union advance. He called out six hundred men for the task. He also quickly mounted a ten-inch gun at Henry and another thirty-two pounder would later be installed. Tilghman would return to Fort Henry. [203]

On January 19, 1862, Confederate General Polk sent out a force of one thousand cavalry to attack the rear of the Union force estimated at four thousand infantry, six hundred cavalry, and two batteries of artillery, which was moving from Farmington to Murray, Kentucky. Tilghman reported that Union General C. F. Smith was at Murray with seven thousand men, including one thousand cavalry and twelve field pieces. Tilghman had control of the hill and was fortifying it as quickly as possible. He had moved six hundred men and three field pieces from Fort Donelson to Fort Henry. [204]

On that same day, Confederate Major General George Crittenden, with the 15th Mississippi, 16th Alabama, 17th, 19th, 20th, 25th, 28th, and 29th Tennessee Infantry and a battery of six cannons, in all about four thousand men attacked Union General George Thomas' Infantry. Confederate Brigadier General Felix K. Zollicoffer's main responsibility was to secure East Tennessee and to protect the railroad from Chattanooga to Knoxville. In September 1861, Zollicoffer made a bold move by seizing the Cumberland Gap, invading Kentucky, and setting up his headquarters at a ford on the upper Cumberland River. With no real opposition to his front, he continued on his march into Kentucky. Union infantry was well entrenched on a densely wooded hill near the Rockcastle-

Laurel county line. Zollicoffer approached the well fortified position and the Union troops attacked and drove Zollicoffer back. The battle between the two forces became known as the Battle of Wildcat Mountain, which was fought on October 21, 1861. In November 1861, Zollicoffer left 5,000 men and his artillery at the Cumberland Gap, and advanced west into Kentucky with 4,000 men, to strengthen control in the area around Somerset. He found a strong defensive position at Mill Springs and decided to make that his winter quarters. He fortified the area, especially both sides of the Cumberland River. Union Brigadier General George Thomas received orders to drive the Rebels across the Cumberland River and break up Major General George B. Crittenden's army. Thomas left Lebanon and slowly marched through rain-soaked country, arriving at Logan's Crossroads on January 17th, where he waited for Brig. Gen. A. Schoeph's troops from Somerset to join him. Zollicoffer took the time to reconnoiter the north bank of the river opposite Mill Springs. The south bank had many advantages, including fresh water, a grist mill, a sawmill, and a supply line by river to Nashville. Zollicoffer was ordered to remain on the south side of the river, but he disobeyed orders and moved his force across the river to the north bank, and put his cannons on the bluffs opposite Mill Springs, called Beech Grove. Zollicoffer's men set to work building cabins, rifle pits, and setting up defenses. Union General George Thomas decided to strike first. On December 31, 1861, Thomas and his men marched forty miles, but the weather turned to rain and the roads soon became a quagmire of mud. What should have taken a few days, ended up taking two and a half weeks. Thomas arrived at Logan's Crossroads on January 17th, 1862. He set up his headquarters at the Jamestown and Columbia roads. Eight miles separated Thomas from his rear column, and to make matters worse, the Fishing Creek was so swollen from the recent rains, Albin Schoepf's brigade was separated from Thomas. He was located on the high bluffs on the east of the creek. Schoepf's men did not link up with Thomas until January 18, 1862. [205]

In early January, Major General George Crittenden, Zollicoffer's superior, had arrived at Mill Springs and taken command of the Confederate troops. A council of war was held, and it was decided that the best defense was to hit the Federals first. There is some evidence that Zollicoffer may have objected to the attack, because Crittenden and Brigadier General William Carroll drank heavily before and during the council of war, and that Zollicoffer doubted their mental capacity to make rational decisions under such conditions. The Confederates formed their lines of march in the rain. Zollicoffer and his four thousand men headed toward Logan's Crossroads. Zollicoffer's men slowly made it down the narrow, twisting road, surrounded by dense woods. The Confederates did not know at the time that some of Schoeph's troops had arrived and reinforced the Union troops which numbered around four thousand men. [206]

On January 19, just shortly after daybreak, the Rebel cavalry under Sanders attacked the 10th Indiana and Wolford's 1st Kentucky Cavalry (U. S). Sergeant George Thrasher, Company C, 1st Kentucky fired the first shots of the battle. Lieutenant Jonathan Miller, Company H was sent to support Company C and was mortally wounded. Union pickets began to retire to a house west of the Mill Springs Road and opened up on the approaching Rebels.

Painting of Union gunboats shelling Fort Henry. (U.S. Naval Academy, Beverly R. Robinson Collection)

Zollicoffer placed his skirmishers and formed his brigade for an attack. The 15th Mississippi drove the Union pickets from the house and ran to the east side of Mill Springs Road, taking cover behind a fence. The 15th Mississippi under Walthall came across an unknown unit in the mist and fog. Walthall cried out "Who are you?" and the other unit gave out the secret password "Kentucky". Walthall thought it was a friendly unit, but it was the 1st Kentucky Cavalry. A rain of fire came down on Walthall's men, but he managed to escape. Walthall, along with the Battle's 20th Tennessee attacked the Yankees and they fell back. Colonel Cummings of the 19th Tennessee moved up the west side of the road, then crossed to form a front with Walthall and Battle. The Confederates overran the 1st Kentucky Cavalry's camp, pushed their way over the fence, and ended up into William Logan's cornfield. The Rebels were on the edge of the 10th Indiana's camp. [207]

Rain and smoke all added to the "Fog of War". It was difficult to make out which side was which. The heaviest part of the battle was raging in a cornfield. The Rebels took cover in a deep ravine southeast of the field, and the Federals took refuge behind a fence to the northwest. Wolford's dismounted cavalry and Speed Fry's 4th Kentucky Infantry rallied their men and kept back the Confederate advance. Thomas arrived on the field and directed movements, taking a position near the intersection of Mill Springs and Somerset roads. Fry began to counterattack, driving the Confederates back across Logan's field, over the branch and up the hillside. The 4th Kentucky reached a fence to take cover. Both sides hammered away at each other. At 7:00 A.M. Fry moved beyond a fence up the hill into a clump of trees. At the same time, Zollicoffer also rode to a clump of trees. He was nearsighted and rode up to a Union officer. The officer was none other than Colonel Speed Fry. Zollicoffer thought that the 19th Tennessee was firing on their own men. He ordered the 19th Tennessee to seize fire and rode to the Yankee officer on the crest of the hill. Zollicoffer pointed to the 4th Kentucky and yelled at Fry "those are our men!" Suddenly a Rebel officer rode up and screamed, "General, it's the enemy!" Fry immediately rode down the hill but turned and fired his pistol. The entire line of the 4th Kentucky fired a volley at Zollicoffer. Zollicoffer, who was clad in a white raincoat, fell from his horse dead. Major H. M. R. Fogg, Zollicoffer's aide, also fell from his horse with a mortal wound. After Zollicoffer was killed, Crittenden took over and rallied his men to attack. Crittenden's men were armed with flintlock rifles that didn't shoot well in the rain, and his men began to retreat. The Federals were equipped with percussion-capped rifles. Union counterattacks on the Confederate right, led by Colonel Samuel P. Carter's brigade, and the left, led by the 9th Ohio Infantry, were success-ful, forcing the Confederates from the field. Crittenden never deployed two Confederate regiments. [208]

By 9:00 A.M. the battle was still raging where Zollicoffer had fallen, but the Confederates were only holding back the Yankees. Thomas moved the 2nd Minnesota into the Union center to relieve the exhausted 4th Kentucky and 10th Indiana. Union artillery from Ohio, under Kenney, fired fifty six rounds into the Confederate line. Standart's 1st Ohio battery also began to rain down death upon the field. They fired an additional twenty rounds. [209]

The 9th Ohio Infantry moved through a field and into the woods west of the Mill Springs Road and flanked Carroll's brigade. The Confederate left collapsed. The 2nd Minnesota attacked the Confederate center, and Battle's and Walthall's troops began to leave the field. Lt. Balie Peyton, Company A, 20th Tennessee tried to rally his men, but they fled for the field. Peyton charged the Union lines with his revolver firing round after round. He fell dead immediately from a hail of fire. Crittenden ordered a withdrawal and had to abandon twelve cannon and large quantities of stores in Beech Grove, and then crossed the Cumberland River by the use of the *Noble Ellis*, a boat provided to Crittenden by General Albert Sidney Johnston. He headed toward Knoxville. Crittenden lost 439 men, while the Federals lost 232 men. The Battle of Mill Springs, along with one at Middle Creek, broke whatever Confederate strength there was in eastern Kentucky. Johnston was slowly losing control of his defense line. [210]

After the Battle of Mill Springs, Union George Thomas took position at Burkesville on the upper Cumberland above Nashville and threatened Johnston's Bowling Green position. Union General Don Carlos Buell thought that Halleck's gunboat flotilla could head up the Cumberland, sail past Fort Donelson and unite with Thomas' troops above Nashville. Union General Henry Halleck, the commander of the Western District, argued for a movement through the center of Johnston's line at the Tennessee river, which would negate attacking Bowling Green, Nashville or Columbus. McClellan wanted to attack at Stevenson, Alabama. Lincoln wanted Nashville. By January Generals Henry Halleck, Don Carlos Buell, and George B. McClellan had adopted General Ulysses S. Grant's plan to attack the twin rivers. Because of the high water, Foote's flotilla could cross the Muscle Shoals on the Tennessee River and destroy the Nashville and Chattanooga Railroad bridges as well as the Memphis and Charleston Railroad. Buell's army would advance to the Cumberland and the gunboats would cut off Johnston's army north of the river and prevent removal of military stores from Middle Tennessee. Halleck wanted a major offensive for February. By January 16, Eads "City Class" ironclads had been completed. [211]

By January 21, there were major problems at Fort Henry. The fort had been built on poor ground and water was quickly rising into the Fort. Tilghman was beginning to get nervous about the conditions. He still had not finished the works on the south side of Fort Henry. The entire fort, together with the entrenched camp is enfiladed from three or four points on the opposite shore, while three points on the eastern bank completely command them both, all at easy cannon range. At the same time the entrenched camp, arranged as it was in the best possible manner to meet the Yankees, was only two thirds completed, and was completely under the control of the fire of the gunboats. Points within a few miles of Fort Henry, which had great advantages and few disadvantages, were totally neglected, and a location fixed upon without one redeeming feature or filling one of the many requirements of a site for a work such as Fort Henry. The work itself was well built in Tilghman's opinion, but an enemy with common sense could control the entire position, since most of the fort was surrounded by high water. [212]

By late January, Ulysses S. Grant and his army, along with Flag Officer Andrew Foote's seven gunboats were beginning to make their move toward Fort Henry and Donelson. The Federal army was pushing into Kentucky. Union General Ambrose Burnside was moving closer to New Orleans. Confederate General Albert Sidney Johnston, who was still in Bowling Green felt the slow noose around his headquarters closing in around him. Johnston's right was exposed to invasion into East Tennessee. The road leading to the city of Nashville was open to invasion from the Union army. His movements were also threatened on the left at Forts Henry and Donelson, and Clarksville. Johnston immediately sent eight thousand troops under Confederate General William Hardee to Russellville, Kentucky to protect Bowling Green. He also sent two regiments of infantry to Henderson Station, fifteen miles from Jackson, Tennessee. He had already sent eight thousand men to Clarksville, Tennessee to secure and drive the Union force back, with the aid from Clarksville and Hopkinsville. Johnston was beginning to sweat. Nashville was in threat of being captured or he himself ran the risk of being outflanked. Nashville was one of the most important cities in the South. It was the South's major producer of food. It was the leading war production center in the West. Approximately ninety percent of the South's copper came from around Ducktown, Tennessee. The Confederacy's largest gunpowder mills lay along the Cumberland River northwest of the city, utilizing saltpeter from the cave regions of East Tennessee. The South's greatest iron production region lay between the Cumberland and Tennessee Rivers. Johnston asked General Samuel Cooper, Adjutant and Inspector General to call up all corps in the country to arms. "No matter what the sacrifice may be, it must be made, and without loss of time. Our people do not comprehend the magnitude of the danger that threatens. Let it be impressed upon them. All the resources of the Confederacy are now needed for the defense of Tennessee." [213] Polk realized that he was exposed and wanted Johnston to send him forty thousand men between Columbus and the Tennessee River. Again the threat against the twin rivers went unnoticed.

President Jefferson Davis ordered Confederate General P. G. T. Beauregard and General John Floyd's brigade of Virginians to General A. S. Johnston. They arrived in January and were sent to Russellville, not Forts Henry and Donelson. Johnston wanted one hundred cannon sent for Nashville and Clarksville fortifications ignoring the twin rivers.

By January 22, the Union force was marching from Murray to Pine Bluff. On January 21, Tilghman reported that Union Colonel John Eugene Smith's force was nine miles of Highland with his whole force. Tilghman pointed out that Smith would cross the river at that point and the road was good to Fort Donelson and Henry. His fear was that Smith would attack one or both forts. By January 23, Tilghman reported that 5,500 Yankees had crossed Eggher's

Ferry. Tilghman sent out 950 cavalry and some artillery to harass the Union force. On January 25, the Union force was within twelve miles of Paducah. Tilghman's troops halted eleven miles from the Yankee's rear, and were ordered to return to Fort Henry. [214]

On January 27, Lincoln issued War Order Number 1 which ordered action. All the Union forces assembled under Union General Don Carlos Buell, and Henry Halleck must move forward on February 22, 1862.

Three days later, Union General Henry Halleck, commander of the Western forces, gave Union General Ulysses Grant permission to attack Fort Henry.

By the end of January, Tilghman had 3,033 officers and men at Forts Henry and Heiman and 1,956 men and officers at Donelson, but 926 men were absent on the Tennessee fort and 1,640 men were missing from the Cumberland fort. Fort Donelson was fortified with the troops from the 30th, 49th, 50th, 57th Tennessee and Captain Frank Maney's light battery. Fort Henry had seventeen cannon, twelve which faced the river. Trenches covered the rear of the fort. Tilghman had also built Heiman with infantry trenches. Tilghman only had light artillery pieces at Fort Heiman. It was enough to hold off a land assault but could do nothing to help Fort Henry against a naval attack. Lieutenant Colonel. J. F. Gilmer, Chief Engineer of the Western Department, thought that Fort Donelson needed more work than Fort Henry. He added more sandbags to the water batteries because of the rising water. A provisional battery was formed and the embrasures were strengthened, including the platforms and traverses. Coffee and cottonseed sacks were filled with earth for sandbags. Captain J. P. Shuster arrived to provide training for the artillerists. A one-thousand-round-bomb-proof magazine was built including a covered way for access to the town's water battery. Ten thirty two-pounders arrived and put into place at the fort. A ten-inch Columbiad arrived and another Columbiad type cannon arrived from Nashville and Virginia, but both did not have the proper pintle and pintle plates. The Columbiad type cannon was re-bored and became a six-point-five-inch cannon. Severe flooding threatened the cannon positions and magazines in Fort Henry. The high water also covered the twenty torpedoes in the river, practically making them ineffective. Things began to look grim for Fort Henry. [215]

On February 1, Foote's gunboats, the Essex, Carondelet, Cincinnati, St. Louis cast off from Cairo, Illinois. The Uncle Sam would become the headquarters. Boats were secured for ten thousand men, four artillery companies, equipment and supplies. Grant stockpiled one hundred thousand rations and six hundred thousand rounds of ammunition. Grant ordered Union General McClernand to organize the First Division from two of the four brigades at Cairo. General C.F. Smith would take his Second Division from Paducah and Smithland. Thirteen steamers would carry the men down river. The next day

Foote would link up with the *Conestoga* and the *Lexington* at Paducah. The four wooden gunboats would advance against Fort Henry in a parallel line, taking leads from signals of the flagship Cincinnati. [216]

On February 3, Grant met with Foote at Paducah and waited for McClernand's men. McClernand arrived that night and was ordered aboard the transports. Twenty-three regiments participated in the upcoming battle. Grant ordered McClernand to Bailey's Ferry, three miles from Fort Henry. Tilghman and Gilmer were both at Dover, and placed Heiman in charge. Neither man arrived to Fort Henry until 11:30 P.M.

On February 4, 1862, at 4:30 A.M., the sentinel at Heiman's three-gun battery announced a rocket signal from the picket at Bailey's Landing, which was immediately answered by a rocket from Fort Henry, when three more rockets went up from the picket, announcing the approach of three of the Yankee's gunboats. Heiman prepared his men at Fort Henry for an attack. The steamers *Dunbar* and *Boyd* were moved to Paris Landing for the two regiments stationed there. Shortly after daybreak, the pickets on both sides of the river reported a large fleet of gunboats, and the smoke from their smokestacks became visible. Heiman directed Captain Ellis, of the 10th Tennessee, with a small escort of mounted men, to move towards the right bank of the river, and Captain Anderson of the same regiment on the opposite bank. Capt. Milner, with his cavalry, were to occupy the several roads leading from Bailey's Landing to the fort, and throw forward a sufficient number of pickets. Colonel Drake was to send two companies of his regiment and a section of Culbertson's battery to the rifle pits for the defense of the Dover Road, about three quarters of a mile from the fort, while Major Garvin occupied the rifle pits across the road leading to Bailey's Landing. Twelve torpedoes sank in the chute in the main channel of the island. Those sunk were useless because of the high water. At 9:00 A.M., the gunboats began to shell the pickets and other buildings near Bailey's Landing. Captain Ellis reported eight gunboats and ten transports, and the transports were disembarking their cavalry.

During that whole time, Tilghman had a large force at work on the epaulements and trying to keep the water out of the fort. The lower magazine already had two feet of water in it, and the ammunition had to be moved to a temporary magazine above ground, which had little protection.

At 12:00 P.M., five gunboats came into view in the main channel. All troops were marched out of range of the gunboats. The gunboats formed in line of battle across the channel about two miles below the fort, beyond the range of the thirty-two pounders.

At 1:00 P.M., the gunboats opened fire with shell and shot, which was returned by Heiman with his rifled gun and the ten-inch Columbiad. The former fired Archer shells. At the third or fourth firing one of the clamps of the Columbiad broke, and the crew of cannon determined not to fire the cannon again. They continued firing the rifled gun. As the boats approached Heiman, the cannoneers opened up with all eleven guns, which continued for a half hour, at which point the gunboats withdrew. None of the enemy's shells which landed in the fort exploded. Heiman reported to Tilghman that the Yankees were landing a large force within three miles of the fort, at Bailey's Ferry, on the east bank of the river, the Union cavalry was at Boyd's, three miles from the Fort, and that more transports were arriving.

Heiman knew he could no longer hold the heights opposite the fort, so he recalled the forces and moved them back into Fort Henry. Tilghman left Fort Donelson with an escort of Tennessee cavalry, under Lieutenant Colonel Gantt, for Fort Henry. Major Gilmer arrived at Fort Henry a short time later. Colonel Heiman of the 10th Tennessee had placed his infantry on the outer works covering the Dover Road with two pieces of artillery, supported by the 4th Mississippi Regiment, under Captain W. C. Red. Scouting parties of cavalry operating on both sides of the river had been pushed forward to within a short distance of the Yankee's lines. Tilghman's force consisted of the First Brigade under Colonel Heiman, which was composed of the 10th Tennessee, the 27th Alabama, the 48th Tennessee, four light pieces of artillery, and the Tennessee Battalion of Cavalry, under Lieutenant Colonel Gantt, numbering about 1,444 men. The Second Brigade under Tilghman consisted of Colonel Joseph Drake (4th Mississippi Regiment), which was comprised of the 4th Mississippi, the 15th Arkansas, the 51st Tennessee, Alabama Battalion, and three light pieces of artillery, the Alabama Battalion of Cavalry, Captain Milner's company of cavalry; with Captain Padgett's spy company; and a detachment of Rangers, under Captain Taylor, totaling 1,215 men. The heavy artillery, under Captain Taylor, numbered seventy five men, who were placed at the guns in Fort Henry. [217]

Tilghman found it impossible to hold the commanding ground south of the Tennessee River with the small force of badly armed men. There were eight Union gunboats and nine transports in the river approaching Fort Henry. All his defenses were commanded by the high ground on which the construction of Fort Heiman was still in progress. Tilghman decided to leave the Alabama Battalion of Cavalry and Captain Padgett's spy company on the western bank of the river, and transferred the force encamped on that side to the opposite bank, the 48th, and 51st Tennessee Regiments were encamped at Danville and at the mouth of the Sandy, and had to be moved from five to twenty miles in order to reach Fort Henry. This movement, together with the transfer of the 27th Alabama and 15th Arkansas Regiments from Fort Heiman across the river, was completed by 5 A.M. on the morning of the 5th. [218]

On February 5, Tilghman asked Johnston for reenforcements so that they could overwhelm the Yankee force approaching. Tilghman was going to concentrate his forces at Fort Henry. More and more transports were landing Union troops on the banks of the river. The gunboats were estimated to have fifty-four guns. Tilghman knew that a joint attack with infantry and gunboats was about to take place. He ordered Colonel Head to hold Fort Donelson and Colonel Sugg's regiments, Tennessee Volunteers, with two pieces of artillery, ready to move at a moment's notice, with three days cooked rations, and without camp equipment or wagon train of any kind, except to carry extra ammunition. Tilghman ordered Head to the Cumberland, and to take position at the Furnace, half way on the Dover road to Fort Henry. Col Head's force consisted of about seven hundred and fifty men. The small force and the poor position at Fort Henry forced Tilghman to concentrate his entire force by land within the rifle pits surrounding the camp of the 10th Tennessee and the 4th Mississippi Regiments. [219]

At 10:00 A.M. on February 5, Tilghman sent out a strong reconnoitering party from Fort Donelson from Bailey's Ferry by way of Iron Mountain Furnace. They advanced only about a half mile when they came up against a Union reconnoitering party. The Confederate cavalry charged the Yankees, and the Yankees fell back, with only one man killed on each side. Very quickly the main body of the Union infantry and a large force of cavalry was met, and Tilghman's cavalry had to fall back. [220]

Upon learning that his cavalry had been forced back, Tilghman ordered out five companies of the 10th Tennessee, five companies of the 4th Mississippi, and fifty cavalry, along with two additional companies of infantry to support Captain Red at the outer works. It was discovered that the Union force had retired. Tilghman returned to camp at 5:00 P.M., leaving Captain Red reinforced at the outer works. The Union troops were again reinforced during the night by transports. Tilghman ordered fifty cavalry under Captain Hubbard of the Alabama cavalry to surprise the Yankees who were still continuing to land on the opposite side of Bailey's Ferry. Rain prevented Hubbard from moving out. [221]

That night Tilghman, Colonel Heiman, Colonel Nathan Bedford Forrest, and other officers called a council of war. General Ulysses Grant finally arrived with his sixteen thousand Federals against General Tilghman's 2,610 poorly armed troops. One third of Tilghman's men were armed with just shotguns and hunting rifles. The 10th Tennessee, one of the best armed units, had only flintlock Tower rifles, imported from England, dating from the War of 1812. The high water in the river was filling the lowland areas which gave Tilghman only one route to retreat. The only route of retreat approached the Yankees and the roads were impossible for artillery, cavalry, or infantry to travel. Tilghman decided that Fort Donelson might be held, if properly re-enforced, even though Fort Henry should fall. The force at Fort Henry was not necessary to hold Fort Donelson. Fort Henry could not make a successful defense of Fort Donelson or hold long enough for the Confederate army at Bowling

Green to change their position so that they could move to Columbus, but if the Confederate army moved from Bowling Green to Columbus, the movement would break the Confederate center, leaving the center of Kentucky open to invasion from Union forces under Don Carlos Buell. The defense of the right wing at Bowling Green depended upon a concentration of Tilghman's entire division on Fort Donelson and the holding of that Fort as long as possible. Tilghman hoped that the delaying action at Fort Henry would give him time for reinforcements to arrive at Fort Donelson and cooperate with his division, by getting to the rear and right flank of the Yankees. Once the reinforcements were in position, they could control the roads over which a safe retreat might be effected. He decided to delay the Yankees as long as possible and retire the command towards Fort Donelson. Tilghman decided to keep his heavy artillery company, which amounted to Company B, 1st Tennessee Artillery, Lieutenant Watts and eighty men and ordered the rest of the command to Fort Donelson. All officers agreed that they must abandon Fort Henry and fall back to Fort Donelson. General Tilghman turned to Captain Jesse Taylor and asked : "Can you hold out for one hour against a determined attack?" Taylor replied that he could. "Well, then, gentlemen, rejoin your command and hold them in readiness for instant motion." [222]

On the early morning of February 6, Captain Padgett reported to Tilghman that five additional transports had landed overnight and that a large Union force was on the west bank of the river. The east bank of the river was also being reinforced. Tilghman learned that the Union force was fortifying three miles below Fort Henry. He wrote to General Leonidas Polk that he did not trust General A. S. Johnston in reinforcing him at Fort Henry. Tilghman also told Polk that he didn't want raw troops, they would get in the way, but it was too late; the major attack was to come that morning.

At 10:15 A.M., Tilghman was informed that Grant's force was within a half mile of the advance works, and movements on the west bank indicated that General Smith was fast approaching. Grant did not know that Tilghman had pulled his force out of the works. Grant had to know that the Fort was reduced before his infantry force could attack or the gunboats had retired to a safe distance. Grant took a position north of the forks of the river road, in dense woods. Muddy roads also impeded his advance.

At 11:00 A.M., Flag Officer Andrew Foote's flotilla was in the line of battle. The *Essex*, the *Cincinnati,* the *Carondelet*, and the *St. Louis* were the first four in line of battle, and the *Tyler*, the *Conestoga*, and the *Lexington* formed the second line of battle. Fort Henry was at eye level with Foote's gunboats. Foote could blast his cannons at point blank range into the fort. Tilghman knew that he could not even try to take on that huge flotilla with success, but his main goal was to delay Grant's assault as long as possible. He had at his disposal ten thirty-two pounders, two forty-two pounders, two twelve pounders, one twenty-four pounder rifled gun, which could hurl a sixty-two pound shell and one ten-inch Columbiad, which could hurl a 128 pound shell. Captain Taylor assigned each gun a particular vessel to fire its guns at, and directed the guns to be kept constantly trained on the approaching boats. Captain Hayden of the Engineers would assist the Columbiad, while Taylor would work the rifled gun. At 11:45 A.M., the Yankee gunboats, at a range of 1,700 yards, opened fire on the Fort. Foote attacked with the iron clad gunboats *Cincinnati*, under Commander Stembel; the flag ship *Essex*; under commander Porter; the *Cardonlet* under Commander Walke; and the *St. Louis* under Lieutenant Commander Paulding; also three gunboats, *Contesga,* under Lieutenant Colonel Phelps; the *Tyler*, under Lieutenant Commander Gwin; and the *Lexington*, under Lieutenant Commander Shirk. All the gunboats steamed ahead toward Fort Henry. Tilghman waited for the first rounds to sail overhead, then he opened fire, which was "gallantly" carried out by his brave small band of men. The gunboats steadily closed upon the Fort, firing very "wildly" until they were within 1,200 yards. [223]

At 12:35 A.M., the Yankee flotilla burst the twenty-four pounder rifled gun disabling every man that manned the piece. The gunboat Essex received a shot in its boiler, which resulted in wounding, by scalding, twenty-nine officers and men, including Commander Porter. The Essex dropped out of line astern, entirely disabled and unable to continue the fight. Tilghman then lost his ten-inch Columbiad, when the priming wire was accidently jammed and bent during loading and spiked the gun, which rendered it useless and all efforts to reopen the vent failed. Several of the thirty-two pounders were also lost. The fire on both sides was horrific. The entire Union flotilla was engaged, doing very little harm to Fort Henry, while Tilghman's shot fell with dead accuracy and great effect. [224]

It soon became apparent that the time was right and Tilghman should retire to Fort Donelson. But, it was equally plain that the men working the batteries at Fort Henry, for the first time under fire, with all their heroism, needed Tilghman's presence. Colonel Heiman, the next in command, had returned to the Fort for instructions. The men working the heavy guns had become exhausted. Another gun became useless by an accident, and yet another by the explosion of a shell immediately after, striking the muzzle, killing two men and disabling several others. Tilghman decided that if he left his men, it would be disastrous to their morale. Tilghman decided to remain until the end and ordered Colonel Heiman to return to join his command and keep the retreat in good order. As soon as Tilghman made his decision to stay, the fight intensified. The gunboats got within six hundred yards, and the accuracy of their rounds improved and began to fall upon their parapets, while the fire of his own guns, which was reduced to seven, was returned with such "deliberation and judgment" that his men scarcely missed a shot. The gunboat *Cincinnati* soon retired. [225]

At 1:10 P.M., the men under Tilghman were to the point of sheer exhaustion and he was left with only four guns. The fire continued with great energy and tremendous effect upon the Union boats. The flag ship *Cincinnati* received thirty-one shots, the *Essex* fifteen, the *St. Louis* seven, and the *Carondelet* six, killing one and wounding nine in the *Cincinnati* and killing one in the *Essex*, while the casualties in the latter from steam amounted to twenty-eight. The commanders of the gunboats turned only their bow into the fort, to avoid exposure of their vulnerable parts. [226]

At 1:30 P.M., Tilghman took charge of one of the thirty-two pounders to relieve the chief of that gun. Tilghman gave the flag ship *Cincinnati* two shots, which had the effect to check a movement intended to enfilade the guns now left to him. It was plain to see that by that point the gunboats were breaching the fort directly in front of his guns, and that he could no longer sustain the Yankee fire without an unjustifiable exposure of the valuable lives of the men who had nobly stood their ground. Several officers, including Major Gilmer, suggested the possibility of surrender. Tilghman declined, hoping to find men enough at hand to continue a while longer. He threw off his coat, sprang on the chassis of the nearest gun, stating that he would work it himself, ordering, at the same time, fifty men of Heiman's regiment to the fort to assist the gunners. Heiman started for the men himself, but before he could reach his own command the gunboats were so close to the fort that further resistance was impossible. Tilghman could not find anyone to assist him, so he threw up a flag of truce, which he waved from the parapet himself. It was 1:50 P.M.. The flag was not noticed at first so Tilghman leaped into the fort and continued the fire for another five minutes, when he was informed by his officers, that the flag in the fort should be lowered. Tilghman said the engagement lasted two hours and ten minutes. Tilghman sent out Major Gilmer and the adjutant general on a boat towards the *Cincinnati*. Tilghman told Heiman to continue the retreat, and to escape to Fort Donelson. Commodore Foote dispatched Commander Stembel and Lieutenant Commander Phelps, with orders to hoist the American flag where the Rebel flag had been flying, and to inform Tilghman that he would see him on board the flag ship. Tilghman came aboard soon after the Union had been substituted for the Rebel flag by Commander Stembel on the fort and possession taken of it. Foote received Tilghman along with his staff, including Captain Taylor, and Lieutenant Watts and Weller, Captain Hayden and Miller of engineers, Captain H. L. Jones and McLaughlin, quartermaster's department, and Acting Assistant Adjutant General McConnico, and fifty men as prisoners. When Tilghman surrendered Fort Henry, he also surrendered a hospital ship, the *Samuel Orr* and the *Patton*, containing twenty invalids, together with the fort and its effects, mounting twenty guns, mostly heavy caliber, with barracks and tents capable of accommodating fifteen thousand men and sundry articles. All of the material, including the fort, was turned over to General Grant upon his arrival, which was an hour after the surrender. Grant was never able to make a successful attack with his infantry on Fort Henry because of the muddy roads and high water, preventing the arrival of his troops until after Foote had taken the fort. [227]

Commander Walke described Tilghman as a "soldierly looking man, a little above medium height, with piercing black eyes and a resolute, intelligent expression of countenance. He was dignified and courteous, and won the respect and sympathy of all who became acquainted with him." [228]

Commander Walke reported that when Tilghman met Foote he said "I am glad to surrender to so gallant an officer," and Foote replied "You do perfectly right, sir, in surrendering, but you should have blown my boat out of the water before I would have surrendered to you." [229] Walke was surprised by the comment, and said that Foote was too much of a gentlemen to say anything calculated to "wound the feelings of an officer who had defended his post with signal courage and fidelity, and whose spirits were clouded by the adverse fortunes of war." [230]

Foote allowed Tilghman and his officers to keep their sidearms, and that both officers and men should be treated with the highest consideration due to prisoners of war, which was promptly and gracefully accepted by Tilghman. Foote turned to Tilghman saying "Come, General, you have lost your dinner, and the steward has just told me that mine is ready." Both officers retired into the gunboat. [231]

Walke took possession of the fort, and saw the Confederate surgeon working with his coat off on the Confederate wounded. The fort gave pity to all who saw it. Blood was on every side of the dead and wounded. The 128 pounder was dismounted and filled with earth by the bursting of one of the Union shells near its muzzle. The carriage of another was broken to pieces, and two men lay dead near it, almost covered with heaps of earth. A rifled gun had burst, throwing its mangled gunners into the water. [232]

Tilghman's delaying action had worked. The main body of the infantry had retreated to Fort Donelson in good order, though they lost about twenty men from sickness due to poor roads. The rear of the army was overtaken at a distance of some three miles from Fort Henry by a body of Yankee cavalry but Major Garvin repulsed the Union force and they retired.

Tilghman was satisfied that he had completed his mission. He had saved his entire command from capture and even managed to seriously damage the flotilla under Foote. If Tilghman had been reinforced, his ability to defend the east bank would have increased. But even Tilghman consented to the fact that the elements were against him. If the attack had occurred just a couple of days later, one third of the fortifications would have been under water, while the remaining portion of the works would have been untenable by the water over the entire interior portion. Tilghman gave high praise to both Colonel Heiman and Captain Dixon, of the Engineers. He also gave praise to Lieutenant Watts, of the heavy artillery, who was acting ordnance officer at Fort Henry. "Lt. Watts is the coolest officer under fire I ever met with." [233] Tilghman even complimented his captors. "I take pleasure in acknowledging the marked courtesy and consideration of Flag Officer Foote, of the Federal Navy; of Captain Stembel and the other naval officer, to myself, officers, and men. Their gallant bearing during the action gave evidence of a brave and therefore generous foe." [234] Flag Officer Andrew Foote returned the compliment by saying of Tilghman "Fort Henry was defended with the most determined gallantry by General Tilghman, worthy of a better cause, who, from his own account, went into the action with eleven guns of heavy caliber bearing upon our boats, which he fought until seven of the number were dismounted or otherwise rendered useless." [235]

Colonel Heiman said of Tilghman that "the self-sacrificing heroism displayed by General Tilghman in this terrible and most unequal struggle challenges the admiration of all gallant men and entitles him to the gratitude of the whole people of the Confederate States. The tact, skill, and untiring energy which characterized his whole course while in command of the defenses of the Tennessee and Cumberland Rivers proved him a most skillful and gallant leader." [236]

After the battle, Foote returned to Cairo for repairs on his gunboats. Grant continued on to the town of Dover and Fort Donelson, on the Cumberland River. General C. F. Smith had possession of the Confederates redan on the western bank of the Tennessee.

On February 7, the Confederate command learned of the fall of Fort Henry and the capture of Tilghman. Colonel Heiman had made it to Fort Donelson with about three thousand men, but he had to abandon the field artillery because of the poor condition of the roads and the high water. Nothing was saved except the small arms. General Polk also learned that the bridges on the Memphis and Bowling Green road over the Tennessee river were not destroyed as was reported. The bridge over the Bear Creek, on the Memphis and Charleston Railroad was threatened. Polk ordered six companies of Colonel Looney's regiment and one section of artillery with Desha's Arkansas battalion, Chalmer's regiment, from Corinth, Mississippi. [237] Phelps captured the Eastport.

General Albert Sidney Johnston also learned of the surrender of Fort Henry. Johnston feared the worst. His line of defense was crumbling before his eyes. "The capture of that fort by the enemy gives them the control of the navigation of the Tennessee River, and their gunboats are now ascending the river to Florence. Operations against Fort Donelson, on the Cumberland, are about to be commenced, and that work will soon be attacked." [238] Johnston was also worried about Fort Donelson and how well it would hold up against Grant's forces. "I think the gunboat of the enemy will probably take Fort Donelson without the necessity of employing their land force in cooperation, as seems to have been done at Fort Henry." [239]

When the South learned of the loss of Fort Henry, Tilghman quickly became the scapegoat. His brave stand at Fort Henry was quickly overlooked. Tennessee blamed a Kentuckian for the loss of their fort.

The force at Fort Donelson amounted to three regiments of General John Floyd's, which was about seven thousand men who were not well armed or well drilled, except Colonel Heiman's regiment and the regiments of General Floyd's command. Johnston knew that if Fort Donelson fell it would open the road all the way to Nashville. Johnston ordered General William Hardee to fall back to Nashville and cross the river. Generals Hardee and Beauregard informed Johnston that they must abandon Bowling Green and fall back to Nashville.

On February 10, Confederate General Gideon Pillow arrived at Fort Donelson. He was not thrilled at what he saw. The works were not complete and he was lacking everything_tools, lumber, and the equipment for artillery, but Pillow thought that he could hold the fort against an assault by infantry, and if given the time he could mount all the guns and resist the gunboats. Pillow asked for reinforcements under General Buckner. [240]

Fort Donelson had six companies of undisciplined infantry, with an unorganized light battery, while a small water battery of two light guns constituted the available river defense. Four thirty-two pounders had been placed, but were not available. By January 25, 1862, the entire battery, except one piece, had been prepared for the river defense; they built the entire field work with a trace of 2,900 feet, and in the most substantial manner constructed a large amount of abatis, and commenced guarding the approaches by rifle pits and abatis. There was also a telegraph line of thirty-five miles that connected Forts Henry and Fort Donelson from Cumberland City to Bowling Green and Columbus, although the line had been cut after the attack on Fort Henry.

In the meantime, General Grant had to decide what to do with Tilghman and the prisoners from Fort Henry. On February 10, General U.S. Grant wrote to Major General Halleck, commander of the Department of Missouri, as to whether Tilghman could be paroled and confined to the limits of Paducah. Grant was informed that parole was a bad idea. Tilghman was from Paducah, so it was decided that Tilghman and his staff were to be sent to St. Louis, Missouri. [241]

General Albert S. Johnston had fourteen thousand men with General William Hardee at Bowling Green, Leonidas Polk had eleven thousand men at Columbus, eight thousand men, were with Buckner and Floyd at Russellville, and two thousand men, were with Clark at Hopkinsville. General Albert Sidney Johnston decided to give up his position and retire to Nashville. Johnston ordered Floyd to support Donelson, but leave an escape route to Nashville. Pillow was to move to Donelson and assume command. Johnston left five thousand men at Fort Donelson and placed Brig. Generals John Floyd, Gideon Pillow, and Simon Buckner in command. He also sent twelve thousand men to take on Grant's fifteen thousand men. Johnston wanted to evacuate all his troops to Nashville, where he assumed the officials in Tennessee were setting up defensive works around the city. Pillow reached Fort Donelson on the February 9, Buckner arrived on February 11, and Floyd arrived on February 13. Floyd again was told by Johnston that he had complete command to make all necessary arrangements for the placing of troops for the defense of the fort, Clarksville, and the Cumberland. Buckner's division consisted of six regiments, two batteries, which made up the right wing, and was posted to cover the land approaches to the water batteries. Colonels Heiman, Davison, Drake, Wharton, McCausland, and Baldwin made up the left wing of the army, which consisted of six brigades. Four batteries were placed along the left wing. General Bushrod Johnson served as chief of staff.

Grant had added eight new infantry regiments, a cavalry battalion, and another artillery battery. Grant had twenty-five regiments at his disposal. Grant's force consisted of the First Division, commanded by General John McClernand. The first brigade was comprised of Col. Richard Ogelsby, comprising the Eighth Illinois, 18th Illinois, 29th, 30th, 31st Illinois, Schwartz's and Dresser's batteries, and the cavalry companies of Captains Warren Stewart, Eagleton Carmichael, James Dollins, and James O'Harnett. The Second Brigade was comprised of Colonel W. H. L. Wallace, which comprised of the 11th Illinois, 20th, 45th, 48th Illinois, and the 4th Illinois cavalry, Col. Lyle Dickey and Taylor's and McAllister's batteries. The Third Brigade Brigade was commanded by Colonel William Morrison, of the 49th Illinois, which was comprised of the 17th Illinois, and the 49th Illinois.

On February 12, Grant's force of fifteen thousand men were approaching Ft. Donelson on Telegraph road. By eleven that morning McClernand's troops were within three miles of the Confederate's pickets. Major John Mudd's scouting party encountered a detachment of the cavalry strongly supported. Major Mudd drove back the cavalry and held his ground until the advance guard of the 30th Illinois arrived. The First Brigade formed in the open fields, while the second and third brigades were also formed within supporting distance. As the advance continued to the right, the Confederate cavalry appeared and made a determined attack, but were repulsed. The Confederate cavalry attempted to make a flank attack to cut off the first brigade from its support. But this attempt failed when the Eighth Regiment and Gumbart's battery fired shells into the Confederate ranks, and the Confederates fell back to their entrenchments.

By mid-afternoon the second division arrived under C.F. Smith. They formed on McClernand's left, in front of the right of the Confederate's works, and McClernand continued with his advance so as to cover the left of the Confederates works in the direction of the town of Dover. The second and third brigades were ordered to climb the steep hills which overlooked the center and right of the Confederate's works and to form the line of battle on the left of the First Brigade. This brought the First and Second Divisions within supporting distance of each other. The artillery was brought to the crest of the hills, Colonel Ogelsby advanced his right upon the Indiana Creek road toward the Confederates center, and arrived at a point where it descends into the valley of the Indiana Creek, the Union troops came into full view of the Confederates tents on the opposite hill. Along the valley and upon the wooded hills enclosing the Confederates were observed in strong force. Colonel Ogelsby ordered up a howitzer from Schwartz's battery to the brow of the hill upon which a portion of McClernand's line still rested. Artillery began to fire, but the distance proved too great for accuracy. Captain Dresser was ordered to bring forward one of his James rifled pieces, which began to fire with accuracy, and drove the Confederates from their tents and cleared the ground in front for a further advance, which was made by the First Brigade.

Colonel Ogelsby deployed the 8th, 29th, 30th, 31st into line of battle and moved forward in front of the Confederates works a half mile to the right, throwing forward the 18th across a hill in the same direction. This movement brought Col. Lawler's regiment within hearing of officers directing the preparation of a battery designed to open fire upon him in the morning. Lawler moved his unit to avoid the battery fire. Col. Wallace moved forward with the Second Brigade and formed into line of battle on the left of the First. The Third Brigade was formed into line of battle on the left of the Second, and the troops camped the night laying on their arms.

On the morning of the 13th, the Confederates opened fire from a battery from then middle Redan No. 2, upon the right of McClernand's line. McClernand refrained from firing back so as to not bring on a general engagement. McClernand returned fire which lasted an hour and a half. Dresser's battery was brought into position near the left of the 18th, and opposite Redan No. 2, and opened fire upon it, which in a few minutes silenced the opposite battery. While this was going on two companies of Colonel Nobel's Second Illinois Cavalry, Col. Dickey's cavalry, and Lt. Powell, with two companies of regular cavalry, made a reconnaissance further to the right and near the Confederate's works at Dover. They reported their findings and McClernand's line was advanced under partial cover of a ridge and woods. McClernand's line advanced towards Wynn's Ferry road and a evacuated Confederate cavalry camp. During the Confederate evacuation, the battery in Redan No. 2 opened fire upon McClernand's men, which was promptly returned by Schwartz's battery, which had been quickly advanced to a position near a farm house farther to the right. The Confederate battery was silenced, but another in the direction of Dover was opened upon McClernand's right, and in turn Schwartz's two pieces, two pieces of Taylor's and three pieces of Dresser's batteries, silenced the Rebel battery.

The batteries also poured a destructive fire into a mass of their infantry, which was seen still farther to the right, driving them into their breastworks. In the mean time, the Confederates had opened fire from several pieces in Redan No. 2 upon the left of McClernand's line, and also from Redan No. 1 upon Mcallister's battery, still farther to the left, on a commanding hill beyond Indiana Creek, where it had been left supported by the 48th. This fire was intended to distract the Federal's attention and prevent their advance to the right. It was attended with no serious effect upon McClernand's left, but carried away a wheel of one of McAllister's gun carriages. It was immediately silenced by McAllister's battery and the portions of Taylor's and Dresser's batteries, which had been brought back to a position near the farm house.

McClernand's right was engaged and within short range of the Confederate's outer works, and the Confederates infantry opposite McClernand's right had been thrown into confusion. McClernand decided to storm Maney's battery in Redan No.2, which lay in front of the Second Brigade and in a position to annoy the Union forces still advancing, and which afforded a cover from which to dash upon McClernand's line at an exposed and weak point. Col. Morrison was ordered to advance his brigade, 17th and 49th, joined by the 48th, Col. Haynie, from the Second Brigade, to make the assault. Colonel Haynie passed down the slope on which they had formed, the assailants, preceded by skirmishers, moved rapidly up the steep hill on the crest of which was the object of attack. Although abatis had been prepared, they made their way under a increasing fire from the Confederates entrenchments to a cleared space in front of them. At this point a heavy cross fire of artillery and small arms poured upon the assailants, yet for an hour they maintained their ground, advancing close to the entrenchments, and firing with deliberate effect. The 45th moved forward under a heavy fire and took position. The assault was renewed. Colonel Morrison was seriously wounded and carried from the field. The Confederates were reenforced by artillery and a large body of infantry, and Colonel Haynie withdrew under the cover of a hill. The attack came at a high cost to McClernand, who lost 147 men during the attack, and had little to show for his efforts.

The four regiments were brought back to the main line and attached to the Second Brigade. Schwartz's and Taylor's batteries were advanced beyond Wynn's Ferry road still nearer to the Confederate's works in that direction, and renewed their fire both upon the Confederate's works and infantry. At 3

P.M. Dresser's battery of James Rifles opened fire from a new position on the crest of the ridge, between Schwartz's and Taylor's batteries and the farm house. Percussion shells exploded inside the fort at a long range.

Dresser's battery was low on ammunition and fell back to re-supply, and McAllister's remaining two twenty-four pound howitzers were brought up the next morning and took its place.

On February 13, 1862, the weather turned cold as snow and sleet began to fall. The night was gloomy from the mingled snow and rain fell which added to the painful discomfort of not having any tents or camp equipment. Food was reduced to hard bread and coffee. Being in point blank range of the Confederates batteries and sharpshooters, camp fires were not allowed. The Confederate threw up new entrenchments, planting new batteries, comprising all the batteries in the fort, and the defenses were strengthened.

On February 14, 1862, the Union troops were cold and cheerless, tried by exposure, and hunger. Anticipating the desire of the Confederates to preserve an avenue of escape along the river above Dover, McClernand dispatched Captain Stewart and Lieutenant Freeman accompanied by a small detachment of infantry, for a reconnaissance of the ground in that direction. McClernand decided to rest his right flank on a creek made impassable by the backwater of the Cumberland. This move further extended his already attenuated line in the face of newly erected batteries and an accumulated mass of the Confederates infantry to the Cumberland river.

On the same day, Foote's gunboats arrived and twelve army transports with ten thousand men on board came into view. Union General Lew Wallace arrived with troops from Fort Henry. Three divisions were formed under Lew Wallace, McClernand, and General Smith. At 3:30 PM, Foote's four iron clad and two wooden gunboats, the *St. Louis*, *Carondelet*, *Louisville*, and *Pittsburg*, with the *Tyler*, and *Conestoga* attacked Fort Donelson. The fight lasted an hour and a half, and the gunboats came to within four yards of the fort. The *Louisville* was disabled by a shot. The two remaining boats, the *Pittsburg* and *Carondelet* were heavily damaged between wind and water. The Confederates quickly renewed the fire as the Union ships drifted down the river helplessly. The *St. Louis* received fifty nine shots, four between wind and water and one in the pilot house, mortally wounding the pilot and others, requiring some time to put her in repair. There were fifty four killed and wounded in the attack. Foote thought that if given fifteen more minutes, he would have captured the two forts. The Confederates brought to bear twenty guns from the water batteries and the main fort on the side of the hill, while Foote could only return fire with twelve bow guns from the four boats. One rifled gun aboard the *Carondelet* burst during the action. Foote was wounded in the battle, and the *St. Louis*, the *Pittsburg*, *Carondelet*, and the *Louisville* were severely damaged.

Colonel John McArthur's brigade, consisting of the 9th, 12th, and 41st Illinois Regiments moved into position during the night and moved to McClernand's right. McArthur's brigade was a reserve to cover the 18th Illinois, and the remaining part so as to extend his line to a point four hundred yards of the creek. Colonel Nobel's and Dickey's cavalry were placed to the rear and still farther to the right. A ten-pound Parrott gun, of Major Cavender's Missouri battalion was brought up, and it was followed by another gun from the same battalion in the morning. Night fell and brought more snow and rain. On the crest of the ridge an earthwork was built for the protection of the battery near the Wynn's Ferry Road. Two of the twenty-pound Parrott guns and two of McAllister's twenty-four pound howitzers were placed under cover of this earthwork in the morning.

During the night a council of war was held between Pillow, Buckner, and Floyd. Since a retreat was now cut off by the extension of the Union's lines to the river, it became evident to the Confederate commanders that if they did nothing they would surely be captured. The generals decided that the army would attempt a breakout. They would drive back the Union right wing with an early morning attack and after clearing the way, they would retreat in the direction of Nashville by the way of Charlotte. Pillow would lead the assault and Buckner would act as the rear guard.

On the February 15, the men awoke and stood at arms. The Confederates had dismantled their fort of its field pieces and planted them within range of McClernand's right and at early dawn the Confederates were discovered rapidly moving in large masses to McClernand's right, clearly indicating the purpose to open their way for escape by a concentrated and overwhelming attack on that part of McClernand's line, and turn his right flank and attack his in reverse.

At six in the morning, the forces under McClernand's command were formed in line of battle. Colonel McArthur's brigade, consisted of the 41st, 12th, 9th with two 10 pound Parrott guns, on the extreme right. Col. Oglesby's brigade, consisted of the 18th, Eighth, 29th, 30th, and 31st, next on the left; the 13th was moved to the rear of the Eighth as a reserve; the Eighth and 29th, supported Schwartz's battery of four guns, posted in their front; Col. Wallace's brigade, consisted of the 11th, 20th, 48th, 45th, 49th, and 17th, next on the left' McAllister's two 24 pound howitzers and a section of the Missouri battery were posted under cover of the earthworks, in front of the 48th; Taylor's battery of four six-pound and two twelve-pound howitzers were posted in front of the 17th; Dresser's battery of three James rifles six-pounders was posted on the extreme left, in front of redan No. 2.

Schwartz's battery of two six- pound and two twelve-pound howitzers were posted in front of the 29th, on the right; three pieces pointing towards Redan No. 3, and one piece left to protect the rear.

The 17th Kentucky, 31st Indiana; and 25th Kentucky, commanded by Col. Charles Cruft, coming up between 9 and 10 A.M. was formed as a reserve in the rear of the 29th, Eighth, and 13th. The 44th Indiana followed about an hour after, and formed in the rear of the 31st. The reenforcement was brought forward by Col. Cruft, in the absence of General Wallace, his division commander. The 18th after a prolonged fight had fallen back because a lack of ammunition, and was replaced with the 13th.

The Third Division, commanded by General W. L. Wallace was formed on the left of the First Division, and the Second Division, commanded by General C. F. Smith, was formed opposite the right of the Confederate's works and extending towards the river below the fort. As the Confederates moved rapidly toward the Union right of McAllister's howitzer's and the Mississippi Parrott's opened fire on different points along the Confederates defenses. Skirmishing and the firing of sharpshooters were now over, and large masses of Confederates, rushing towards his right, were met by the 18th and 9th and immediately after by the 12th, 41st, and Eighth, before the Confederates had time to deploy into line.

The Confederates succeeded in forming a line and obtaining the desired range for their artillery. A fierce struggle developed. In the course of this struggle two companies of the 29th, under Lieutenant Colonel James Dunlap, immediately supporting Schwartz battery, became detached and hotly engaged. Several times repulsed, the Confederates returned to renew the conflict. When the ground had been strewn with the dead and wounded of both parties, the 9th, 12th, and 41st failed ammunition and unsupported by their artillery, which had not been brought into action, fell back before the pressure of overpowering and reformed a short distance in the rear.

Colonel Oglesby reported that Colonel McArthur had fallen back, exposing the 18th to flanking fire. Col. McArthur was wounded, the batteries were closely pressed, his supply of ammunition was running out, and unless he was supported the First Brigade must fall back. McClernand sent a message to Grant for help, but Grant was not at his headquarters but at Andrew Foote's gunboats.

The left was uncovered, the 18th and 8th and 29th became the point of concentrated attack, which was directed both against their front and the flank of the 18th. Assailed by a cross fire from three batteries, comprising ten guns, Schwartz's battery replied with 146 rounds, continuing to fire grape and canister for two hours. One of his guns became disabled by a shot carrying away the trail of his carriage; it was replaced by another cannon from the rear. Lieutenant Gumbart was next wounded. The 18th was hard pressed in the front and upon the flank and driven to rely upon ammunition taken from the dead and wounded to continue a fight that had raged for three hours. They were forced to yield and fell back to a new position, where they could be supplied with ammunition and food. The 13th rushed forward and took their place, instantly changing their line obliquely to the right to shield their flank and together with the 8th and 29th, continued until all of them were forced to fall back.

Colonel Ogelsby had lost 836 killed, wounded, or missing during the fight. The 8th had lost 242. The field was strewn with dead and wounded of both sides. A short time before this McClernand advised Colonel Ogelsby that the 25th Kentucky, in executing his order to file past the 8th into position, through mistake fired into a portion of that regiment and into the 29th and Schwartz's battery, causing some disorder.

Schwartz's battery was unsupported by the retirement of the 29th, and the 31st rushed to its defense, and at the same moment received a combined attack of the forces on the right and of others in the front, supposed to be led by Buckner. Colonel Logan formed his right wing of his battalion at an angle with his left. In this way he supported the battery, which held the Confederates at bay until his regiment's supply of ammunition was exhausted.

Lieutenant Colonel John White and Captain James Williamson, who had fought in the battle of Belmont, fell. Colonel Logan and Lieutenant Charles Capehart, his adjutant, were wounded.

The 31st was without the means of defense, so the 11th was brought up and took their place, and engaged the Confederates, with the 20th, 45th, 48th, 49th and 17th were advanced and thrown into the fray. Assailed both in front and upon the flank with increased fury and threatened by the Confederates cavalry hovering in the rear of the right, the battle became desperate for the Union soldiers. McClernand asked Major General Wallace for help. He replied that he would like to but was unable to do so because Grant had given orders that no unit was to move from their position without Grant's permission. McClernand sent a plea for help to General Smith, who also declined. McClernand wrote to Colonel Wallace to rely upon himself and maintain his position at all hazards until reinforcements arrived. He did so, repulsing and driving back the Confederates in front to their entrenchments. McAllister's, Taylor's, Dresser's, and Schwartz's batteries and a section of a battery under Major Cavender's Missouri battalion, poured a destructive fire upon the Confederates line, while the infantry, and the 20th led by Col. Marsh, charged and pursued. At one point McAllister's battery was exposed to a cross fire of artillery and closely pressed by the Confederates infantry, which forced the battery to fall back. At this critical juncture Col. Smith, of the 45th, rushed forward with a detachment of his men, and drove the Confederate back, and rescued McAllister's battery. The 11th had lost 328 men killed, wounded, or missing. The brigade had lost 534 men killed, wounded, or missing. Lt. Col. William Erwin, of the 20th, and Lt. Col. Thomas Smith, of the 48th, fell while charging. Lt. Col. Jasper, of the 45th, was also wounded.

It was 11:00 A.M. and the Confederates had directed the combined attack of nearly all his forces against it; yet even under these circumstances the battle was won by the Second Brigade as against the Confederates in their front. Unfortunately this partial victory was fruitless. In the meantime the Confederates on the right, having turned the flank of the Second Brigade, whose ammunition was nearly exhausted, advanced both his infantry and cavalry to attack it in reverse. To avoid this McClernand ordered Colonel Wallace, also Colonel Oglesby, to withdraw their commands and reform and resupply. The order to retire failed to reach Lieutenant Colonel Ransom, and the 11th stood their ground until the Confederates, assailing them from the front and rear, was forced to fall back. Colonel Ransom was seriously wounded, but would not leave the field.

McClernand's entire command fell back some four hundred yards from the left of their position in the morning, the Second Brigade was reformed in line of battle upon the ground that McClernand had previously selected, at right angles with their first lines. The First Brigade was moved in the rear of the Second Brigade. The men were supplied with ammunition and provisions. McClernand reconnoitered the Confederates position and found them falling back in confusion, their officers endeavoring to bring them to a halt. The Confederates in their entrenchments were moving out.

By 1:00 P.M. the way out of Fort Donelson laid open. McClernand's division ceased to exist. At the same time, General Grant arrived at his headquarters. General Wallace, whose division was formed near the ground selected for McClernand's second line, filed to the right, and formed a portion of his fresh troops in front of McClernand's second line and in close supporting distance of it, resting the left upon a section of Taylor's battery, which Captain Schwartz posted so as to command the road leading back to his former position. The remainder of the battery was placed a short distance in the rear, to guard against a flank approach either from the right or left.

From this position Captain Taylor opened fire with canister and was soon after joined by Lt. Wood, with a section of Williard's battery, who also opened a fire in the same direction, and generously renewed Capt. Taylor's failing stock of ammunition. Several of the Confederates afterwards found dead some four hundred yards above in the road were supposed to have been killed by the fire of these guns.

Colonel L. F. Ross, of the 17th, came up and took command of the regiment. General Wallace, having formed the line, and also opened fire of musketry in the same direction, which was mainly answered by a fire of artillery from redan No. 2 and of infantry in the thick woods in front and to the left of his line. About the same time Dresser's battery was advanced under McClernand's order upon the same road to a position in front, and opened fire intended to command the approach to their present position across Indiana Creek and to silence the guns of the Confederates in that direction. This fire was continued and returned with much spirit for some time. One of the shots from redan No. 2, scathing a tree close to Lt. Harrison Barger, which stunned him.

By 1:30 P.M. the Confederate attempt to push out of Fort Donelson failed. Pillow ordered Buckner back to the entrenchments. Buckner felt that the time was right to break out. He discussed it with senior general Floyd. Floyd found Pillow and asked why they had given up the Wynn Ferry road after they had already secured it. Pillow said he wanted to regroup. Floyd and Pillow thought that Grant was being reinforced with 20,000 troops, and both decided to fall back to the fort.

Wallace decided not to counterattack. The second engagement served to discourage the Confederates from any further attack. The Yankees rested upon their arms until about 1:30 P.M. when Grant ordered an attack. He knew the Confederates were trying to break out and ordered that the right must be retaken. Grant ordered the Second Division into motion and sent them toward Buckner's old works. Only three battalions of the 30th Tennessee held these works. McClernand sent Major Mudd, 2nd Illinois Cavalry, to reconnoiter to the right and front. Mudd went forward through thick woods and across a field covered with snow in that direction, and found a detached body of Confederates. About the same time the 8th Missouri and 11th Indiana came up and formed on the right of General Wallace's line, advanced in the same direction.

Major Brayman, McClernand's adjutant, and others reported hearing command in the woods a short distance in front and to the left of Taylor's battery and the discovery of other hostile indications farther down in the valley of Indian Creek; McClernand ordered Colonel Wallace to form the Second Brigade in line of battle, resting their right upon the battery and their left near Indian Creek. This position covered the space between Taylor's battery and the right of General Smith, and protected the left of the second line of battle from flank attack.

The sound of General Smith's muskets was soon heard, indicating an attack upon redan No. 1 in his front. Soon after Col. Webster, chief of Grant's staff, came with intelligence that the 30th Tennessee had retired before the assault of General Smith and that he was already leading his men into this redan, which he firmly held. Colonel Webster also brought Grant's orders to press the Confederates at all points. General Wallace had met the Confederates and was pressing them with success, and requested McClernand send forward five or six regiments to his right for the purpose of reinforcing him. McClernand ordered forward a detachment. At the same time McClernand ordered the 46th Illinois to move forward to the right and near the road to support General Wallace's left and also ordered Colonel Ross, with the Third Brigade of McClernand's division to advance directly in the same road. The object was to command the space between General Wallace's left and McClernand's former position on the ridge in front of the Confederate entrenchments. Colonel Ross pushed forward to the point occupied by McAllister's battery in the morning, retaking the former position of the Second Brigade and throwing forward his skirmishers, who drove straggling parties of the Confederates to cover of their works. The loss of this brigade in killed, wounded and missing was 149.

The forces of the Confederates engaged by General Wallace had been driven back by his assault. Buckner's main force joined the 30th Tennessee along the second ridge and stopped the Federal assault. Nightfall ended the fighting. The battle ended after ten hours of fighting. The Federals had managed to break the Confederate outer defenses which protected the main fort.

The field, with its dead and wounded, was in Union hands, and the entrenched position of the Confederates again were surrounded, cutting off their escape route. While holding his ground, Grant ordered the withdrawal of the First and Third Divisions to a compact position on the Confederate's left where they were to camp for the night.

Around one in the morning, Floyd called another council of war. All regimental, brigade and divisional commanders attended. The escape was planned for three hours later. Confederate Colonel Nathan Bedford Forrest also joined the meeting. The river road was impassable. Buckner proposed surrender. Floyd agreed. Pillow was the last to agree but he would escape. Buckner would remain at the Fort to surrender. Forrest did not agree to surrender. He gathered his men and offered to lead anyone who wanted to escape to follow him. Five hundred cavalry and two hundred infantry rode out of Donelson to Lick Creek, then to Dudley's Hill, then to the road to Cumberland Iron Works.

On the 16th McClernand and General Wallace made preparations for a renewed attack upon the Confederate's works. Buckner was at the Dover hotel waiting for Grant and General Wallace. Buckner was hoping for better surrender terms since he was an old friend of Grant, but Grant quickly told Buckner that it would be unconditional surrender. Grant promised to provide rations for Buckner's men and the officers would be allowed to keep their sidearms and servants. The enlisted men would keep their clothing and blankets. The surrender was final. Word of the surrender got back to the commanders in the field. McClernand discovered that the Confederates had surrendered and led his division down to the water battery and the main landing at the fort. Captain Stewart and Schwartz had been the first of the Federal arms to enter the town of Dover.

A national salute was fired by Taylor's battery and the American flag was planted on the fort. McClernand's entire command was encamped at Dover. Of the eight thousand men McClernand's division that had been engaged,

1,519 were killed, wounded, or missing. The Union army had seized thirteen thousand prisoners, twenty thousand stand of arms, sixty pieces of cannon, and huge supplies of animals, wagons, ordnance, commissary stores, and quartermaster's stores.

The Confederate soldiers in the Fort could not believe their ears when they had heard that the Confederate officers had surrendered. The men's morale was high and they thought they were about to fight another battle when they learned of the surrender.

The surrender came as a huge blow to the Confederates. Kentucky was lost. Middle and Western Tennessee was now denied to the South. Missouri was threatened. Union troops could march into Middle and Western Tennessee without a shot being fired. The rivers were open to invasion. The Mississippi was open invasion from both ends. Admiral David Farragut was moving north toward New Orleans. Foote and his gunboats were moving south toward Island No. 10 along the Mississippi.

When Tilghman decided to turn around and rejoin his artillerymen at Fort Henry, he left a void in the military command structure at Fort Donelson. As a commanding general of both Forts Henry and Donelson, Tilghman's responsibility was to leave his artillerymen to defend Fort Henry long enough, so that his delaying action could secure the safe arrival of his men to Fort Donelson. Instead, Tilghman delegated himself as a subordinate commander and took control of an artillery piece at Fort Henry, which placed his life at risk. Although Tilghman was brave and courageous at Fort Henry, his true responsibility was to command his remaining troops at Fort Donelson. Because Tilghman surrendered at Fort Henry, Johnston was forced to fill his vacancy by appointing some of the worst men to command Fort Donelson. General John Floyd was a political general, who had no knowledge of the surrounding area. Because of General Buckner's military experience, he was the better choice to command Fort Donelson, but again he was not aware of the area and the men at the fort had never been under his command. Tilghman knew the area and knew the men under his command. The resulting mayhem with the command structure at Fort Donelson could have been avoided if Tilghman had remained in control of Fort Donelson.

CHAPTER FOUR

Prison Life and the Fall of the River Forts.

After the surrender at Forts Henry and Donelson, the big question on Grant's mind was what to do with the fifteen thousand prisoners. Three thousand prisoners were sent to Springfield, Illinois, Indianapolis, Indiana and to Chicago, Illinois. The prisoners from Fort Henry were sent to Paducah. Grant recommended parole for Tilghman, but when the War Department found out that Tilghman was from Paducah, they quickly realized that parole would be a huge problem for Union General William T. Sherman's control of the city. The War Department decided that the prisoners would be sent to Cairo, and then to Alton, Illinois. Tilghman was temporally imprisoned in Louisville, Kentucky on February 16, 1862, at which point he was informed that he was to be moved to Alton. But Union Secretary of War Edwin Stanton and Union General George B. McClellan didn't want the Confederate officers to be paroled or exchanged. The Confederate officers would be considered prisoners of war. The senior officers would be sent to Fort Warren. President Lincoln wanted Confederate General Buckner, Kentucky Confederate General Roger Hanson, and Tilghman taken out of Kentucky quickly as possible. [242]

On the February 18, Union General George B. McClellan informed Tilghman that he was to be sent to Fort Warren along with General Buckner. Fort Warren was located on George's Island on the Boston Harbor. It was a fort with pentagonal walls and gun emplacements and was originally a training camp for state volunteers and garrisoned the 14th Massachusetts Infantry. It held a few smugglers and political prisoners from Maryland and the border states. In August 1861, two thousand Confederate prisoners arrived from Governor's Island in New York City. Luckily Tilghman was sent to the elite of Northern prisons. Food was sufficient, entertainment and exercise yards were provided, and discipline was maintained. [243] Both Generals were to be disarmed and closely guarded and not allowed to communicate with anyone. The order was handed down that if they tried to escape the prison guards would put them in irons. The police in each city along their route was put in charge of Colonel Cutts, who assisted in guarding the prisoners. The prisoners were to be treated kindly and made as comfortable as reason permitted. One hundred and ten officers were under guard and started for St. Louis on February 26, 1862. [244]

On March 3, 1862, Tilghman and Buckner arrived at Fort Warren, along with fifty other field officers. Both Generals were kept in separate apartments and were allowed no conversation with any prisoners. The Generals were put on the same footing as other prisoners of war. They were not allowed to write or receive any letters, which must have been hard for Tilghman considering he had a wife and children at home. [245]

On May 13, 1862, the *Boston Gazette* reported that General Tilghman's mother and her sister came to Boston and rented a room at the Revere House, for the purpose of visiting General Tilghman at Fort Warren. There was some difficulty in obtaining the required permission to see her son, but Mrs. Tilghman and her sister, Mrs. Lowry, were allowed to visit Lloyd. The first exclamation on meeting him was "Oh my rebel son!" and during the conversation she said: "When I heard you were taken, I thanked God that you were rescued from secession influences, and were I to hear there was any chance of your being exchanged, I would go on my knees to the President to prevent you from again joining the rebels, for I had rather you remain here during your life than to know you were among the traitors of the country." [246]

By May 21, the Confederate Secretary of War, George Randolf made an inquiry to Union General Irvin McDowell as to how Tilghman and Buckner were being treated. The Confederate War Department had heard that Buckner and Tilghman were confined in dungeons and wanted a response from the proper authorities if this was true. Union General Irvin McDowell was surprised that the letter was sent to him, and immediately referred it to the War Department in Washington. By May 24th, General Irvin McDowell made some inquiries and said that Generals Buckner and Tilghman were not in dungeons. The Union Secretary of War, Edwin Stanton, even became involved, and inquired to Colonel J. Dimick, commander of Fort Warren, as to how the Generals were being treated. Dimick flatly denied that Tilghman and Buckner were in dungeons and said that they were in separate basement rooms. They talked to no one except Dimick and his staff and they had one hour each day for exercise on the ramparts separately. [247]

Northern newspaper reports added fuel to the fire, and again raised the question of how Tilghman and Buckner were being treated in prison. For example, the *Boston Journal* reported that: "150 rebel prisoners at Fort Warren, which will probably be increased very soon, three only are kept in close confinement: Charles Keene, a privateer, and Generals Buckner and Tilghman. Keene is only allowed out at 5:00 a.m. (reveille), to march with his tub, flanked by two of the guard, across the parade ground and back to his cell. The two Generals are allowed, separately, to go out one hour each day, between 9 and 10 o'clock." [248] The Confederate newspapers quickly picked up on this report, and the editorials were laced with comments like "Our Generals in close confinement in a fort, while the Yankee generals are allowed their liberty and suffered to lounge and luxuriate at our best hotels." [249] The Kentuckians were also enraged by this newspaper report. Mrs. Buckner wrote to H.C. Burnett asking him if the report were true. Burnett informed Mrs. Buckner that the report was untrue and that G. W. Randolf, the Confederate Secretary of War, assured Burnett that Buckner and Tilghman were not in close confinement. Captain Stephen F. Chipley, of the Second Kentucky Infantry, who had been paroled from Fort Warren recently, informed Burnett that Generals Buckner and Tilghman had been placed in solitary confinement in rooms that had the windows closed up. Chipley went on to say the generals would not be able to open the windows until each of them pledged that they would not speak to or recognize anyone. Chipley reported that the only reason why the windows were allowed to be opened was because a surgeon had certified that unless the windows were opened the general's health would give way and in all probably death would ensue. Chipley also reported that the officers and privates were not allowed to salute Generals Tilghman and Buckner. General Buckner was not allowed to write to anyone or to see anyone. Burnett reported to Confederate Secretary of War G. W. Randolf that "there are thousands of true men in Kentucky and all in our Army from that State who feel a deep interest in all that concerns these generals, and many of them believe that there has not been that attention upon the part of the authorities to their treatment by the Federals which justice and humanity and their services to the Confederacy demanded." [250]

Randolf wrote Burnett back informing him that the fact of bad treatment of Generals Buckner and Tilghman was denied by the U.S. Government, but Major Cosby, General Buckner's assistant adjutant general, who was also just paroled, said that yes, General Buckner was not allowed to correspond with prisoners, but he was kindly treated, well lodged, and allowed to take the air on the ramparts of the fort. It was also reported that Colonel Dimick, the commander of Fort Warren, was very friendly with Buckner. The issue was finally brought to a close with the assurance of Colonel Dimick himself, and Major Cosby's report. [251]

During the time Tilghman spent in prison, the repercussions from the fall of Fort Henry and Donelson were being felt in the Western Theater. Once Fort Henry and Fort Donelson had been taken, Grant was free to move into Tennessee. He arrived at Pittsburgh Landing, Tennessee in March. Union General

Henry Halleck, Commander of all forces in the West, ordered Union General Don Carlos Buell's army at Nashville to join Grant at Pittsburg Landing, and then to attack Corinth, Mississippi. Confederate General Albert Sidney Johnston concentrated his forces at Corinth to oppose Grant. By the end of March, he had 44,000 men, commanded by Lieutenant General Leondias Polk, Major General John Breckinridge, General Braxton Bragg and Major General William Hardee. They would be facing Ulysses Grant's 39,000 men. Reports came in confirming that another Union army was approaching the area and Johnston knew that he must attack Grant before Union General Don Carlos Buell's 36,000 men reached Pittsburg Landing. Grant assumed that Johnston's army was still in Corinth and did not expect an attack, so no defensive plans were formulated and no trenches or earthworks were dug. Sherman set up his headquarters at a place called Shiloh church. Since Grant assumed that there would be no attack, he placed Sherman's raw recruits in the advance position. Because of rain, and a lost division under Bragg, Johnston was not able to reach Pittsburg Landing until April 6th. [252]

Johnston's troops were less than two miles from the Federal camps. At 5:00 A.M. on Sunday morning, April 6, 1862, Union Major James Powell of the 25th Missouri and three hundred men scouted the area, colliding with Confederate Major Aaron Hardcastle's 3rd Mississippi Infantry Battalion, the advance guard of Wood's brigade, attached to Hardee's Corps. The Confederates began to fire on Powell and his troops. Powell and his men stood their ground as reinforcements were brought up from the brigade. Jesse Appler of the 53rd Ohio deployed his men, but soon fell back before the massive Confederate onslaught. Cleburne began to advance, his goal being to seize the crossroads at Shiloh church. Braxton Bragg moved up to support William Hardee. Grant called for Buell's troops, who had arrived in Savannah the day before, and were on the east bank of the river. Grant also called for Lew Wallace to get his men ready to move out. At 9:00 A.M., Grant rode from his headquarters to the front. By 10:00 A.M., the Confederates had driven through the camps of three Union divisions, sending the surprised blue-clad soldiers reeling back toward the river. Union General Benjamin M. Prentiss's division was pushed back almost a mile. The Confederates stopped at Prentiss' camp and began to eat the food that Prestiss's men had been cooking for their breakfast. This gave Prentiss time to take up a good defensive position on high ground along a sunken road. About 1,000 men formed along the road, which was about a mile behind their original position. Other units formed on either side of Prentiss: Hurlbut sent two brigades on his left, and W. H. L. Wallace aligned three brigades on Prentiss' flanks, two on Prentiss' right and one to his far left, beyond Hurlbut. To the right of Wallace were two brigades of McClernand's division and then Sherman's division. These troops made a desperate attempt to slow the Confederate advance. Union General

Ulysses Grant looked over the new line and ordered Prestiss to "maintain that position at all hazards." [253]

Cheatham's division advanced upon the new Federal line, and when they came within 150 yards, the Federals unleashed their artillery. At 30 yards, Union Colonel William Shaw and his14th Iowa fired at the oncoming Confederates. The Confederate line fell back. On Cheatham's extreme right, Union Brigadier General Jacob Lauman's brigade of Hurlbut's division took on the Confederates. His men opened fire on the Rebels at one hundred yards, but the Confederates approached until they were within ten yards of the 31st Indiana before they were stopped. The Rebel troops under Braxton Bragg continued crashing and screaming through the woods, toward the Federal position. Bragg ordered the men of the 4th, 13th, and the 19th Louisiana and the 1st Arkansas to attack the Federals on the sunken road. Charge after charge, twelve in all, were made against Prentiss' position, and each was repulsed with great slaughter. "It's a hornet's nest in there!" cried the Rebels, recoiling from the blasts of canister, case shot, and the fire from the 8th Iowa's eight hundred rifles. By 2:30 PM, after two hours of fighting, the Confederates were no closer to taking the Federal lines at the Hornet's Nest than they were at the Sunken Road, and the Confederate onslaught began to grind to a halt. There were massive problems on the field. There was no overall Confederate commander, and no coherent plan of attack. The Confederates had 17,000 men against Grant's 4,000 men under Prentiss, but the Confederate troops were sent in piecemeal. Orders were given and then countermanded by different generals. At some points along the line Confederate companies halted because there were no further orders for them. Beauregard was in the rear and did not know what was going on at the front and only sent men where he heard fighting. Corps commanders reduced themselves to small unit commanders. [254]

A Confederate attack led by General Albert Sidney Johnston broke through Union troops in the Peach Orchard on Prentiss left, led by the Kentucky troops under Gen. John C. Breckinridge, and the Rebels pushed back the troops on his right, leaving what was left of Prentiss's division without support. Johnston led the Kentucky Confederate troops toward the Peach Orchard, but about half way there he was struck in the leg by a bullet that severed a major artery and the blood was flowing into his boot. Johnston soon became disoriented and dismounted. Johnston had a field tourniquet in his pocket, but his officer's didn't know how to use it, and earlier in the battle he had sent his personal surgeon Dr. Yandell away to tend to the wounded soldiers. General Johnston soon bled to death. [255]

After Albert Sidney Johnston's death, General P.G.T. Beauregard took command of the Rebel forces. Beauregard now was obsessed with the Hornet's Nest also. He could have gone to the flanks, and driven the Federals right into the river at Pittsburg Landing, but he chose not to. Beauregard soon massed the largest assembly of cannon in the war up to that point, 62 in all, and he aimed them at point blank range at the Hornet's Nest and the Sunken Road. At about 4:00 PM, he began a bombardment with shell and canister. The Hornet's Nest exploded under the fire, but still Prentiss and his men held on, their lines bending back into a horseshoe shape as more and more pressure was applied to their flanks. By 5:30 they were completely surrounded and being attacked on all sides. Unable to do any more to obey Grant's order to hold his position, Prentiss ordered cease-fire and surrendered his remaining 2,200 men at 6:00 PM. However, his gallant defense had given Grant the time he needed to construct a new line to the rear. Grant's new line ran inland at a right angle from the river above Pittsburgh Landing northwest toward Owl Creek. The line was three miles long and strongly defended. Colonel J.D. Webster grouped cannon on the left of the line while Sherman and McClernand protected a road that ran north parallel to the Tennessee River. Lew Wallace arrived at 7:00 PM and set up at the far right of the new line. Colonel Jacob Ammen's brigade, from Buell's corps arrived. The division commander, Brigadier General William Nelson and his men followed Ammen's brigade across the river and took their positions on Grant's new line. [256]

The Confederates had been fighting for twelve hours and were exhausted and hungry, having not eaten since 3:00 A.M.. Many of the Confederates refused to go on and sat down in the abandoned Federal camps and began to eat. Bragg and Polk tried to rally the men for one more attack before darkness set in. Bragg, on the left, could only gather Chalmers' troops and John Jackson's men, who were already out of ammunition. Bragg's two divisions tried to rush the new line, but Federal artillery ripped Bragg's men to pieces. Polk and Hardee, on the right, fought with Sherman's and McClernand's troops, but were not successful in capturing any of them. As twilight settled, Beauregard suspended the assault on the Federals, and recalled Polk and Bragg. [257]

During the night, Nathan Bedford Forrest's cavalry scouted the Federal lines. Forrest reported to Hardee that Grant had about 45,000 men, against their 20,000 Confederates. Grant decided that he would attack the Confederates the next day. [258]

On April 7, 1862, the Union forces pushed forward at about 7:30 A.M. and the outnumbered Confederates were pushed back. Grant took back most of the ground he had lost the previous day. Cleburne put up some resistance around Shiloh Church, leading an attack on Sherman's men, but his soldiers became entangled in the thick undergrowth, and soon his lines were decimated by the Federals. Confederate Brigadier General Sterling A. M. Wood tried to hold Shiloh Church, but his left crumbled and as his flanks became exposed to Federal fire, he pulled back. At 2:30 P.M., Beauregard ordered a withdrawal to Corinth. An hour later, the Confederates began to withdraw. The Union troops were just as exhausted as the Confederates and did not pursue them. On April 8th, Nathan Bedford Forrest's cavalry, the rear guard for the Confederates, was overtaken by Sherman's skirmishers. Forrest led a charge against them, but outdistanced his men in the process and soon realized that he was alone against 2,000 Federals, all aiming their rifles at him. Forrest was shot in the side by a Federal soldier. The bullet lodged against Forrest's spine, but somehow he managed to pick up a Federal soldier and use him as a shield and ride back to his own lines. Forrest was the last man to be injured in the Battle of Shiloh, the first great bloody battle of the war. Union losses were 13,047. Confederate losses were 10,694.

Halleck arrived at Pittsburgh Landing on April 11, and removed Grant from field command. Halleck personally organized the army into a 100,000 man force, with 200 cannon, and arrived on the outskirts of Corinth on May 28th. Beauregard, outnumbered two to one, tried to trick Halleck into thinking that Confederates had more men than they actually had, by sending trains in and out of Corinth. Each time the train arrived the town's people and soldiers would give a great cheer as if a new train load of soldiers had arrived. The ruse worked well and bought Beauregard enough time to safely escort his men out of town. On May 30, the Federals entered a deserted Corinth and seized the Memphis & Charleston railroad. Confederate President Jefferson Davis said "this railroad was the vertebra of the West", and now it was in Federal hands. [259]

On March 2, Beauregard had ordered Leonidas Polk to pull out of Columbus, Kentucky. Beauregard didn't believe Columbus could hold against a Union assault. The Tennessee and Cumberland River were now open to invasion by Grant. Confederate General Beauregard, who was now assigned to command, selected Island No. 10, sixty miles below Columbus, as the strong place where the possession of the Mississippi River was first to be contested.

Island Number 10 below the mouth of the Ohio River. It was an important part of the Confederate river defenses at New Madrid, Missouri. The area was strongly fortified with one hundred and fifty pieces of artillery, and garrisoned by nine thousand Confederates. The weakest part to the Confederate's defenses was New Madrid.

On February 21, 1862 Union General John Pope landed at Commerce and began his march to the town of New Madrid. The march was not easy; the area was surrounded by swamps. The men had to drag pieces of artillery and wagons by hand, but Pope and the Army of the Mississippi arrived at New Madrid on March 3, 1862. Pope found five Confederate regiments of infantry and several companies of artillery, and an earthwork with fourteen heavy guns about a half mile below the town. Pope discovered another work at the upper end of the town with seven pieces of artillery, with entrenchments between the works. Six gunboats were anchored along the shore between the upper and lower redoubts. The approaches to the town were covered by direct and cross fire from at least sixty guns of heavy caliber. Pope knew it would be impossible to take the works, so he waited for his heavy guns to arrive. Pope also established smaller caliber guns to cover the river below in order to blockade the river, and to cut off reinforcements from the Confederates. Pope selected Point Pleasant, twelve miles below the city, to set up the blockade. [260]

By March 12, 1862, the Confederates reinforced Island No. 10 with nine thousand infantry artillery and nine gunboats. The fleet was commanded by Commodore Hollins; the land forces were commanded by Generals McCown, Stewart and Gantt. On that same day, Pope's siege guns arrived and were delivered to Colonel Bissell, Engineer Regiment. The battery was placed eight hundred yards in front of the Confederate's main work at New Madrid. On March 13th, Pope fired on the Confederate work. Captain Mower, First U. S. Infantry, was placed in charge of the siege guns. Colonel Morgan, commanding the 10th and 16th Illinois, was to build the battery and construct the trenches. Both were supported by Stanley's Division, consisting of the 27th and 39th Ohio, under Colonel Groesbeck, and the 43rd and 63rd Ohio under Colonel Smith. [261]

On March 14, Pope's batteries fired on New Madrid's works. The Confederates replied with their entire heavy artillery on land and water. Captain Mower was ordered to fire only on the gunboats. Mower disabled several of the Confederate gunboats and dismounted three of the heavy guns in the Confederate's main work. One of Pope's twenty-four pounders was disabled when a Confederate round struck the muzzle of the gun. Pope extended his trenches toward the bank of the river.

During the night a huge thunderstorm broke out and continued until morning. Just before daylight a flag of truce approached Pope's batteries with information that the Confederates had evacuated their works. Captain Mower was the first to plant his flag on the works.

Pope captured thirty-three pieces of artillery, several thousand small arms, with hundreds of boxes of fixed ammunition, and tents for 10,000 men. The guns were turned on the Confederates. One gunboat and ten large steamers were cut off from below. Island Number 10 was cut off from reinforcements and supplies from below.

Pope's force came under the fire from sixty cannon. Pope's success had forced the Rebel defenders into a small peninsula formed by the winding river, called New Madrid Bend. Impenetrable swamps extended east of New Madrid bend, and the Rebel forces, concentrated at both Island No. 10 and the nearby Tennessee bank, were trapped between the flotilla upriver and Pope's force

120

down river. Pope used the guns at New Madrid in batteries placed at several important locations along the river. His lines were extended seventeen miles along the river. The Confederate gunboats challenged the new batteries along the river and came to within three hundred yards. The Confederate gunboats were repulsed with the loss of one gunboat, and several badly damaged.

The Union flotilla had been firing at long range from the gunboats and mortar boats at Island No. 10 but with no effect. On March 16, Pope was ordered to construct a road through the swamps to a point on the Missouri shore opposite Island No. 10 and to erect batteries at that point. It was determined that a canal would work better than a road. For nineteen days Pope's men worked on the canal. It was finally completed on April 4th. The nine mile long canal was not deep enough for the gunboats, but did allow for barges to cross, bringing in a fresh division, which increased Pope's force to 23,000.

During the night Captain Walker, commander of the *U.S.S. Carondelet*, steamed his gunboat past the batteries at Island No. 10. Although many shots were fired at the gunboat, none of them struck the ship. The gunboat arrived at New Madrid on the 5th.

On April 6, General Granger, Colonel Smith, and Captain Marshall were to make a reconnaissance of the river below, and Captain Walker was to take these men down the river to ascertain the character of the banks and the position and number of the Confederates batteries. The *Carondelet* destroyed a Rebel battery on the Tennessee shore that helped protect the Rebel escape route from Island No. 10.

That night the *U.S.S. Pittsburgh* was ordered down to New Madrid. The gunboat made it through the gauntlet of fire unscathed and linked up with the *U.S.S. Carondelet*. On the morning of April 7, Pope's heavy artillery fired on the Confederate's batteries and the two gunboats ran down the river and joined in the battle. At 12 o'clock the Rebel batteries had been silenced. The steamer containing Paine's division moved out from the landing and began to cross the river. As soon as Pope began crossing the river, the Confederates began to evacuate their position along the bank and the batteries along the Tennessee shore opposite Island No. 10. The Confederate force was moving toward Tiptonville. General Paine's division was ordered to stop his boats and were to land immediately on the opposite shore and push toward Tiptonville.

At 9 P.M. the small force at Island No. 10 found themselves deserted and were surrounded. They surrendered to Commodore Foote. The rest of the Confederate forces were driven by Paine into the swamps; it was not until 4 A.M. the Confederates realized they were cut off and unable to resist, surrendered.

Pope captured three generals, 273 field and company officers, 6,700 privates, 123 pieces of heavy artillery, thirty-five pieces of field artillery, seven thousand stand of arms, tents for twelve thousand men, and numerous amounts of ammunition and supplies. The left flank of the Confederacy's western defenses had totally collapsed and was in Union hands. The same day that Island No. 10 surrendered, the Union also made another victory at New Orleans.

Ninety miles below New Orleans, Louisiana stood Fort Philip, an old Spanish earthwork fort which stood on the Mississippi River's east bank, and was armed with seven hundred men and fifty-three guns. On the west bank stood Fort Jackson, a massive masonry stronghold with sixty-seven guns and another seven hundred men. Fort Jackson was under the command of Lieutenant Colonel Edward Higgins, a former officer of the U.S. Navy. All the land forces were under Brigadier General Johnson K. Duncan. Both forts were surrounded by impenetrable marches and well stocked with supplies and ammunition. Below the forts, Confederate engineers sunk eight hulks across the river that were anchored and chained together, which would create a barricade to impede Union ships and hold the Union ships under the fire of the fort's waterfront batteries. The Confederates also filled flatboats with pine knots, ready to be set ablaze and cut loose to drift downstream into the Yankee's wooden war ships. Also waiting for the Union warships would be four Confederate vessels, two of them ironclads; the *Louisiana* and the *Manassas*. The whole naval force was under Commander John K. Mithcell, C. S. N.

The reason for the extreme measures were to protect the important city of New Orleans. New Orleans was the largest urban area in the Confederacy with 170,000 people. It was also the Confederacy's most important port.

In January of 1862, Admiral David Farragut was given command of the Western Gulf Blockading Squadron. Farragut arrived at Ship Island with the *U.S.S. Hartford* on February 20, 1862. By the middle of March 1862, Farragut had assembled his fleet which consisted six steamers belonging to the mortar flotilla. They were the *Harriet Lane, Owasco, Clifton, Westfield, Miami, Jackson;* besides the mortar schooners. The *Brooklyn* and the *Mississippi* also joined the fleet. In all Farragut had twenty-four wooden ships and nineteen schooners. On April 16, Farragut moved up with his fleet to within three miles of the Confederate forts. The mortar vessels was hidden under the thick woods on the right bank of the river. The mortar schooners had been camouflaged with brush on the mast-heads so that the Confederate gunners could not distinguish them from the trees. The leading vessel was placed to within 2,850 yards from Fort Jackson and 3,680 yards from Fort St. Philip. On each schooner was mounted one massive thirteen-inch mortar. On April 18, the signal was given to fire at the forts. Each schooner was instructed to fire once every ten minutes. The moment the schooners opened fire, the forts opened up with a fury. The firing continued until sundown. The Union forces had fired two hundred and forty shells into the forts. The next morning, the firing commenced.

On April 20, two steamers, the *Pinola* and the *Itasca*, were detailed to break the chain. Both ships were discovered and the Confederate gunners from Fort Jackson fired upon the two gunboats. The schooner's mortars were ordered to redouble their fire to help the two gun boats. In Farragut's words, "Commander Porter, however, kept up such a tremendous fire on them from the mortars that the enemy's shots did the gun boats no injury, and the cable was separated and their connection broken sufficiently to pass through on the left bank of the river." [262]

For nearly five days, the Union fleet had fired 16,800 shells into the Confederate forts. One of the schooners had been lost, and the men were exhausted.

At 2 A.M., Farragut decided to run the gauntlet of the forts. His main fear was the *Louisiana*. The *Louisiana* had sixteen mounted heavy guns, with a crew of two hundred men, and was equipped with a shot-proof gallery from which sharpshooters could fire at an enemy. Luckily for Farragut, the *Louisiana's* engines were not completed, and she was tied to the river bank and could only use one broadside and three bow guns. The first ship to sail down the gauntlet was the *Cayuga*, commanded by Lt. N. B. Harrison. It made it past the broken chain. While passing the forts, the Hartford was struck thirty two times in the hull and rigging. Three men were killed and ten wounded.

The *Brooklyn*, under Captain Thomas Craven, followed the *Hartford*. The *Brooklyn* was attacked by the *Manassas*, commanded by Lieutenant Warley, but did little damage. She was then attacked by a large steamer, which received her broadside at a distance of twenty yards, and drifted out of action in flames. The *Brooklyn* was struck seventeen times in the hull. Nine men were killed and twenty-six wounded.

The battle was pretty much over when the large ships passed the forts. The *Itasca*, the *Winona*, and the *Kennebec* were the only ships that did not proceed down the gauntlet, because they were slow steamers, and it was daylight, which would have made them Confederate targets.

Farragut's loss was thirty-seven killed and one hundred and forty seven wounded. The ships which suffered the most were the *Pensacola*, which took thirty seven hits; the *Brooklyn*, which took thirty five hits; and the *Iroquois*, which took twenty eight hits. The Federal ship *Varuna* was lost.

Farragut told his men to "Push on to New Orleans". Farragut's fleet steamed up the river, but on the way encountered the Chalmette batteries. The Chalmette batteries were on both sides of the river and mounted twenty heavy guns. They also had one thousand infantry at their disposal. But Farragut's fleet swept past the batteries and met no further resistance. Farragut arrived in New Orleans on April 25 at 1 P.M. The "Queen City of the South" was open to the conquerors without resistance. Large angry crowds came out to greet Farragut and his seventeen warships, and the accompanying smaller gunboats. Confederate General Lovell had retreated and had left the city to its civil authorities. Farragut was not prepared to occupy the city, which was a job for Butler and his infantry, who were yet to arrive on transports. But Farragut sent two brave men through the angry citizens towards City hall, where both men were met by the mayor and members of the city council, who had no other choice but to surrender.

While the city was surrendering, Lieutenant Commander Guest was sent with a flag of truce to Fort Jackson calling for both of the forts to surrender, since Farragut was in New Orleans. General Duncan refused to surrender until he had heard from New Orleans.

On April 26, the Federal schooners were ordered to get under way, proceed to Pilot Town, and resupply with ammunition. Six of them were ordered to cross the bar and proceed to the rear of Fort Jackson, and be ready to open fire.

The next day five mortar vessels appeared in the rear of Fort Jackson and the U.S. Steamer *Miami* landed Union troops close to Fort Philip. The garrison mutinied since they had heard that New Orleans had surrendered and there was no use in fighting. The men refused to obey orders and had spiked the guns, and forced their officers to surrender. The Confederates also abandoned Fort Pike and Macomb, which guarded the passes to Lake Pontchartrain and Fort Livingston, which was the entrance to Barataria Bay.

On April 28, Duncan sent a flag of truce and came on board the *Harriet Lane* proposing to surrender Forts Jackson and St. Philip. General Duncan and his companions left the *Harriet Lane* and went ashore. In less than ten minutes, the Confederate flags were hauled down, and both forts were delivered over to the Union officers. Commander Mitchell set the *Louisiana* on fire. The *Louisiana* soon exploded and sank below the waters. The *Defiance* and the *McRae* were also destroyed. Mitchell tried to escape capture by boarding a steamer. The *Harriet Lane* saw Mitchell and his men trying to escape and headed for the steamer Mitchell was on. The order was given for the *Harriet Lane* to fire on the flag pole, carrying Mitchell's flag. The Confederate flag was immediately taken down, the steamer was stopped and Mitchell surrendered.

On May 1, the Federal army under Benjamin Butler occupied New Orleans. The Battle for New Orleans was over.

After capturing Island No. 10 Union General John Pope and Flag Officer Andrew Foote made plans to capture Fort Pillow. Fort Pillow was the last major stronghold between Island No. 10 and Memphis, Tennessee. In February 1862, Confederate General Leonidas Polk sent Brigadier General John Gillepigue to command Fort Pillow. Confederate General P. G. T. Beauregard sent thousands of slaves to improve the entrenchments at Fort Pillow. By

April 10, 1862, Foote and Pope's 20,000 men were ready to attack, but Pope's men would be sent to Corinth, Mississippi, and he was left with only 1,500 men. [263]

On May 9, Capt. Charles H. Davis replaced Foote, who had never quite recovered from his wound. Davis had seven ironclads, sixteen mortar boats, and a wooden gunboat. Most of the ships were anchored five miles above Fort Pillow, at a place called Plum Run Bend. The *Cincinnati* and *Mortar No. 10* were anchored a few miles down river, firing two-hundred-pound shells at Fort Pillow. The Confederates decided to attack the Union flotilla on May 10, 1862, with their eight gunboats: The *CSS General Sterling Price, Sumter, General Bragg, General Earl Van Dorn, Little Rebel, General Jefferson Thompson, General Beauregard*, and the *Colonel Lovell*. [264]

The Rebel boats left their moorings at 6 A.M. and proceeded up the river passing a sharp point, which brought all the Confederate ships into view of the Union flotilla. The Federal gunboat, *Cincinnati*, was guarding a mortar boat, that was shelling the fort. The Confederate ship *General Bragg*, under the command of Captain W. H. H. Leonard, came at her; the *Cincinnati* firing her heavy guns, retreated toward a bar where the depth of water would not be sufficient for the Rebel boats to follow. The *Bragg* boldly continued receiving fire from nearly the whole fleet, and struck the *Cincinnati* a violent blow that stopped her further flight, then rounded down the river under a broadside fire and drifted until her tiller rope, which had gotten out of order, could be readjusted. A few moments after the *Bragg* struck her blow the *General Sterling Price*, commanded by Officer J. E. Henthorne, ran into the same boat a little aft of her starboard midship, carrying away her rudder, stern post, and a large piece of her stern. This threw the *Cincinnati's* stern to the *Sumter*, under the command of Captain W. W. Lamb, who struck her, running at the utmost speed of his boat. The *General Earl Van Dorn*, under the command of Capt. Isaac D. Fulkerson, running in the rear of the *Price* and *Sumter*, directed his attention to the *Mound City*, at the time pouring broadsides into the *Sterling Price* and *Sumter*. As the *Van Dorn* proceeded to fire her thirty-two pounder and silenced a mortar boat that "was filling the air with its terrible missiles." The *Van Dorn*, still holding on the *Mound City* midship, in the act of striking the *Mound City* sheered, and the *Van Dorn* struck her a glancing blow, making a hole four feet deep in her starboard forward quarter. At this juncture the *Van Dorn* was above four of the Yankee's boats. The *Mound City* soon sank. [265]

The Union boats took positions where the water was too shallow for the Rebel boats to follow. Since the Confederates guns were too short in range and "inferior in number and size," [266] Captain J. E. Montgomery, commanding the Confederate River Defense, recalled his ships. The Confederate flotilla made it back to Memphis to the cheers of the crowds. The Union warships did not follow. The Battle of Plum Run Bend was over. The Confederates lost only two men, and managed to sink two of the Union's most powerful ironclads. [267]

On May 19, Union Brigadier General Isaac F. Quinby, commanding the District of the Mississippi, proceeded to the flotilla above Fort Pillow. The troops under Colonel Fitch would be reinforced by Quinby's companies, which consisted of eight companies of the 47th Indiana, four companies of the 34th Indiana, two companies of the 54th Illinois, four companies of the 2nd Illinois Cavalry, and a section from each of the two companies of the 2nd Illinois artillery, three pieces of Captain De Golyer's Michigan battery, and one half of the Missouri company of Volunteer Sappers and Miners. With Fitch's troops it brought the Union force to around 2,500. Quinby made a reconnaissance of the area and deemed a frontal attack by land on the fort was impossible. [268]

On May 30, 1862, Beauregard pulled out of Corinth, Mississippi to Tuscumbia River, Alabama. Beauregard sent a message to Brigadier General Villepigue telling him that he wanted to draw the Yankees farther into the interior, where he could strike a blow, which could not be done at the present location. Beauregard ordered Villepigue to withdraw from Fort Pillow for Grenada.

On June 4, the Yankees found Fort Pillow evacuated and entered the Fort. After the evacuation of Fort Pillow, the Confederate soldiers were sent to Memphis on transports. The Confederate fleet was short of coal and fell back to Memphis on the 5th, with the intention of returning to Island No. 40. When Beauregard learned that Corinth, Mississippi was occupied by Union General Henry Halleck, he ordered the evacuation of troops from Fort Pillow and Memphis on June 4, 1862. The city could not be defended by land. On June 5 at 10 P.M., the tugs, which were on picket duty above the city, reported the Union tugs in sight. This was discredited, but the Confederate gunboats anchored in the channel of the river, prepared for a battle. Federal ships started to advance south on the Mississippi.

Confederate Commodore Montgomery and Confederate Brigadier General Jeff Thompson, of the Missouri State Guard, were put in joint command of the river defense by General Beauregard. The Confederate River defense consisted of the Navy Rams, *General Beauregard*, *General Bragg*, *General Price*, *General Earl Van Dorn*, *General Thompson*, *Colonel Lovell*, *Sumter*, and *Little Rebel*.

At 4:00 A.M. on June 6th Union Captain Charles Davis, commanding the Union ironclads, moved toward Memphis, from Island No. 45, two miles south of the city. He had under his command the *Benton*, *Louisville*, *Carondelet*, *Cairo*, and *St. Louis*, which was later joined by the *Queen of the West* and the *Monarch*, commanded by army Colonel Charles Ellet. Davis' fleet captured the Confederate transport ship *Sovereign* north of the city.

At 12:30 A.M. on June 6, Montgomery requested two companies of artillery to be sent aboard at daybreak. All of Montgomery's men were at the depot awaiting transportation to Grenada. Thompson immediately ordered the companies to prepare for battle. At dawn Thompson was awakened with the information that the Union boats were in sight of Memphis. Thompson hurried on board to consult with Montgomery. He instructed Thompson to hurry his men to Fort Pickering Landing, and sent a tug to bring them up to the gunboats, which were advancing to attack the Union boats. Thompson hurried his men to the place indicated, but before they could reached their boats, it was already too late. In an hour and a half, the Confederate ships had been either destroyed or driven below Fort Pickering. Thompson marched back to the depot to await orders.

Thompson saw a large portion of the engagement from the river banks, and he said that many of the Confederate boats were handled poorly or the plan of battle was very faulty. The Union rams did most of the fighting, and were handled better than the Confederate gunboats. The Union guns and sharpshooters were constantly employed, while the Confederate boats were without either. The *Colonel Lovell* was injured and sank in the middle of the river, when the *Queen of the West* rammed her. *Colonel Lovell's* Captain James Delancy, and a number of others, swam to shore. The *Beauregard* and the *Sterling Price* were running at the Union ship *Monarch* from opposite sides when the *Monarch* passed from between them, and the *Beauregard* ran into the *Price*, knocking off her wheel and entirely disabling her. Both were run to the Arkansas shore and abandoned. The *Little Rebel*, the commodore's flag ship, was run ashore and abandoned after she had been completely riddled with shells. The *Bragg* was also badly shelled and run aground. The *Little Rebel* had its machinery blasted by Union cannon fire and the boat was run aground by the ramming of the *Monarch*. The Union gunboat *Benton* set the *Thompson* on fire with her cannon shots, and the *Thompson* soon exploded. The battle continued down the river out of sight of Memphis, and it reported that only one of the Confederate boats, the *Van Dorn*, escaped.

The only casualties on the Union side was Colonel Charles Ellet who had been severely wounded by a pistol bullet that hit his knee. He died several days later. The Confederates lost about 180 men, and between 70 to 100 were captured.

Immediately following the battle, Colonel Ellet's son, Medical Cadet Charles Ellet, Jr. officially received the surrender of the city from the Mayor of Memphis. The Indiana Brigade, commanded by Colonel G. N. Fitch, then ordered his troops into the city. The capture of Memphis was the last of many captures along the Mississippi, since the fall of Forts Henry and Donelson. Memphis was an important commercial and economic center on the Mississippi. It also opened up another section of the Mississippi to Union shipping.

LLOYD TILGHMAN

While Tilghman was in prison, the Union forces managed to take the Tennessee, Cumberland and parts of the Mississippi River. All of the Union achievements were from the fall of Fort Henry and Donelson. Union forces would soon move on one of the most important river cities on the Mississippi river: Vicksburg. When Tilghman was finally exchanged and set from free from prison life, he would face his next mission: the protection of Vicksburg.

CHAPTER FIVE
Release From Prison

On August 16, 1862, Confederate General Braxton Bragg issued Special Order No. 153, in which Tilghman was to proceed to Vicksburg, Mississippi and take command of all "abolition and Confederate officers and soldiers who may be in the vicinity for the purpose of being exchanged or paroled." [269] Tilghman was to establish a camp near Vicksburg at some suitable point on the railroad where the men could be amply supplied. Tilghman would then immediately organize the Confederate prisoners who had been exchanged. Tilghman was to retain the men in the original companies and regiments in which they were enlisted. [270]

On August 17, Confederate Chief of Staff for Department No. 2, Thomas Jordan issued Special Orders No. 155, which spelled out how newly paroled prisoners were organized. Brigadier General Tilghman played a large role in how they were organized. Regiments that enlisted for twelve months would be reorganized under the provisions of the "Act to provide for the public defense" approved on April 16, 1862. Furloughs would not be granted. Brig. General Tilghman had the military command of the camps of rendezvous and instruction for exchanged and paroled men of Department Number 2. When the Union and Confederate prisoners were exchanged, Brigadier General Tilghman was to report to Major General Earl Van Dorn. All officers and men captured at Fort Donelson, New Madrid Bend, and Island No. 10, between the ages of 18 to 35 who were not on duty with other regiments would be escorted to Jackson, Mississippi, to report to General Tilghman. All prisoners of war within the limits of the department taken from the Yankees would be sent under escort to Jackson, Mississippi to be turned over to Brigadier General Tilghman. [271]

On August 27, 1862, by Special Order No. 118, Tilghman was exchanged for Union General John Reynolds. Buckner was exchanged for Brigadier General G. A. McCall. Tilghman and Simon Buckner and ten thousand exchanged men were then ordered to Jackson, Mississippi. General Tilghman had the difficult task of equipping, clothing, and arming the men and forming them into artillery, cavalry, and infantry units. [272]

By September 14, 1862, Major General Sterling Price and his Army of the West had captured Iuka, Mississippi, near the Tennessee border. Price's orders were to prevent Union troops in northern Mississippi, commanded by Major General's Grant, E. O. C. Ord, and William S. Rosecrans from moving into Tennessee. Bragg was in the process of moving his Army of Mississippi, and General Edmund Kirby Smith's Army of East Tennessee into Kentucky. Union General Grant feared that Price's army would move north to reinforce Bragg's army, and take total control of Kentucky and eliminate the only Union force, commanded by Union General Don Carlos Buell. Grant ordered Ord's eight thousand men to move northwest toward Iuka, and General Rosecrans nine thousand men were to move to from the south toward Iuka. Both Generals were to attack Price. The attack would not begin until September 19, 1862.

While the Union forces were moving in on Price at Iuka, Tilghman had four thousand men arriving in Jackson, Mississippi. Tilghman was already facing problems of who was in charge of forming the newly released men into units. Bragg sent his staff officer to oversee Tilghman. Tilghman wrote to George Randolf, Confederate Secretary of War, that he was getting tired of Bragg's staff officer breathing down his neck. Tilghman wrote: "You will settle the vexed question where the troops are to go ultimately and relieve me of the embarrassments of Bragg's staff officer. I can organize men promptly and more efficiently. Can you give me full and sole control? I cannot communicate with Bragg and matters are all at cross purposes." [273] George Randolf told Tilghman that he was to take his orders from General Earl Van Dorn as to how the troops were to be reorganized, since he was the senior officer present. [274]

Tilghman hunted down arms for his men anywhere he could get them. He wrote to Confederate General Sterling Price and asked if he could have his arms and where were they. Officers were asking Tilghman to get their sidearms and swords back from the Yankees. Many of the officers found out that the sidearms were at Columbus or Camp Chase, Ohio, which had been sent to Vicksburg, and they wanted them returned as soon as possible. Another task that Tilghman had to handle.

On September 18, 1862, Price was informed of Ord's men approaching Iuka. General Van Dorn immediately ordered Price to join his forces at Rienzi. The next day Grant changed his plans, telling Rosecrans to attack Price first, not Ord. Ord ordered Price to surrender. Price began to evacuate Iuka and collided with Rosecrans' men, southwest of the city. Price attacked Rosecrans. [275]

Confederate Brigadier General Lewis Little's division was called away from Ord's front to join in the battle against Rosecrans. At 2:30 P.M., Price sent Brigadier General Henry Little to charge Rosecrans' position. Little seized the Federal guns of the 11th Ohio battery, and overwhelmed and put to flight the 80th Ohio Infantry. Price then ordered Little to send forward his entire division, but Little was killed by a Yankee bullet before he could give the order. The confusion caused by Little's death allowed Rosecrans to deploy the bulk of his men. The Federals recaptured the guns of the 11th Ohio battery but were again driven off. Hebert took over command of the division. Hebert attacked Union General Charles Hamilton's division, Rosecrans' force, along the Jacinto road, which was located 1.5 miles south of Iuka. Ord did not attack, claiming that he did not hear any fighting. Rosecrans would fight the battle alone. Darkness ended the battle.

The next day Price and his Army retreated south along the Fulton road. Price joined General Van Dorn's forces. The Federals lost 825 men, 141 killed. The Confederates lost 693, with 86 dead. [276]

By September 22, 1862, 10,368 non-commissioned officers and privates had been exchanged. On General Bragg's orders, General Sterling Price immediately wanted five thousand of the exchanged men, since he had arms for them. Tilghman refused to send them, and General Price refused General Tilghman's request for arms. General Price wanted the men because of a huge Federal force that was on its way to Vicksburg from Memphis. Grant was beginning his direct assault upon Vicksburg. Another Federal force was coming from New Orleans. President Jefferson Davis would have to settle the dispute between the feuding Generals.

While this feuding was going on, Tilghman was still in charge of exchanging the Federal prisoners that the Confederates had. Tilghman was corresponding with Major General Ben Butler who was in New Orleans, Louisiana. All Union officers were sent to Vicksburg. Several of these officers were captured at the battle of Iuka, Mississippi. Tilghman also pointed out that the Federals had General Charles Clark , C. S. Army, who was wounded at the Battle of Baton Rouge and in Federal hands. Tilghman requested that he be exchanged as quickly as possible. Tilghman also pointed out the prisoners taken at Forts Saint Philip and Jackson. Butler asked Tilghman how many men were involved in the exchange that involved Union prisoners. Tilghman wrote Butler that it was between 25,000 to 30,000 prisoners. The prisoners captured at the Battle of Munfordsville, Kentucky, which was fought in August 1862 during the Kentucky Campaign, and Cave City, Kentucky numbering 6,000 and 1,800 were to be delivered at Vicksburg. Tilghman wrote to Butler that he thought Baton Rouge would be an excellent site for the exchange. On October 3rd, Butler wrote back to Tilghman informing him that all prisoners held by the United States would be paroled and sent to Tilghman. The prisoners would leave by steam boat on October 8, and would arrive at Baton Rouge. Butler also asked if the Eighth Vermont which was captured by General Taylor be exchanged. Brigadier General Clark was with his family in New Orleans and was in much better health and was allowed to leave New Orleans whenever he felt ready. All prisoners who were captured at Forts Jackson and Saint Philip would be exchanged and sent to Tilghman. [277]

By October, Union General Ulysses Grant was moving his force out toward Vicksburg. General Daniel Ruggles wrote to Major General Earl Van Dorn who was in Holly Springs, that a 5,000 man Union force with three companies of cavalry and two batteries were leaving New Orleans. The call was sounded for all men to be ready in Vicksburg and that Tilghman should join the force to combat the Yankees. [278]

After the Battle of Iuka, Generals Van Dorn and Price planned the attack on Corinth, Mississippi. Corinth was defended by two sets of earthworks that guarded the northern approach to town. Confederate Major General Earl Van Dorn's 22,000 men left Chewalla, Tennessee, at dawn, on Oct. 3, 1862. Marching ten miles south to Corinth, Mississippi, they assaulted Major General William Rosecrans' twenty-three thousand Federals in these works. The Confederates, a combined command of Van Dorn's and Major General Sterling Price's troops, intended to take the town, regain control of the Mobile and Ohio and Memphis and Charleston railroads, and organize an invasion of Tennessee. [279]

Van Dorn believed Rosecrans thought that the Confederates were moving against Northern railroad lines. Rosecrans, unsure of Confederate intent, recalled all his troops within the Corinth lines. Van Dorn's attack, calculated as a surprise, depended on three divisions, under Brigadier General's Dabney Maury, Louis Hebert and Major General Mansfield Lovell, rushing the town's western works on a broad front and carrying them by shock. [280]

Driving in Union pickets, Confederates lines were formed with Lovell's division on the right and Maury's and Hebert's on the left. As the Federals approached the pickets, three earthquake tremors occurred, frightening the troops. Van Dorn, conscious of his men's morale, urged commanders to show firmness in the assault. [281]

Federals manned a chain of field forts on Corinth's western perimeter. A four-hundred-yard expanse of felled timber surrounded them. Corinth sat over a half mile to the rear, surrounded by a second fortified line. Rosecrans posted only half his troops in the works. When a brigade of skirmishers rushed into the lines on October 3, crying that Confederates were about to attack, the defenders were ill-prepared for the massive attack that ensued. Lovell's three divisions of Confederates crashed into the Union works, manned by Brigadier General Thomas Davies Federal division.

Confederates dressed ranks in the fallen timber, rushed forward, carried the works, and drove the Federals toward their interior lines. All three of Davies' brigade commanders were wounded_Brigadier General Pleasant Hackelman would later die of his wounds. Van Dorn's troops pursued, but 90 degree heat, fatigue, and water shortages slowed them. An hour's halt was called for rest, allowing the Federals to reinforce a second line outside the interior fortifications. A renewed Confederate assault failed. Rosecrans' men, holding a compact front, gave stiffer resistance. As daylight faded, Van Dorn consulted with Price, and the battle was stopped. Lovell had performed poorly in the October 3 fighting. Price claimed that a reliable performance from him might have made a last assault successful.

At 10:00 A.M., the battle would begin, with Hebert attacking and flanking the Union right and, at the same time Maury was to rush on the Union center, and Lovell would advance from the southwest to roll up the Union left. Three artillery batteries on high ground west of town would soften up the Federals starting at 4 AM.

But at 4 A.M., the Confederate cannons were smothered by heavier Union guns. Hebert reported sick after his advance was delayed, and his replacement, Brigadier General Martin E. Green, lost an hour fumbling with instructions. Maury's unsupported troops escalated their skirmishing with the Federals to pitched proportions, bringing enemy artillery fire down on Confederate positions. The Southerner's center advanced and Green's division followed.

At 9:30 Lovell's troops skirmished but did not move forward. He never appeared at the front or ordered an attack. Maury's and Green's men fought into the Federal lines, Maury's piercing them and charging into Corinth itself. Without Lovell's support on the south, the breakthrough was thrown back by the Union troops. Confederates in Colonel W. H. Moore's brigade managed to break through the Federal line, capture a redoubt and overrun a battery. The 20th Arkansas fought in the streets of Corinth until their colonel was killed. They were soon cut off, and caught in a crossfire by Union troops. Rosecrans soon regained his lost ground, and by 11:30 A.M., the fighting was over. [282]

On the Confederate's right-center, Confederate Brigadier General John Moore led five regiments against Battery Robinett. Colonel William P. Rogers, commander of the 2nd Texas, was in the vanguard of the assault. The Southern troops briefly took possession of the work. Rogers was killed, and three of Moore's regimental commanders had fallen. A counterattack by four Federal regiments recaptured the battery, and the Confederates fled to the rear. [283]

By noon, the Confederates had withdrawn toward the road north to Chewalla. Nearly a third of those engaged in the October 4 fighting were casualties. Lovell's division reported few. Rosecran's troops, badly shaken, did not pursue. A two day Confederate retreat took Van Dorn's troops to Ripley.

Rosecrans lost nearly 2,500 killed and wounded in the two day fight. Confederates lost 2,470 dead and wounded, and another 1,763 missing in battle or deserted during the retreat to Ripley. [284]

133

LLOYD TILGHMAN

By October 11, 1862, Confederate General Earl Van Dorn had twelve thousand men at Holly Springs, General Price had twelve thousand men ten miles away. Tilghman joined Van Dorn's forces. Grant's forces were concentrating in their front, and advancing toward Ripley and also from Grand Junction. The Confederates were desperate for musket caps, cartridges, lead, and cannon ammunition. Lloyd Tilghman said there were no ammunition or arms for the exchanged prisoners at Columbus or anywhere. Tilghman said that arms were going to Price and Pettus, but not him. This was drastically slowing down his process of arming his men and sending them out for combat. [285]

By October 24, Tilghman had completed the reorganization of the exchanged prisoners. Union General Grant's headquarters was at Jackson, and the Confederates held Holly Springs. By the end of October, Grant was ready to move south. Grant massed his army around Grand Junction, midway between Memphis and Corinth.

CHAPTER SIX

The Vicksburg Campaign

On November 2, 1862, Union General Ulysses S. Grant began his campaign against Vicksburg. Vicksburg was the most important city to the Confederates because it occupied the first high ground coming close to the river below Memphis. From there a railroad runs east, connecting with other roads leading to all points of the Southern States. So long as Vicksburg was held by the Confederates, the free navigation of the river was prevented. Grant's mission was to follow the Mississippi River, maintaining his supply line, until he reached Jackson. Once he arrived in Jackson, his men would cut the railroad line linking it with Vicksburg.

Grant ordered Union General Charles Hamilton and his three divisions to leave Corinth and head for Grand Junction. He also ordered Union General James McPherson to leave Bolivar and head for the Grand Junction. [286]

Union General McPherson commanded Grant's left wing and General C. S. Hamilton commanded the center, while Sherman was at Memphis with the right wing. Confederate General John Pemberton was fortified at the Tallahatchie River, but occupied Holly Springs and Grand Junction on the Mississippi Central Railroad. McPherson and Hamilton approached Grand Junction. Hamilton camped behind Scott Creek, two and a half miles south of Grand Junction. McPherson's right wing was west of Hamilton. Lauman's and Quinby's divisions headed for Lamar. Colonel Amory Johnson's brigade, McPherson's division, formed his brigade a mile and a half down the Holly Springs road, and relieved Union Colonel Albert Lee's cavalry. It would not be long before both sides clashed. Union Colonel Lee's men dismounted and formed parallel to Holly Springs road. Lee's men charged and attacked Confederate Colonel William Jackson's cavalry. The Federal cavalrymen poured huge volleys into Jackson's flank. The cavalry under Lee had Colt revolving rifles, which could fire six rounds of ammunition and were dismounted, but the Confederate cavalry had only shotguns, which were highly inaccurate and produced a scattering effect. The Confederate cavalry were on horseback, which made the task of aiming at the enemy difficult. After the skirmish Lee was to ride to Hudsonville and Colonel Lauman's division were camped at Lamar to wait for Union Colonel Quinby's arrival. At Hudsonville, Lee's cavalry again clashed with Jackson's Confederate cavalry. During the two fights the Confederates lost 130 men, sixteen killed. On November 9, Quinby entered Lamar, and McPherson prepared to advance to Coldwater. McPherson saw ten thousand men from the hills south of the river and decided to turn back. Pemberton retired his infantry and artillery south of the Tallahatchie. [287]

On November 10, 1862, the Federals were massing toward Holly Springs. Price had evacuated Holly Springs, but Confederate General Pemberton countermanded that order. The Confederates occupied Coldwater, and Abbeville. Pemberton had four divisions: Price had 10,000 men in two divisions: Brigadier General Dabney Maury, Brigadier General John Bowen. Brigadier General Albert Rust was commanding Lovell's division, who was sick at Holly Springs. Tilghman's division was made up of the released prisoners. Rust had six thousand men in three brigades; five batteries, four guns each. Tilghman had four thousand men in two brigades; two batteries, two guns each. At Abbeville there were twelve thousand militia to hold the line at Tallahatchie. There were no entrenchments at Coldwater, and only rifle pits at Holly Springs. There were no heavy cannon. Price was positioned on the hills north of Abbeville, Maury's division covered the bridges and Bowen's left flank at Wyatt. Lovell's Corps was on Price's right near the ford at the mouth of the Tippah, and the twelve thousand militia of the State Troops marched from Abbeville to Oxford. [288]

The Yankees were on the move; ten thousand soldiers went to Mobile, Alabama. There would be a movement towards New Orleans and General Samuel Curtis was to reinforce Helena, Arkansas and move on Grenada, and move into Little Rock, Arkansas if possible. Six regiments had left for Memphis, and six more were to follow. The Third Regular Cavalry and other regiments of cavalry, including artillery, were to join Union General William T. Sherman in LaGrange, Tennessee. Grant's forces were repairing the railroads in Holly Springs, so that rations could be sent to his men by rail.

While the Confederates were at Abbeville, a Court of Inquiry was held. Brigadier General Bowen made charges against General Van Dorn for his conduct during the Battle of Corinth, which was fought back in October. General Tilghman sat on the Court of Inquiry board. Other members of Court of Inquiry board were Generals Sterling Price and Dabney Maury. General Bowen made specific charges. There were two charges. The first charge was Neglect of duty, and was broken down into several specifications.

The first specification was that "Major General Earl Van Dorn, command-ing the troops of the Confederate States Provisional Army in the District of Mississippi and East Louisiana, including the force known as the Army of the West, did concentrate the greater portion of said force and undertake an important expedition against the enemy at Corinth, Miss., where they (the enemy) were strongly fortified and in formidable numbers, fully prepared for a stubborn resistance, without due consideration or forethought; and did utterly fail and neglect to discharge his duties as a general commanding an army in the following particulars, first: By failing to provide himself with a proper map of the approaches and plan of the work to be attacked. Second: By eschewing entirely the services of an engineer officer and failing to recon-noiter the position before the attack. Third: By marching his troops to the attack with an insufficient supply of commissary stores to maintain them, depending entirely upon captures from the enemy to enable the occupation of the place if taken. Fourth: By marching the troops in a hasty and disorderly manner, hurling them upon the enemy with an apparent attempt to take a command by surprise whose outposts had been engaged with his (General Van Dorn's) advance for thirty-six hours before attack. All this at or near the towns of Ripley and Corinth, Miss., on or about the 1st to the 3d of October, A.D. 1862." [289]

In the second specification, Bowen claimed that "Major General Earl Van Dorn, after the troops of his command had driven the enemy from their exterior line of entrenchments at Corinth, Miss., October 3, 1862, did fail and neglect to perform his duty as a general commanding an army by delaying the attack upon their inner works until the next morning, thereby affording them ample time to receive re-enforcements, of which advantage they fully availed themselves.

Specification 3.--In this, that Maj. Gen. Earl Van Dorn did fail and neglect, as a general commanding, by suffering the enemy to receive large reinforcements on the nights of October 3 and 4, at Corinth, Miss., without his knowledge, when he, the aforesaid General Van Dorn, was present inside of their works with a victorious army and in hearing of the noise made by their wagons and artillery carriages, and did further neglect to ascertain the strength and location of the enemy and their entrenchments, which he ordered to be taken by assault in the morning." [290]

In the Second charge Bowen accused Van Dorn with Cruel and improper treatment of officers and soldiers under his command. In the first specifica-tion Bowen said that "Maj. Gen. Earl Van Dorn, commanding the aforesaid army in the expedition against Corinth and on his retreat from the same, did cause long, tedious, and circuitous marches to be made, and either through ignorance of the route or neglect repeatedly march and countermarch over the same road, and did have a large command moving to and fro without any apparent reason while the men were foot-sore, wearied, and starving. This on the retreat between Corinth and Holly Springs, Miss., on or about October 6, 7, and 8, 1862." [291]

In Specification two, Bowen claimed that "Maj. Gen. Earl Van Dorn, commanding as aforesaid, did allow one or more trains of cars, freighted with wounded soldiers from the battlefield at and near Corinth, Miss., to be detained without any necessity at Water Valley, Miss., during one or more entire nights, said wounded soldiers having been herded in said cars at Holly Springs without blankets or nourishment and many with undressed wounds, no surgeon, officer, nurse, or attendant with them, thus causing an incredible amount of useless suffering and creating disaffection among the troops."

After hearing all the evidence, Tilghman, Price, and Maury deliberated, all the members including Tilghman, found no justification for the charges, and Van Dorn was found not guilty. [292] It was not long before Van Dorn would be replaced.

On November 27, 1862, General John Pemberton knew the Yankees were at Helena and ordered troops at Columbus, Pocahatoula, and Jackson to proceed to Vicksburg.

The next day Pemberton had been informed that the Union force based at Delta had struck inland, taking the Coffeeville road and the Union cavalry, under Col. Albert Lee, had reached the Tallahatchie. He was also aware of the Union troops under General C. C. Washburn were heading for the Mississippi Central railroad.

Two days later, on November 29, Colonel Albert Lee's Union cavalry was at Ebenezer Church. Pemberton ordered his men to evacuate the Tallahatchie line. General Lovell was to march to Yocona at Taylor's Depot and Colonel Jackson's cavalry was to cover the roads leading south from the Tallahatchie and the Tobytubby, Wyatt, and Tippah Fords. Griffith's 1,200 Texans with four of McNally's Arkansas battery left Tobytubby. At Oakland, the Confederates learned that the Federals under Major General C. C. Washburn were heading for Coffeeville, and that the Federals had retired on the Charleston and Mitchell's Cross Roads.

On November 30, 1862, General Tilghman's tents were burned by orders of Pemberton, as Tilghman was evacuating Abbeville. A court of inquiry was held. Major General Lovell told Tilghman that the tents were heavy and wet, and they were to be thrown out on the road to allow the wagons to pass over the bad roads and keep up with the train. Tilghman was exonerated for burning the tents. Tilghman was ordered to report to Confederate Major General Lovell. [293]

By December 1, 1862, the Confederates had abandoned the Tallahatchie line. Grant's headquarters was at Holly Springs. Pemberton retired behind the Yalobusha. Union General C. C. Washburn returned to Mitchell's Cross

Roads. The 28th Mississippi Cavalry attacked the Union outpost, guarding the crossing of the Yocona, manned by two companies of Colonel Spicely's command. Washburn ordered Major Burgh and Captain Walker to support the infantry. The mountain howitzers opened fire on the Confederates. The Mississippi cavalry broke and ran. Washburn decided to raid Coffeeville. Colonel Griffith's Texans rode out of Coffeeville and proceeded to Grenada and Preston. The Confederates pulled out of Tallahatchie and fell back to Oxford. [294]

On December 2, the Texas troops reached Preston, but the Federals had already left. Griffith remained at Preston. The village covered Pemberton's left flank. By that evening Washburn decided to attack Coffeeville. Colonel Spicely was to abandon Oakland. Six hundred infantry and a section of guns of the 1st Iowa battery were to proceed with the cavalry. Griffith's men had rode to Oakland and waited for the Union troops. The 3rd Texas cavalry was north of the road to Mitchell's Crossroads. The 3rd Texas would attack the Union troops in the flank and rear. The 6th Texas led by Captain Jack Wharton guarded the Charleston road. The 27th Texas Cavalry took position at the junction. Major Broocks and three companies were along the road to Mitchell's Crossroads. The Indiana troops deployed. A fight broke out and Colonel Hawkins came to Brooks' support. The Texans pushed the Indiana troops back. Two hundred yards to the rear, Walker deployed his men dismounted. Walker called for help. The mountain howitzers were brought forward. Griffith's men charged, and the 27th Texas broke the Federal line and the Indiana troops fled. Two mountain howitzers were captured. Another section of mountain howitzers was placed on the field and raked the 27th Texas. They came to a halt. Wharton and the 6th Texas dismounted. Griffith's left was in danger of being turned. The Texans returned to their horses and withdrew. At Oakland the Texans re-formed. The Union cavalry resumed their advance. Griffith ordered a retreat. One mountain howitzer was left behind. Two miles east of Oakland, Griffith again reformed. Colonel Thomas Stephens brigade, which was the left flank of Washburn's line, entered Oakland. Washburn halted. Washburn camped in Oakland and on the 4th he evacuated Oakland and reached Coldwater and linked up with General Hovey's command. On December 5, Hovey headed for Delta and reached his destination on December 7th.

Meanwhile Pemberton had withdrawn fifty miles to the Yalobusha. Hovey had outflanked the Confederates out of their fortified position. Colonel Albert Lee's Union cavalry was at Tallahatchie, near Wyatt's Ferry and was to join the main Union force at Oxford. Colonel Hatch's brigade was near Old Waterford. North of Oxford Confederate Brigadier General Louis Hebert's brigade had blocked the road. A skirmish broke out and the Confederates pulled back. Lee's cavalry continued to harass Pemberton's rear guard. By nightfall Oxford was in Colonel Lee's hands. Sherman was to march to Abbeville.

On December 3, Colonel Theophilus Dickey, Chief of the Union Cavalry, ordered Hatch's brigade, consisting of eight companies of the Second Iowa Cavalry forward on the Coffeeville road. Union Colonel Albert Lee's cavalry brigade was to take a road to the east of the one followed by Hatch. At 7 A.M. Hatch left Oxford. Lee's men crossed the Yocona on the Paris road. Lee and Hatch were to meet at Coffeeville. General Logan's infantry reached Oxford and relieved the cavalry. [295]

The next day on December 4, 1862, Colonel Mizner, of the 3rd Michigan Cavalry and 6th Illinois Cavalry, headed down the Water Valley road with the 3rd Michigan and one gun of Co. G, 2nd Illinois Artillery. He was to reinforce Hatch. Colonel Dickey with one gun, moved out to overtake Colonel Lee north of Water Valley. Hatch's brigade crossed the Yocona at Prophet Bridge. Colonel William Jackson's Rebel cavalry was sent to destroy the bridge. The Confederates were pushed back to the north edges of Water Valley. The Rebels fell back to Coffeeville, pursued by Hatch's brigade. The Federal troops chased the Rebels four miles below Water Valley. [296]

The Yankees were outflanked and withdrew from Water Valley and took position on a ridge northeast of town. Hatch told Colonel Prince to dismount eight companies of the 7th Illinois and Major Datus Coon of the 2nd Iowa of four rifle companies to dismount. Two regiments of Confederates also dismounted, and charged. Mounted Confederates attacked Hatch's flanks. Hatch repulsed Jackson's attack. The Rebels fell back. The Confederates were reinforced and made another charge. Ricker's battalion of the 5th Ohio charged the Confederates left. Colonel Prince extended his left and outflanked Jackson's right. The Federals counterattacked. The Rebel's sharpshooters were in the woods to his rear and attacked. The 2nd Iowa was mistaken for Rebels and fired upon. Hatch left the 7th Illinois to hold the ridge and with Coon's and Ricker's battalions, withdrew up the Prophet's bridge road. The Rebels retired from Water Valley. On that same day Grant moved his headquarters from Abbeville to Oxford. [297]

On December 5, 1862, at 2:30 P.M., Union Albert Lee's cavalry brigade, with the 7th Kansas cavalry in the lead, overtook the Confederate rear guard. Colonel Dickey saw Jackson's rebel cavalry to his right. Mizner and Hatch were deployed as skirmishers to the right and left of the column. Mizner sent two companies to the right, while Hatch ordered two companies of the 7th Illinois to the left. Dickey rode to the front. One mile from Coffeeville, the cannon of Company G, 2nd Illinois artillery unlimbered and fired several shells. General Lovell, commander of the First Corps, had sent a division of Tilghman's to check the advance. Lovell rode with Tilghman to the front and sent the First Brigade, under Brigadier General Baldwin on the right of the main road leading into Water Valley, and Colonel A. P. Thompson and the 3rd Kentucky were sent on the road leading out of Coffeeville to the west of the main road, to watch the left flank. Artillery was brought up. Company A, Pointe Coupee Louisiana artillery, under Captain Bouanchaud, placed four guns in the rear of Baldwin's troops, and three hundred yards to the Louisiana's battery was placed Hedden's Kentucky battery of two ten-pound Parrott rifles. Soon an artillery duel broke out between the 2nd Illinois artillery and Hedden's artillery and Pointe Coupe's artillery. Tilghman's rifled guns soon silenced the Yankee cannon. [298]

General Tilghman then asked permission to advance on the enemy. Permission was given and Tilghman ordered the 14th Mississippi, under General Ross, which had been in reserve, to take position on the extreme right of his line. The cavalry under Colonel W. H. Jackson was also made ready, and moved to the rear of the main line. General Rust, with two brigades on Tilghman's right, was also made ready. Tilghman then ordered Colonel Thompson, General Rust, and General Ross to advance. As soon as they got within two hundred yards, the Yankees opened up on the Confederates. Colonel A.P. Thompson ordered the 9th Arkansas, and the 8th Kentucky to return fire, and press the enemy. Colonel Dickey shouted for Lee to face his column to the rear. Mizner and Hatch were to form lines on each side of the road to cover the retreat of the skirmishers. At 3:30 P.M. Dickey told Hatch to send four companies of dismounted men to reinforce Lee's brigade. Hatch sent the 7th Illinois cavalry. Even though the Yankee's made two stands, they were quickly driven off. The first was defended by Mizner's men, the second by Hatch's men. As Mizner's men rushed to the rear, Hatch threw his dismounted rifle company into line. Major Coon of the 2nd Iowa waited until the Confederates were within twenty yards, then unleashed three volleys from their Colt Repeating Rifles into the oncoming Confederates. The Rebels outflanked the Union soldiers and Hatch's men retired to the next ridge. As the blue clad soldiers fell back they fought a holding action, using their Colt Repeaters and Sharps carbines. The Yankees were then pushed to the edge of an open field, where the Blue Coats mounted their horses and retreated. When they reached the edge of a wooded area, they dismounted and began to fire at the exposed Confederates who were pursuing them across the open field. [299]

General Tilghman feared that General Rust had not moved far enough to cover his right flank and he immediately ordered Lieutenant Barbour, commanding his body guard, to move to the extreme right. As soon as Lieutenant Barbour moved into position, was he was immediately fired upon by the Yankees. Tilghman sent the 14th Mississippi to Barbour's assistance. The Mississippi troops pushed back the Federals and killed Colonel McCullough of the 4th Illinois. The Yankees by this time had been pushed almost three miles from Coffeeville, and commanded the high ground outside of town. Two rifled cannon were unlimbered by the Yankees. The heaviest fire was directed down upon the 8th Kentucky and 9th Arkansas, but the Confederates pushed on. At one point it seemed as if Colonel Hatch's brigade would be encircled by Tilghman's men, but Hatch ordered the 2nd Iowa, company E, to charge. The brigade filed into the field on the left, and a company of dismounted cavalry rallied and held their position until Hatch could escape and rejoin the main Union column. Soon Tilghman's men overran the Yankee position. [300]

Their objective of pushing back the enemy was complete, and General Tilghman ordered his men to halt and cease fire. The Confederates killed thirty four Union soldiers, including Lt. Colonel William McCullough, and Second Lieutenant Thomas Woodburn. They captured seventeen prisoners. The Confederates lost seven killed, and forty three wounded. The besting of Grant at the Battle of Coffeeville was in a small measure, General Tilghman's pay back for the defeat he suffered at Grant's hands at Fort Henry. The Confederates returned to Coffeeville. The Yankees retired to Water Valley. [301]

On December 8, 1862, Grant ordered Sherman to Memphis, Tennessee. Once Sherman had arrived in Memphis he was to take command of all troops there and the portion of General Curtis forces east of the Mississippi River. As soon as Sherman had broken the troops into brigades and divisions they moved down the river to the vicinity of Vicksburg and with the gunboat fleet under Flag Officer Porter proceeded to destroy Vicksburg. Halleck ordered Grant not to hold the country south of the Tallahatchie, but to collect 25,000 troops at Memphis by the 20th for the Vicksburg Campaign. Pemberton's force in Grant's front was the main part of the garrison at Vicksburg, while Grant's force was the defense of the territory held by the Union forces in West Tennessee and Kentucky. Grant hoped to hold Pemberton in his front while Sherman would get in Pemberton's rear and into Vicksburg. [302]

Grant's plan was if Pemberton could not be held away from Vicksburg he was to follow him, but Grant would not abandon the railroad north of Yallabusha. If the Confederates should fall back Grant would follow him even to Vicksburg. He was to hold the road to Grenada on the Yallobusha and cut loose from there, expecting to establish a new base of supplies on the Yazoo or at Vicksburg, with Grenada to fall back upon in case of failure. [303]

The Union army halted at Oxford. On December 18, Grant was ordered by Washington to divide his army into four corps, with General McClernand to command one of them and to be assigned to the operations down the Mississippi. [304]

On December 20, 1862, Confederate General Earl Van Dorn appeared at Holly Springs and captured Grant's secondary base of supplies, along with 1,500 men commanded by Colonel Murphy of the 8th Wisconsin. During the same time, General Nathan Bedford Forrest raided the railroad between Jackson, Tennessee and Columbus, Kentucky. Grant was cut off from all communications with the north for more than a week, and it was two weeks before rations or forage could be issued from stores. Grant decided to abandon his campaign into the interior with Columbus as a base, and returned to La Grange and Grand Junction destroying the road to his front and repairing the road to Memphis, making the Mississippi river the line over which to draw supplies. Pemberton was falling back at the same time. [305]

Grant sent his cavalry to drive General Earl Van Dorn from Holly Springs. All wagons were to collect and bring in all supplies of forage and food from a region of fifteen miles east and west of the road from Grant's front back to Grand Junction, leaving two months' supplies for the families of those whose stores were taken. [306]

General Pemberton managed to make it back to Vicksburg before General Sherman got there. This would lead to a show-down between General Sherman and General Pemberton.

CHAPTER SEVEN

The First Attack on Vicksburg

hickasaw Bluffs was located on a series of broken hills touching the Mississippi River at Vicksburg extending into the interior in nearly a direct line and has right angles with the general course of the river. The Yazoo touches the base of these hills at a point twelve miles in the interior known as Snyder's Mill, then diverging from them, empties into the Mississippi some six miles above the city. There is between the hills and the Yazoo a triangular shaped area of bottom land, densely wooded, with the exception of one or two plantations on it, and intersected with bayous and low, swampy ground. Skirting the hills from Snyder's Mill down to near the Mississippi is first a swamp and then an old bed of the Yazoo, containing a lot of water, and only to be crossed with out bridging at three points, where torrents from the hills have borne along sufficient matter to fill up the bed. From the termination of this old bed to the Mississippi a belt of timber is felled, forming an abatis. There was a continuous obstacle twelve miles long, formed of abatis and water, skirting the hills and but a short distance from them, terminated at one end by the heavy batteries and field fortified position of the mill and at the other end by the heavy batteries and field works above Vicksburg. Through this obstacle there are but three natural passages. [307]

The base of the hills were determined as the proper lines of defense, and an advance of Confederate troops was made to guard the three natural approaches to it by throwing up earthworks, felling timber, etc.

Union General Ulysses S. Grant's plan to capture Vicksburg involved a two-prong attack. Grant with his force would move down the Mississippi Central Railroad and then drive west to capture Vicksburg. At the same time, Sherman would be transported down the Mississippi under protection of the transports and gunboats of Admiral Porter, and would disembark seven miles up the Yazoo River and attack Vicksburg north of the city.

144

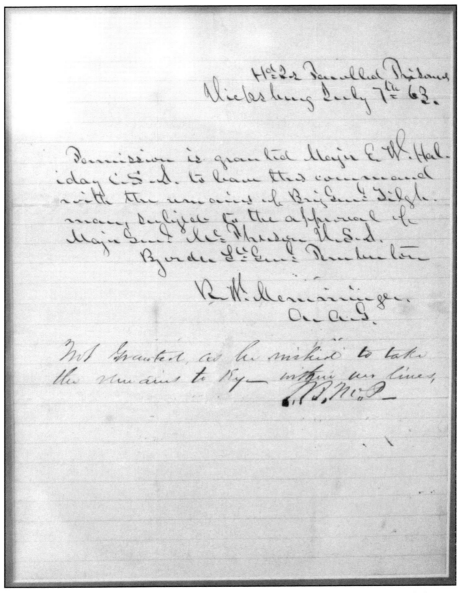

Original letter sent by General James McPherson sending the remains of Confederate General Lloyd Tilghman to Kentucky after the siege of Vicksburg. The letter was written by Union General McPherson, initialed endorsement by Confederate Major R.W. Memminger, A.A.G., who was Adjutant General to Confederate General John Pemberton, who commanded the Vicksburg fortress. The letter reads: "Headquarters, Paroled Prisoners-Vicksburg, July 7, 1863, permission is granted Major E.W. Haliday, C.S.A., to leave this command with the remains of Brig. General Tilghman subject to the approval of Major General McPherson, U.S.A. by order Lieut. Gen. Pemberton-R.W. Memminger, A.A.G." (The CWBWT Museum, photo Bryan Bush)

Confederate General Lloyd Tilghman's home in Paducah, Ky. (photo Bryan Bush)

Interior view of the Tilghman House Museum Ballroom

Paducah Tilghman High School, Paducah, Kentucky

LLOYD TILGHMAN

State of Kentucky Historical Marker in front of the newer Tilghman High School. The original Augusta Tilghman High School was located on South 10th Street, now known as Walter C. Jetton Boulevard

Paducah Tilghman High School, formerly known as the Fighting Rebels, now known as the Tornados

State of Kentucky Historical Marker. Tilghman's monument is in the background, Paducah, Kentucky

Confederate General Lloyd Tilghman's Monument located in the circle park on Fountain Avenue, Paducah, Kentucky.

Confederate General Lloyd Tilghman's Monument, Paducah, Kentucky.

Inscription on Confederate General Lloyd Tilghman's Monument, Paducah, Kentucky

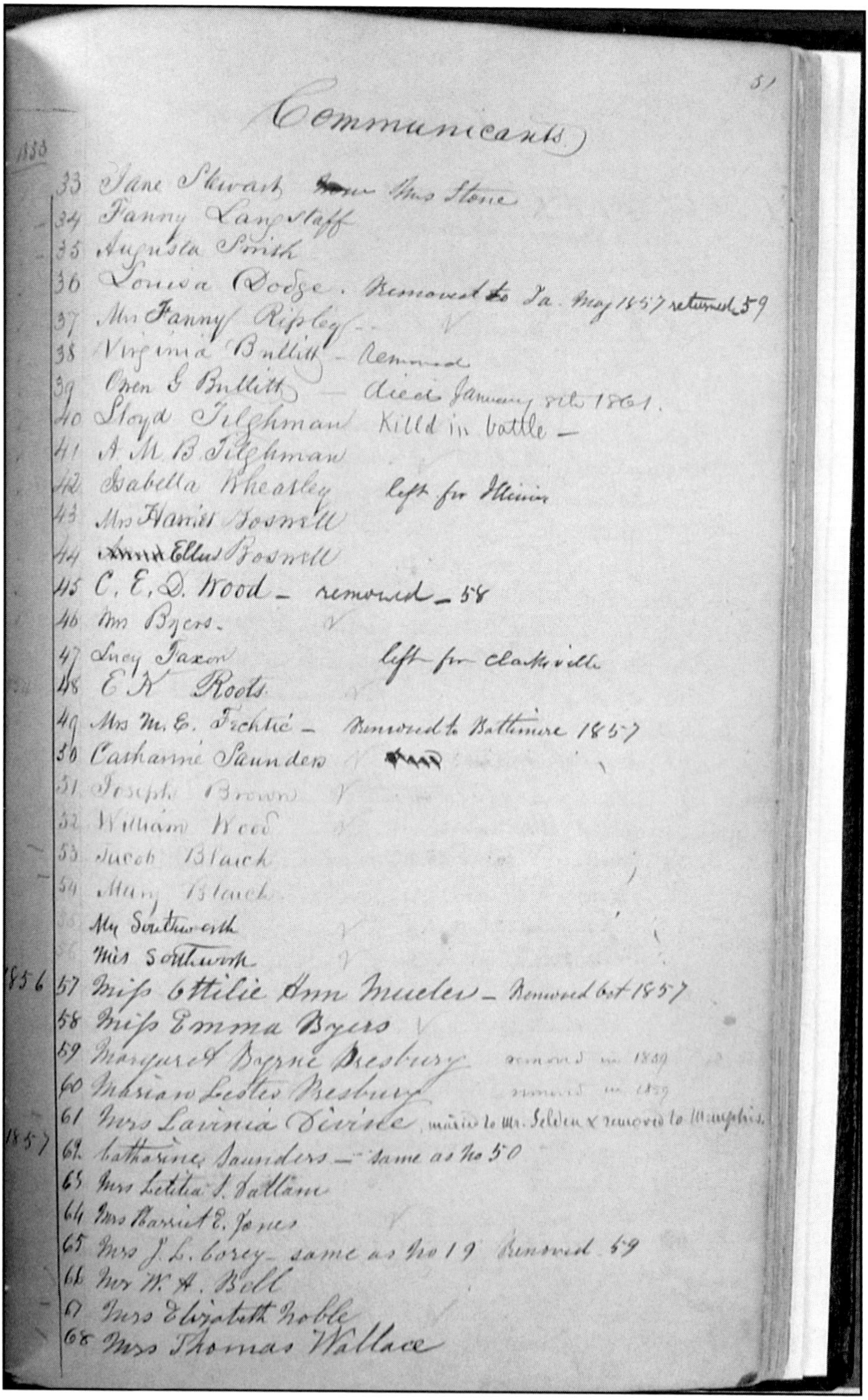

Communicants

51

1853

33 Jane Stewart, ~~now~~ Mrs Stone
34 Fanny Langstaff
35 Augusta Smith
36 Louisa Dodge. Removed to Pa. May 1857 returned 59
37 Mrs Fanny Ripley
38 Virginia Bullitt — Removed
39 Owen G Bullitt — died January 8th 1861.
40 Lloyd Tilghman killd in battle —
41 A M B Tilghman
42 Isabella Wheatley   left for Illinois
43 Mrs Harriet Boswell
44 ~~Annie~~ Ellen Boswell
45 C. E. D. Wood — removed — 58
46 Mr Byers.
47 Lucy Faxon   left for clarksville
48 E N Roots
49 Mrs M. E. Fechtie — Removed to Baltimore 1857
50 Catharine Saunders
51 Joseph Brown
52 William Wood
53 Jacob Black
54 Mary Black
Mr Southworth
Miss Southworth
1856 57 Miss Ottilie Ann Mueler — Removed Oct 1857
58 Miss Emma Byers
59 Margaret Byrne Presbury   removed in 1859
60 Marian Lester Presbury   removed in 1859
61 Mrs Lavinia Deville, marie to Mr Selden & removed to Memphis.
1857 62 Catharine Saunders — same as No 50
63 Mrs Letitia S. Hallam
64 Mrs Harriet E. Jones
65 Mrs J. L. Corey — same as No 19 Removed 59
66 Mr W. A. Bell
67 Mrs Elizabeth Noble
68 Mrs Thomas Wallace

154

Left: Burial Records of Charlie Tilghman, who died on May 16, 1859. Charlie Tilghman was the infant son of Lloyd Tilghman

Right: Baptism Records in Paducah, Ky., showing the baptism of Charlie Tilghman, who was baptized on April 26, 1859, which was witnessed by Lloyd Tilghman and Augusta Tilghman, Lloyd Tilghman's wife

Opposite page: Historical Records, Paducah, Ky. Tilghman is listed 40th as one of the members of the church in Paducah

Columbiad, Seacoast, 10 inch, sleeved to 8 inch rifle, iron. Common name 10 inch Rodman. Located in a cemetary in Ohio.

Model 1832, 32 pounder located at Columbus-Belmont State Park, Columbus,

156

Columbiad, Seacoast, 10 inch, Model 1861. Commonly known as 10 inch Rodman.
Made in Selma, Alabama, located in Cairo, Illinois. The large caliber cannons, such
as this Columbiad were used very often in fortifications.

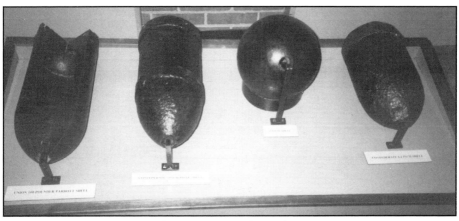

Artillery shells from large caliber cannons, Richmond, VA.

Confederate General Lloyd Tilghman Monument located at Vicksburg, Mississippi. (Photo courtesy of the Vicksburg National Military Park)

Brigadier General John Cook's wine goblet and dice. The wine goblet would have been sliver plated at one time and would have been part of a set of probably six more goblets and a pitcher.

159

General Lloyd Tilghman

On December 23, 1863, the Confederates learned of Union General William T. Sherman's advance fleet and by 10 P.M. they knew that seventy-four transports, and twelve gunboats were in the vicinity of Yazoo River.

At daylight on December 25, 1863, the troops under Confederate General Martin Smith were ordered into the trenches. Sherman chose his point of debarkation at a point on the Yazoo, twelve miles up, on an island formed by the Yazoo and the Mississippi Rivers and a system of bayous or old channels. Sherman's infantry force consisted of 32,000 men. George Morgan's, A. J. Smith, Morgan Smith and Steele's division were ready to move out on the 27th. [308]

The Confederates had surmised that the attack would be focused on the center of the Confederate line, in order to gain the high ground. The infantry force under Brigadier General Lee was placed at the most exposed points along the line, with orders to hold until reinforcements arrived. The brigades of General Barton, Gregg, and Vaughn arrived on the 26th, bringing the Confederate forces to fourteen thousand men. By daylight on the 27th, all the Confederate troops were in position, with all the exposed points covered in force, and the whole front being watched by skirmishers. [309]

The Confederate line on the right was held by General Lee, General Barton in the center, and General Vaughn on the left. General Gregg was between Barton and Vaughn. The order was for each brigade to draw reinforcements from the one immediately on its left, the left itself to be reinforced by fresh arrivals from the interior or from the reserve.

Sherman's whole army was distributed in four columns, The first column was under General Steele and located above the mouth of the Chickasaw Bayou. The second column was under General Morgan, with Blair's brigade of Steele's division, located just below the same bayou. The third column was under General Morgan L. Smith and was on the main road from Johnson's plantation to Vicksburg, with orders to bear to his left, so as to strike the bayou about a mile south of where Morgan was ordered to cross it. The final column was the division under General A. J. Smith, who was to keep on the main road.

Early on December 28, Steele's command marched along the country road from Vicksburg to Yazoo City, all along the foot of the hills, and was met by the Confederates. He tried to cross the bayou, but came under the watchful eyes of the Confederates rifle pits, batteries, and a frowning hill. Steele's men soon became engaged with the Confederates, along with the other columns. He soon came to the conclusion that it was impossible for him to reach the country road with out a heavy loss to his men. Sherman ordered Steele to retrace his steps and to board the steamboats to the southwest side of Chickasaw Bayou and was to support General Morgan's division. Steele arrived that night to Morgan's position. [310]

Also during the night, Morgan's division made a bridge from his pontoon boats and crossed the bayou, which was thought to be the main bayou but was only an inferior one, and turned out to be useless. Sherman ordered Morgan to cross over with his division and carry the line of works to the summit of the hill by a determined assault. On the 28th, General Morgan advanced De Conroy's brigade and engaged the Confederates, and heavy firing of artillery and musketry opened up on both sides all along the line. Morgan moved his column until he encountered the real bayou but was checked by the Confederates. [311]

During the attack, General Smith, while reconnoitering, was shot in the hip by a rifle bullet. General D. Stuart replaced him. General Stuart tried to pass over his division whenever he heard General Morgan engaged on his left.

To his right General A. J. Smith had placed Union General Stephen Burbridge's brigade of his division next to Stuart, with orders to make rafts and cross over a portion of his men to dispose his artillery so as to fire at the Confederates across the bayou and produce the effect of a diversion. His other brigade, Landram's, occupied a key position on the main road, with pickets and supports pushed well forward into the tangled abatis within three fourths of a mile of the Rebels forts and in plain view of the city of Vicksburg. [312]

Sherman's plan for the 29th was to break the center near Chickasaw Creek, at the head of the bayou of the same name, and once in position to turn to the right (Vicksburg) or left (Drumgould's Bluff). Sherman had not heard from Grant or from General Banks. Sherman did not know that Confederate General Earl Van Dorn had destroyed the Union Holly Springs base, and Grant had to fall back to Tennessee. Confederate General Nathan Bedford Forrest had also demolished fifty miles of Union railroads and telegraph lines, cutting off all communication with Sherman and Grant. Sherman felt the time was right to assault the hills in front of Morgan. The orders were for Morgan's division to carry the position to the summit of the hill; Steele's division to support him and hold the country road. General A. J. Smith and M. L. Smith was to cross the sand pit, undermine the steep bank of the bayou on the farther side, and carry at all events the levee parapet and first line of rifle pits, to prevent a concentration on Morgan. [313]

At daylight on the 29th, the attack began and was attempted along the whole line. In front of General Lee the attack was the fiercest, since it was conducted on open ground, thus taking advantage of their superiority of numbers. The assaulting force moved from their concealed position in the woods, advanced rapidly on an open space of four hundred yards, and made a determined attack upon Lee's entrenched position. Taken in the flank by the artillery and met in front by a withering sheet of musketry fire, the Yankees struggled up to within a short distance of the Confederate line, when they wavered, stopped, and fled in panic and confusion, stewing the ground with their dead and wounded, leaving the Confederates in possession of four regimental colors, over 300 prisoners and 500 stand of arms. [314]

In front of General Barton, the assault, although not made in such numbers, was persisted in with a tenacity indicating a determined purpose to succeed. Five different assaults were made against the advance work, each time they were repulsed with losses, and from daylight until sunset the troops were under a severe fire from musketry and artillery.

The large abatis in front of General Vaughn, together with the batteries in position in the line to his rear, stopped Sherman's attack cold, and was repulsed. Sherman's men were met with sharpshooters. A few shots from Vaughn's 12 pound and 24 pounders drove the Yankee's back into the woods. [315]

During the night, Sherman visited with Admiral Alexander Porter and after serious consideration, Sherman knew that he could not break the Confederate center. Sherman came up with another plan of attack. Admiral Porter would cover a landing at some high point close up to Drumgould's batteries and Sherman would hold the ground and send ten thousand men and assault the batteries on the Confederate right. Success would give Sherman the possession of the Yazoo River and place him in connecting distance of Grant. [316]

On the 30th, the Yankee fire dropped off, and permission was given for them to bury their dead and care for their wounded on the 31st. The Confederate loss was 63 killed, 134 wounded, and ten missing. The loss of the Yankees was at 208 dead, 1005 wounded, and 563 missing. [317] On that same day, Major General Stevenson arrived and relieved General M. L. Smith.

The next day ten thousand men boarded the ships. The attack was to take place at 4 A.M., but General Steele arrived with a note from Admiral Porter, informing Sherman that the fog was so dense on the river that the boats could not move, and the expedition must be moved to another night.

On January 1, Porter sent another message to Sherman telling him that the moon would not set until 5:25, so the landing must done during the day, which was obviously too hazardous. Sherman knew that an attack during the day on Dumgould's batteries would have been suicide. One third of Sherman's army was already on transport and the rest of his army was camped in a low, swampy, timbered ground, a quagmire after heavy rains. Sherman decided not to stay any longer. [318]

By January 2, 1863, all the troops were loaded on their transports. The Confederates during this whole time massed infantry and cavalry; artillery crowned the summits of the hills, and field batteries appeared everywhere along the country road. Sherman could hear Confederate rail cars arriving and departing all the time, and large reinforcements were arriving. Sherman decided to move his men to Milliken's Bend. Porter held the Mississippi from Vicksburg and the Yazoo up to Drumgould's Bluff, but both positions were not in Union hands. On January 4, 1863 Sherman handed over control of the troops without a protest.

After the failure of Grant to take Chickasaw Bluffs, Union Major General John McClernand took command of the Union forces used during the attack at Chickasaw Bluffs. McClernand was going to attack Fort Hindman, which formed the key to Little Rock, the capital of the State of Arkansas, and the extensive country drained by the Arkansas river, and from which Confederate detachments were sent forth to obstruct the Mississippi River. A government transport, the Blue Wing, with military stores, was captured by a Confederate gunboat. The Rebels took it to Fort Hindman at Arkansas Post. McClernand's force arrived at the mouth of the White River on January Eighth, 1863. The plan of attack was for the 15th Corps under Major General Sherman to take Arkansas Post by the rear until the right of the corps had reached above the river above the post, being careful to guard against a surprise rear attack, and to keep his command clear of the range of the Union gunboats. The 13th Corps under Brigadier General Morgan would follow the 15th and form on its left.

Arkansas Post was established by the French in 1685 and was located at a horseshoe bend in the Arkansas River about one hundred and twenty miles northwest of Vicksburg, Mississippi. Fort Hindman was a square earthwork fort, which was built within the Arkansas Post, upon the bank of the river, at the head of the horseshoe bend. The exterior sides of the fort, between the salient angles, were three hundred feet in length; the faces of the bastions two sevenths of an exterior side and perpendiculars one eighth. The parapet was eighteen feet wide on the top the ditch was twenty feet wide on the ground level and eight feet deep, with a slope of four feet base. A banquette for infantry was constructed around the interior slope of the parapet; also three platforms for artillery in each bastion and one in the curtain facing north. On the southern face of the northeast bastion was a case mate eighteen by fifteen feet wide and seven and a half feet high in the clear, the walls of which were constructed of three thickness of oak timber sixteen inches square, and the roof was revetment of iron bars. This case mate contained a nine inch Columbiad. A simple case mate constructed in the curtain faced the river, containing an eight inch Columbiad, and still another nine inch Columbiad was mounted in the salient angle of the southeast bastion on a center pintle barbette carriage. All of these guns commanded the river below the fort. Besides these were four three-inch Parrot guns and four six-pounder iron smooth bore guns mounted on field carriages on the platforms in the fort. The entrance of the fort, secured by a traverse, was on its northwest side, and from the salient angle of the northwest bastion extended a broken line of rifle pits west for seven hundred and twenty yards toward the bayou, intersected by wooden traverses. Along the rifle pits six field pieces were mounted, of which three were rifled, below the fort were the rifle pits and levee. The levee was pierced with six guns and lined on the inside by rifle pits. The second line of rifle pits, with intervals left for six guns, extended across the high land from the river to the swamp, its near approach being obstructed by an abatis of fallen timber, and still nearer the fort was a deep ravine entering the river at right angles and extending inland in different arms in front of the left of the Union line. In front of the center line was an open field. [319]

On January 9, at 5 P.M. McClernand's thirty-thousand man force landed on the left bank of the river, at Notrib's farm. Brigadier General Thomas Churchill, C. S., learned that a fleet of 70 or 80 transports were passing into the Arkansas River, and that their objective was to attack Arkansas Post. Churchill immediately set out to strengthen his position. He ordered out his entire force, which numbered 3,000, to take position in some of the lower trenches about 1.25 miles below the fort. The Second Brigade, under Colonel Deshler, and the Third, under Colonel Dunnington, occupied the works, while the First Brigade, under Colonel Garland, was held in reserve.

The next day on January 10, 1863, General McClernand requested that Admiral Porter advance the gunboats and open fire on the Confederate works in order to divert their attention while the land forces should gain the positions assigned to them. The admiral advanced his boats and opened a cannonade on the fort, which was continued for an hour. At 10 P.M., January 10, Colonel Stewart, chief of cavalry, reported to McClernand that he had pushed his reconnaissance west to the Confederates cantonment of log huts and beyond the bayou, and that there was nothing in the way of an advance to that point. He also captured one hundred prisoners. Churchill had realized that he was being flanked by the cavalry and thought it wise to fall back under the cover of the guns of the fort to an inner line of entrenchments. McClernand ordered Sherman to gain the bayou. General Steele's division had re-crossed the swamp, and General Osterhaus camped near the landing in a position commanding the neighboring approaches across the swamp and covering the transports against attack from the opposite side of the river. Colonel Lindsey's brigade had landed nine miles below Notrib's farm, at Fletcher's Landing, on the right bank of the river and had taken position and planted a battery on the bank above the fort, cutting off the escape or reinforcements of the Confederates by water. [320]

By 10:30 A.M. on January 11, the two corps were in position to attack. General Steele's division formed the extreme right of the line, reaching the bayou. General Stuart's and A. J. Smith's divisions were formed on its left. One brigade of General Osterhaus' division, Colonel Sheldon commanding, formed the extreme left of the line, resting upon the river, in full view of the fort. Another brigade of the same division, Colonel De Courcy commanding, was held in reserve near the transports, while the remaining brigade of the same division, Colonel Lindsey commanding, was disposed on the opposite side of the river. A section of twenty-pound Parrot rifles were posted by General Osterhaus near the river bank, within eight hundred yards of the fort, concealed by fallen trees from the view of the Confederates, while two sections of the Illinois Mercantile Battery were masked and held in reserve. [321]

At 1 P.M. the gunboats opened fire, immediately followed by the fire of artillery along the right wing of McClernand's line, and soon after by the fire of artillery along the left wing. At the sound of the cannon fire, the Union infantry attacked across open fields toward the Rebel breastworks that protected the rear of the fort.

By 1:30 P.M. Hovey's and Thayer's brigades and Giles A. Smith's and T. K. Smith's brigades, of General Sherman's corps, had crossed in double quick time a narrow space of cleared ground in their front and gained position in a belt of woods extending irregularly by some three hundred yards to the Confederate rifle pits. Sherman was stopped for a short time by rifle and artillery fire from the Confederate works. Sherman's men "boldly" resumed and continued their advance, supported by Blair's brigade, who served as a reserve, until they approached within short musket range of the Confederate lines. Sherman's men found shelter in some ravines, which were covered by underbrush and fallen timber. Hovey was wounded by a shell fragment, but continued. General Thayer lost his horse. Hoffman's battery was advanced to within two hundred yards of the Confederate entrenchments and fired into three different positions. It was 3 P.M. [322]

The twenty-pound Parrot rifles on the river bank enfiladed two faces of the northeast bastion some of their shots penetrated the embrasure of the case mate and with the gunboats, silenced the gun inside the fort, and also the lighter gun in the north curtain and the gun en barbette in the southeast bastion. General A. J. Smith's division had passed to the front and neared the Confederate works. Three ten-pound Parrot rifles under Blout had exploded a caisson within the Rebel entrenchments. [323]

General A. J. Smith deployed nine regiments of General Burbridge's and Landram's brigades, supported by three regiments, which were held in reserve. General Burbridge and Landram's troops steadily moved forward, and drove the Confederates toward open ground to their front and right of the Union defenses. Seeking shelter behind some cabins, Colonel Guppey, 23rd Wisconsin, was ordered to charge and dislodge the Confederates, which he did, forcing the Confederates to flee their entrenchments. Smith continued his attack until they got to within two hundred yards of the fort. [324]

Meanwhile Colonel Sheldon, under General Osterhaus, had ordered Cooley's battery within two hundred yards of the right of the Confederate defenses. Both artillery and infantry fired heavily into the Confederate ranks until the rifle pits in front were cleared. The 120th Ohio charged to the east of the fort, but failed in taking it because of a deep ravine.

Colonel De Courcy's brigades were now ordered up to support General Sherman and took position on the right. It was 3:15 P.M. and the guns of the fort had been silenced. McClernand ordered a final assault.

Union General Stephen Burbridge's brigade, with the two regiments of Landram's which had been sent to its right, and the 120th Ohio, went forward under a deadly fire to the Rebels entrenchments. The 16th Indiana, with the 83rd Ohio, and the 120th Ohio were the first to enter the fort. General Burbridge was at the entrance of the fort and was halted by the guard, who denied that they had surrendered until he called their attention to the white flag and ordered them to ground arms. General Churchill and Colonel Dunnington met with McClernand and surrendered the post, its armament, garrison and all its stores. [325]

Farther to the Rebel's left, their entrenchments were stormed by General Sherman's command, who ordered General Steele to push forward one of his brigade along to the bayou and cut off the Confederate escape route. Colonel Lindsey, with his brigade, moved down the opposite shore and opened an oblique fire from Foster's two twenty-pound Parrots and two ten-pound Parrots into the Confederates line of rifle pits, carrying away their battle flag. The Third Kentucky was on board of one of the gunboats to cross the river to the fort, but by the time they got there, the fort had already surrendered. [326]

At 4:30 P.M. after three and a half hours of fighting, the battle was finally over. Seven stands of colors were captured, including the garrison flag. McClernand had also captured five thousand prisoners, seventeen cannon, three thousand stand of arms, 130 swords, fifty Colt pistols, 1,650 rounds of shot, shell, and canister, forty-six thousand rounds of ammunition, and numerous amounts of stores. McClernand lost 129 killed, 831 wounded, and 17 missing. Churchill lost one hundred and forty men. Churchill said after the battle: "In no battle of the war has the disparity of forces been so unequal. The enemy's force was fully 50,000, when ours did not exceed 3,000, and yet for two days did we signally repulse and hold in check that immense body of the enemy." [327] But the Union got what they wanted: a victory. The North had been unsuccessful on several different battlefields and this was the victory needed to boost the moral of the Union war effort. [328]

On January 29, Grant traveled to Young's Point, Louisiana, just below Milliken's Bend, where Sherman and McClernand had established their headquarters. Grant assumed command of all the armies in the field. Grant kept the Memphis and Charleston Railroad, while he abandoned the Mississippi Central Railroad. Columbus was the only point between Cairo and Memphis, on the river, left with a garrison. All troops and guns from the posts on the abandoned railroad and river were sent to the front. The real work began and the siege of Vicksburg was about to take place. The problem Grant faced was to secure a footing upon dry ground on the east side of the river from which the troops could operate against Vicksburg. But Vicksburg would not be an easy city to take. From south of Cairo the Mississippi River runs through a rich valley of many miles in width, bound on the east by land running from eighty up to two hundred feet above the river. On the west side the highest land is but little above the water. The land is made up of bayous filled with water. It is impossible to turn the bends with vessels of any length. Marching across the country with Confederates was impossible.

In January the Union troops took their position opposite Vicksburg. The rains had raised the water table and there was no possibility of a land movement until March, so Grant decided to keep his men busy and continued to work on a canal that has been started by Brigadier General Thomas Williams the previous June. The purpose of the canal was to cut across the mile-wide peninsula formed by the horseshoe bend of the Mississippi at Vicksburg and thus bypass the port's defenses. Grant knew the canal would not work, but Lincoln wanted the canal finished. The canal was only thirteen feet deep and eighteen feet wide when it was abandoned, so Sherman and his men would have to widen it to sixty feet. Four thousand men were working on the canal, but the river rose suddenly and broke a dam at the upper end, which had been put there to keep water out until the excavation was completed. [329]

On January 30, Grant ordered General McPherson to cut the levee at Lake Providence. If they were successful in opening a channel for navigation by this route, it would carry the Union forces to the Mississippi River through the mouth of the Red River, just above Port Hudson and four hundred miles below Vicksburg by the river. [330]

On February 4, Grant visited General McPherson on the progress on Lake Providence. The work had not progressed as to allowing the water from the river into the lake, but the Union troops had succeeded in floating a small steamer from the river into the lake. The steamer allowed the Union army to explore the lake and bayou. Grant soon realized that there was scarcely a chance of the river ever becoming a practicable route for moving troops though the Confederate territory. The Confederates held Port Hudson, below the Red River debouches, and all the Mississippi above to Vicksburg. The Red River, Washita, and Tenas were all navigable streams, on which the Confederates could place small bodies of men to obstruct the Union army's passage. Grant went ahead and let the work be continued, because he felt that keeping the men busy was better than leaving them idle. This work was abandoned when the canal proved a failure. [331]

Lieutenant Colonel Wilson was sent to Helena, Arkansas to examine and open a way through Moon Lake and the Yazoo Pass. Formerly there was a route by way of an inlet from the Mississippi River into Moon Lake, a mile east of the river, then east through Yazoo Pass to Coldwater, along the latter to the Tallahatchie, which joins the Yallabusha about two hundred and fifty miles below Moon Lake and forms the Yazoo River. But a strong levee across the inlet had left the only entrance for vessels into this rich region the one by way of the mouth of the Yazoo several hundreds of miles below. On February 2nd, the levee was cut. The bayous filled with water and much of the country overflowed. This pass left the Mississippi river but a few miles below Helena. [332]

On February 17, Confederate General W. W. Loring left Jackson, Mississippi for the purpose of finding some suitable place on the Yazoo or Tallahatchie to erect earthworks and place obstructions on the route the Yankees were planning to steam down. Loring decided that the two rivers from Yazoo to one hundred miles above would be the position for defensive works. A line of works composed of cotton bales and earth were thrown up, exceeding from the Yazoo to the Tallahatchie, and a raft was constructed and placed on the Tallahatchie on their right.

By February 20, the Federals knew the location and number of the Confederate troops in Granada, Vicksburg and Port Hudson. A soldier from the 4th Illinois Cavalry, who was captured by the Rebels and later paroled at Jackson, Mississippi, stated that there were few troops at Grenada, and very few along the line of the Mississippi Central Railroad. At Jackson, General John Adams of Tennessee was in command, but at the post there was only one or two regiments. Rebel gossip put the Confederate forces at Port Hudson and Vicksburg at sixty thousand. The soldier from the 4th Illinois was sent back by the way of Meridian, and over the Mobile and Ohio Railroad. At the point between Jackson and Meridian large machine shops were being constructed. Vast quantities of cotton marked "Confederate States" were piled along the road. Great amounts of sugar had been shipped from Vicksburg and to Jackson and other points near. At Jackson, five large cotton houses were filled with the hogsheads. Along the Mobile and Ohio Railroad hardly any troops were stationed; a single train of two or three cars ran over the road each day for local accommodations. About ten miles north of Okolona were two regiments of cavalry. Three miles north of Okolona a bridge was destroyed and the trains stopped at the town. At Jackson there were about twenty Federal officers and seven hundred Federal soldiers, who were kept in close confinement. The Confederate authorities paroled and sent north by rail twelve men each day. [333]

The report sent by Colonel Albert Lee, commanding the Union cavalry, to General Grant mentioned that three members of the Seventh Kansas Cavalry were captured and Tilghman had put them in chains, hand and foot. Union Colonel Albert Lee asked Captain Henry Binmore, Adjutant General of the

16th Army Corps, if he could capture three Rebels and do the same to them and then ask to open a correspondence with Tilghman. [334]

On February 24, 1863, Union General Ross, with his brigade of 4,500 men on transports, moved into the new water way. The Rebels had obstructed the navigation of Yazoo pass and the Coldwater by felling trees into them. The tree removal required a lot of labor, but it was finally accomplished. The men dragged the sometimes twenty-ton trees out of the way with rope cables, five hundred men to the cable. [335]

Other obstacles faced the Union soldiers and their boats. Some of the river bends were so tight that the vessels were unable to maneuver past them under their own power, so the ships had to be hauled with hawsers. The trees were so thick that they formed giant canopies. The ships' smoke-stacks got entangled in these tress and down went the stacks. The upper works were also carried away by the overhanging trees.

On March 8, 1863, Tilghman reported that Union forces were advancing down from the Tallahatchee River. Tilghman asked Pemberton to send troops to Yazoo City with some heavy guns and a force to keep the advance party in check. He also reported that a large number of boats including the Prince of Wales was sent down with bacon and corn. Pemberton told Tilghman to hold his force and be ready to move at a moment's notice. He told him to draw in his cavalry if the Yankees to continue to advance on the Tallahatchie. [336]

The Union forces were approaching a fortification at Greenwood, where the Tallahatchie and Yallabusha unite and the Yazoo begins. This island was fortified and manned with cannon and 1,500 men under General W. W. Loring. The fort was constructed with cotton bales and sandbags. It was named Fort Pemberton. No land approach was possible. Fort Pemberton rose slightly above the water. The channel was also blocked by old ships that had been sunk. Grant thought that two more feet of water would flood the fort. Another cut was made in the Mississippi levee, directly opposite Helena. It did not flood the fort as expected. [337]

General Loring reported that Yankees were landing two miles on the opposite side of the Yalabusha. Loring had already ordered Tilghman to Chockachuma with his command to Yazoo City. Loring asked Pemberton to send additional troops and heavy arms to Yazoo City as quickly as possible in order to block the river and resist the Union advance. Loring reported to Pemberton that two iron-clads and seven other gunboats, including a mortar, and twenty-one transports filled with seven thousand infantrymen and artillery, comprised a fleet commanded by Generals Walker and Slack and Commodore Hull. Their objective was Yazoo City, with a view to operate in the rear of Vicksburg. [338] The Yankees also seemed to be aware of the number of Confederate troops at Yazoo City. Loring swung the raft across the Tallahatchie and the Confederate States steamer *Star of the West* sank behind it. Captain John Myrick was placed in command of the batteries. The Yankees attacked Loring's forces with one gunboat, the *Chillicothe*, a land battery and a thirteen-inch mortar. The gunboat steamed around the bend of the river in their front, as though it was going to rush the raft and destroy it. A well placed shell from their thirty-two pounder fell upon the *Chillicothe*'s turret, and the gunboat slowed down. This was followed by a solid shot from an eighteen-pounder rifle, which also struck, and the *Chillicothe* backed up the stream until her hull was hidden around the bend, saving her bow and that portion of which contained the gunboats eleven-inch guns. The Chillicothe then opened fire, and the fire fight was kept up for an hour, when the gunboat withdrew, having been struck several times by three of their guns. At four o'clock the fight was resumed by another gunboat, which was the *DeKalb*. After two hours of fighting, the boat withdrew. The Yankee troops were landed. During the day, Colonel T. N. Waul, who was commander of the post, sent out skirmishers, who engaged a large body of Yankee infantry and cavalry and drove them back to their transports. On the night of the 11th, the Yankees erected a cotton bale battery at the point marked, about seven hundred yards from the large Confederate rifled 6.4 inch bore gun, with a view to dismounting it. A naval thirty-pound battery was placed in the cotton bale battery. [339]

On the 12th, the naval forces were not able to attack. However, that night, another thirty-pounder cannon was added to the Union battery. Loring could not attack because of a lack of ammunition.

On the 13th, at 10:00 a.m., the *Chillicothe*, *Baron De Kalb*, the land battery, and the thirteen-inch mortar boat attacked the Confederates. The Confederates opened up all their guns at the Yankees. The fight was kept up all day. The Yankees landed their forces, but were not able to capture the city. Night ended the battle. During the engagement, an eleven-inch shell from the *Chillicothe* passed through the parapet, displaced a cotton bale, and ignited a tub of cartridges in the magazine of the Whitworth gun. The fire was lit from the fuse of the eleven-inch shell. Fortunately the shell did not explode. But Lieutenant J. Q. Wall of the Pointe Coupe Artillery was slightly wounded, and fifteen of his men were burned, some badly. A shell did explode over the heads of his gunners, and three men were wounded, one of whom later died. Loring's troops worked the whole night, repairing the parapet, erecting heavy traverses, and strengthening the works. The Yankees were not able to see if any effect had been made on the Confederates. Tilghman told Pemberton that he suggested to Loring to place the regiment and battery at Dodd's Ferry, rather than Chocachuma. The Confederate troops then could meet the Union forces at Dugan's and Chocahuma. General Tilghman was in command of the Confederate forces, and there was still the 6.4 inch rifled gun to contend with. [340]

On Saturday the 14th, the Yankees attacked at 4:00 P.M. with their land batteries and a gunboat for about a half hour. The next day, on Sunday the 15th, the Yankees reinforced and so did the Confederates.On Monday the 16th, The Yankees were preparing for a grand assault with their entire force upon Loring's works. The gunboat *Chillicothe* got into position, bow on, at 1,220 yards and, with their land batteries and sharpshooters, the battle began. In about twenty minutes, a shot from one of Loring's heavy guns penetrated the *Chillicothe* and injured the ship so badly that the assault was abandoned and the ship withdrew, leaving the land batteries and sharpshooters to keep up the fight until sunset. Loring lost one killed and four wounded, and sixteen severely burned by the explosion of their magazine.[341] On Friday the Yankees abandoned their breastworks and commenced a rapid retreat up the river. Thus ended the Battle of the Tallahatchie.

Loring remarked that the Union expedition was Grant's plan to attack Vicksburg in the rear. It was to move rapidly down the Yazoo to the mouth of Sunflower; there he would await another expedition down that river; the two united were to meet a third up the Yazoo; the three were to travel by raft at Snyder's Bluff, then turn on Vicksburg. Grant's plan failed. Grant would have to find another way to attack Vicksburg.

On March 14, 1863, Admiral Porter, along with Grant, explored another possible route. Steele's Bayou empties into the Yazoo River between Haines Bluff and its mouth. It was narrow, very tortuous and fringed with heavy tree growth, but was very deep. It approached to within one mile of the Mississippi at Eagle Bend, thirty miles above Young's Point. Steele's Bayou connects with Black Bayou, Black Bayou with Deer Creek, Deer Creek with Rolling Fork, Rolling Fork with the Big Sunflower River, and the Big Sunflower with the Yazoo River about ten miles above Haines bluff. Porter's five gunboats and four mortar boats reached as far as Deer Creek, but trees made the progress slow. The gunboats made their way through without damage. The transports were another story. Grant returned to his headquarters to hurry up reinforcements. Sherman on the 16th took with him Stuart's division of the 15th Corps. They took large transports to Eagle Bend on the Mississippi, where they landed and marched across to Steele's Bayou and re-boarded the transports. The river steamers, with their tall stacks and light guards extending out, were torn off by the trees. The gunboats got too far ahead. Porter with his fleet got within a few hundred yards of where the sailing would have been clear and free from the felled trees, when he encountered Rebel sharpshooters, and his progress was brought to a halt. Obstructions lay in front of his gunboats. The Rebels had sent 4,000 men to take on the Union force.[342]

Sherman went back to clear the Black Bayou and to hurry up reinforcements. On the 19th Sherman received word that Porter had been attacked by sharpshooters and was in trouble. Sherman's reinforcements tried to reach

Porter through the Black Bayou with their steamer, but the progress was so slow they decided to land and march on foot. The troops marched twenty-one miles and reached Porter. The vessels were backed out and returned to their rendezvous on the Mississippi and ended the fourth attempt to get in the rear of the Mississippi. The canal building was also abandoned on March 27th. [343]

On March 29, McClernand with his corps of four divisions marched from Richmond, Louisiana to New Carthage, hoping that he might capture the Grand Gulf before the balance of the troops could get there, but the roads were bad and just a little above water. Some miles from New Carthage the levee to Bayou Vidal was broken in several places, overflowing the roads for two miles. By April 6, McClernand had reached New Carthage with one division and its artillery.

Milliken's Bend, and Young's Point, bayous enter the Mississippi at Carthage twenty miles above the Grand Gulf. The Mississippi levee cuts the supply of water off from the bayous, but all the rainfall behind the levee at these points is carried through the same channels to the river below. In case of a crevasse in this vicinity, the water escaping would find its outlet through the same channels. Grant determined to open the channels. If the plan was successful, Grant could have a route for his transports that veered away from the Confederates batteries. There was a good road in the back of the levees, along the bayous, which could handle troops and artillery and wagon trains. Grant began to clear the route from trees and let the water in from the river. This work continued until the waters of the river began to recede and the road to Richmond, Louisiana emerged from the water. The waters began to recede and the roads crossing the peninsula behind the levees of the bayous were emerging from the waters. The troops were concentrated from distant points at Milliken's Bend preparing for the final move. [344]

On April 16, Admiral Porter was ready to start on his trip to run the gauntlet of the Vicksburg batteries. The first of the gunboats was the *Benton*, then the *LaFayette*, then the *Sterling Price*, the *Louisville*, *Mound City*, *Pittsburgh*, and the *Carondelet*. Next came the transports, the *Forest Queen*, *Silver Wave*, and the *Henry Clay*, each towing barges loaded with coal for the gunboats and transport ships when they were below the batteries. The gunboat *Tuscumbia* brought up the rear. The Confederate batteries immediately opened up on the Union fleet. A battery between Vicksburg and Warrenton fired across the intervening peninsula, which was followed by the upper batteries, and then the batteries all along the line. The gunboats ran close under the bluffs, delivering their fire at short ranges. They were under fire for two hours and every ship was struck several times, but with little damage to the gunboats. The *Henry Clay* was disabled and deserted. [345]

The Confederates had known of the Union fleet's approach. They prepared bonfires on the east side and fired houses on the point of land opposite the city on the Louisiana side. Luckily no one on the transports was killed.

On April 17, Grant visited McClernand at New Carthage and saw that McClernand's men were progressing too slowly. McClernand had found a new route from Smith's plantation to Perkin's plantation, eight miles below New Carthage. Four bridges were built across the bayous. Grant returned to Milliken's Bend on the 18th and on March 20th he issued orders for his commanders. Major General John McClerand would command the 13th Corps, and would be the right wing of the Union Army. Major General William T. Sherman would command the 15th Corps and would be the left wing of the Union line. Major General James McPherson would command the 17th Corps, and would comprise the center. Two of McPherson's divisions were to march out immediately. Sherman was to follow McPherson. Two of his divisions were at Duckport and Young's Point, and the third under Steele was under orders to return from Greenville, Mississippi.

Grant needed more supplies for his three corps, so six more steamers ran the batteries on April 22, 1863. Twelve barges were in tow with supplies. Five made it through, but one sank. About half the barges made it.

On April 24, Tilghman, who was at Canton, reported that a regiment of cavalry was approaching from Carthage. Tilghman had moved out with the 54th Alabama and a section of artillery. He also had the Eighth Kentucky, about one hundred strong. He asked for some cavalry. Pemberton told Tilghman to call in the 50th Alabama. He was also to order Major Cummins to fall back to Canton. If General Featherstone was to call for a battery, Tilghman was to supply him with one. Tilghman was also to mount the 8th Kentucky, but did not send them to Carthage, but drew in his other regiments to Canton. He was to keep out scouts, and if the Yankees were approaching points named by Tilghman, he could move by railroad more rapidly. Tilghman employed half of his command to intercept the Yankees should they attempt to retreat by Carthage. Tilghman was to employ active citizens, well mounted, to act as scouts, and keep Tilghman advised of the Yankees movements. [346]

Tilghman reported back to Pemberton that seven hundred Yankee cavalry were at Philadelphia, Neshoba County. Cummins fell back behind the Yockanockany River, with the train at Laflore's Ferry.

On that same day Grant's headquarters was located at Perkin's plantation. Grant sent out reconnaissances in boats to determine whether there was high land on the east shore of the river where the Union forces might land above Grand Gulf. There was none. The troops were sent in the direction of Hard Times, twenty two miles farther down river and nearly opposite Grand Gulf. Grant had lost two steamers and six barges, so only ten thousand men could be transported. All the troops, except what could be transported by transports, had to march. Three large bayous had to be crossed. Bridges were soon built across them. [347]

On April 25, Tilghman was ordered by Pemberton to Durant, where he was to leave the rail cars and move toward Rockport. [348] Two days later, on April 27, Tilghman was ordered to leave a guard at Big Black bridges, and move to Canton. He was then ordered by Pemberton to come at once to Jackson and bring his smallest regiment. [349] Union General McClernand's Corps was at Hard Times, and McPherson was following closely behind. Sherman created a diversion by moving his corps up the Yazoo and threatening an attack on Haines Bluff.

The next day, Union Brigadier General Stephen G. Burbridge, commanding the First Brigade, 10th Division, 13th Army Corps, was ordered to embark four of his regiments and the 17th Ohio Battery on transports and barges to proceed to Grand Gulf. He was to proceed to Hard Times Landing, opposite the Grand Gulf.

On April 29, Pemberton moved Tilghman from Jackson, Mississippi to Edward's Depot with two regiments; the 26th Mississippi and the 15th Mississippi, and one light artillery battery. Meanwhile, Union General James McClernand and his ten thousand men were ordered to load on transports and barges. The plan was to have the navy silence the guns at Grand Gulf, and have as many men as possible in order to storm the earthworks. Union Admiral Alexander Porter made the attack with his eight gunboats. For five and a half hours the attack was kept up without silencing a single Confederate cannon. Porter withdrew. The navy lost eighteen killed and fifty six wounded. McClernand landed his troops on the west bank. The navy and transports ran the batteries successfully. The troops marched across. By morning the Confederates saw Grant's whole fleet moving down the river three miles below them. The troops landed at Bruinsburg, a few miles above Rodney, from which point a good road led to Port Gibson. [350]

The next day, on April 30, Tilghman was at Big Black Bridge. Tilghman's force consisted of 1,550 men. Tilghman's force was comprised of units from the 15th and 26th Mississippi, 19th Arkansas, and the 27th Alabama, J. M. McLendon's Battery, four guns and two twelve-pound howitzers of Captain Schuler Lowe's company. [351]

On that same day, McClernand's corps and one division of McPherson's corps had landed at De Shroon, Louisiana, six miles above Bruinsburg. Grant had twenty thousand men under General McClernand's 13th Corps and two brigades of Logan's division of the 17th Corps under McPherson on land. Bruinsburg is two miles from high ground. The bottom at that point is higher than most of the low land in the valley of the Mississippi and a good road led to the bluff. McClernand reached the bluffs before sunset and pushed on, hoping to reach Port Gibson before the Confederates could reach the city.

Port Gibson had roads leading to Grand Gulf, Vicksburg, and Jackson. Mc-Clernand met the Confederates five miles west of Port Gibson at Thompson's plantation. [352]

Early the next morning seven thousand Confederates under General John Bowen took a strong position. He hoped to hold Grant's forces off until General W. W. Loring could reach him, but Loring did not arrive in time. Two brigades of McPherson's corps followed McClernand and were ready to take position on the battlefield, when the 13th Corps could move out of the way. Bowen selected an area where the road to Port Gibson divides, taking two ridges. McClernand divided his force. They were separated by a ravine. One flank could not reinforce the other. McClernand put the divisions of Hovey, Carr, and A. J. Smith upon the right branch and Osterhaus took the left. On the left, Osterhaus had been repulsed. As soon as the road could be cleared of McClernand's troops. General John Smith's brigade, McPherson's corps, was ordered to support Osterhaus and to move to the left and flank the Confederates out of their position. This movement carried the brigade over a deep ravine to a third ridge and when Smith's troops were seen through the ravine, Osterhaus was directed to renew his frontal attack. It was success-ful. The Confederates were in full retreat on their right, and the left soon followed. Grant's force came to within two miles of Port Gibson. Bowen had lost nearly one third of his command. [353]

On May 1, Tilghman was ordered by Pemberton to quickly reach Edward's Station with his two regiments, and wait for Loring's force. He was to take no artillery with him. He was then ordered to Grand Gulf. The order was again countermanded and Pemberton ordered Tilghman to march to Port Gibson. Pemberton ordered Loring to Edward's Depot then to Port Gibson to join Tilghman. Loring would then take command of operations there. Tilgh-man would be placed in command of Tracy's brigade and his own regiments there. The other regiments of Tilghman's and Buford's brigades would go to Vicksburg and be ordered to Grand Gulf. Tilghman was then informed by Pemberton that Loring would take the Pointe Coupe Artillery from Jackson. That was all the artillery that was to go. Pemberton then wrote to Tilghman to move at once with two regiments to join Bowen. He was to take forage at Edward's Depot. [354]

On May 2, the Yankees had bridged the Bayou Pierre, to the east of Port Gibson, and were moving on the Jackson Road. Pemberton realized that if Grant should arrive at the junction before he did, he would be completely cut off, and would have no entrenchments in his rear. Pemberton decided to abandon Grand Gulf and fall back in the direction of Jackson or Vicksburg. Pemberton consulted with Loring and Tilghman. Both Generals recommended that Pemberton was to move. General Loring requested that Pemberton put the army in motion, while he would conduct the retreat. It was reported that

General John Bowen had retreated back to Grand Gulf, and the road was open to the Yankees. [355] The Yankees were approaching Big Black. Tilghman was ordered to hold back the Yankees and kept them in check. Tilghman then burned the bridge and fell back. On that same day, General McClernand ordered General Stephen Burbridge to proceed to Port Gibson, where he had the pleasure of raising the stars and stripes. The rear guard of the Confederates were retreating. McPherson reached Hankinson's Ferry and seized the ferry boat, and sent a detachment across and several miles north on the road to Vicksburg. When they reached the junction of the road going to Vicksburg with the road from Grand Gulf to Raymond and Jackson, Logan with his division was turned to the left towards Grand Gulf. McPherson met the largest Confederate force since the Battle of Port Gibson and had a skirmish nearly approaching a battle, but the road Logan had taken enabled him to come upon the Confederates right flank, and they soon fell back. McPherson was ordered to hold Hankinson's Ferry and the road back to Willow Springs with one division. McClernand, who was in the rear, was to join in this as well as to guard the line back down the bayou. [356]

On the 3rd, Grant reached Grand Gulf and found the city abandoned. While he was there, Grant received a message from General Banks, who was on the Red River. He reported that he could not be at Port Hudson before May 10th and then with only fifteen thousand men. Grant was planning to secure Grand Gulf as a base of supplies, detach McClernand's corps to Banks and cooperate with him in the reduction of Port Hudson. The news from Banks forced Grant to adopt a different plan. To wait for Banks cooperation would have detained Grant's men for a month. The reinforcements would have not amounted to ten thousand men after losses from casualties and river guards at all high points close to the river for three hundred miles. The Confederates would have quickly reinforced and strengthened their positions. Grant decided to move independently of Banks, cut loose from his base, destroy the Confederate force in rear of Vicksburg and surround the city. Grand Gulf was given up as a supply base. Grant foraged from the surrounding countryside for his supplies. He found beef, bacon, poultry, mutton and molasses in abundant supply. Grant kept the local mill stones grinding corn night and day. While the troops were awaiting rations, Grant ordered McClernand and McPherson to make reconnaissances with the idea of leading the Confederates into believing that the Union forces were intending to cross the Big Black and attack the city at once. [357]

On May 6, 1863, Sherman, with his two divisions, arrived at Grand Gulf bringing Grant's force to thirty-three thousand men. At his headquarters at Lanier, Tilghman was informed that sixty federals were heading for Edward's Station. His scouts had seen Osterhaus' observation post. The scout also told Tilghman that four thousand to five thousand Union cavalry were seen along a road that would take them to Big Black Bridge. Tilghman immediately sent out a patrol, but there were no Federal troops to be found heading for Big Black. [358]

The next day Sherman ordered a forward movement and was directed to order up Blair. Hurlbut was ordered to send four regiments from his command to Milliken's Bend from Memphis to relieve Blair's division, and on the 5th he was ordered to send Lauman's division to join the army. McPherson gathered his troops north of the Big Black and was heading on the road to Jackson via the Rocky Springs, Utica, and Raymond. McPherson and McClernand were both at Rocky Springs, ten miles from Hankinson's Ferry. McPherson remained there until the 8th, while McClernand moved to Big Sandy and Sherman marched from Grand Gulf to Hankinson's Ferry. [359]

On the 9th, McPherson moved to a point within a few miles west of Utica; McClernand and Sherman remained where they were. On the 10th McPherson moved to Utica, Sherman to Big Sandy; McClernand was still at Big Sandy. The 11th, McClernand was at Five Mile Creek; Sherman at Auburn; McPherson five miles advanced from Utica. May 12th, McClernand was at Fourteen Mile Creek; McPherson at Raymond after a battle. McPherson's troops had crossed the Big Black at Hankinson's Ferry. Grant planned to get to the railroad east of Vicksburg and approach from that direction. McPherson's troops were withdrawn, and the movement east to Jackson began. [360]

McClernand's troops were kept with its left flank on the Big Black guarding all the crossings. Fourteen Mile Creek was reached and crossings effected by McClernand and Sherman with little loss. McPherson was to the right of Sherman, extending to Raymond. The cavalry was used to find roads, cover the Union advances and to find the most practicable routes from one command to the other so they could support each other. Grant decided to place his army between Pemberton's army and fight him in detail. Grant's line was parallel with the Jackson and Vicksburg railroad. The right was at Raymond eighteen miles below Jackson, McPherson commanding; Sherman was in the center on Fourteen Mile Creek; McClernand was to the left also on Fourteen Mile Creek, and his pickets thrown ahead within two miles of Edward's station. McClernand's left wing was on the Big Black River. [361]

McPherson encountered the five thousand strong with two batteries under General Gregg, about two miles from Raymond. Logan was in advance with one of his brigades. He formed his line of battle. McPherson ordered the road in the rear to be cleared of wagons, and the balance of Logan's division and Crocker's to come forward. Logan got his division into position for an assault before Crocker could come up, and attacked the Confederates, carrying the Confederate's position easily, sending Gregg retreating from the field. McPherson lost sixty-six killed, 339 wounded, and 37 missing. The Confederates lost 820 men who were either killed, wounded, or captured. [362]

With the victory at Raymond, Grant decided to turn his force toward Jackson. Pemberton was now on Grant's left. A force was also collecting on Grant's right, at Jackson, the point where all the railroads communicating with Vicksburg connect. All the Confederate supplies of men and stores would come by that point. Grant had to destroy all the possibility of aid to Vicksburg if he was to succeed in capturing the city. He decided to cut loose from his base and move his whole force east. [363]

Grant ordered McPherson to move on Clinton, ten miles from Jackson. Sherman was to march to Raymond. McClernand was ordered to march with three divisions by Dillon's to Raymond. One was left to guard the Big Black River.

On the 13th General Joseph Johnston arrived at Jackson from Tennessee and immediately assumed command of all Confederate troops in Mississippi. McPherson arrived at Clinton with the advance and immediately set to work destroying the railroad. Sherman's advance reached Raymond before the last of McPherson's command had left the town. McClernand withdrew from the front of the Confederates at Edward's Station and reached his position. Later that night McPherson was ordered to move one division of his command to Clinton, one division a few miles beyond Mississippi Springs, following Sherman's line, and a third to Raymond. He was also ordered to send his siege guns, which were large caliber cannons, ranging from twenty-four pounders and twenty-pound Parrott rifle cannons, with the troops going by the Mississippi Springs. Grant had a force confronting Pemberton if he should come out to attack his rear. [364]

On that same day, Confederate Major General Bowen, in command of his division, spotted the enemy advancing. Loring's division was ordered to reinforce him. Confederate General Carter Stevenson arrived with his division and took a very strong position one mile south of Edward's Depot. The Confederate left was positioned on the railroad and the Confederate right was not far from Baker's Creek. Union General McClernand withdrew from the front of the Confederates at Edward's station. McPherson was then ordered to march on Jackson in the morning. Sherman was given the same order, but he was to march on the direct road from Raymond to Jackson, which was south of the road McPherson was on. McClernand was ordered to move one of his divisions to Clinton-one division a few miles beyond Mississippi Springs following Sherman's line, and a third to Raymond. [365]

The next day, General Pemberton ordered a council of war, in which he read a dispatch from General Joseph Johnston, which stated that the Union forces of two or three divisions was at Clinton, nine miles from Jackson, Mississippi, and he advised a movement. During the council there was much discussion as to what to do next. Two generals wanted to move at once upon the road to Clinton; two of the generals wanted to remain or fall back; three wanted to strike at the communications of the Yankees, keeping the

Confederates route open with the bridge over Big Black River, and fighting. Pemberton did not agree with Johnston's proposal, but wanted rather to move in the Union force's rear.

Pemberton decided that the army would move out in the morning at 8 A.M. and cross Baker's Creek at a ford; the move was prevented by high water. But by 4 P.M. they crossed a creek upon a bridge a short distance above the ford. By dark Loring's division was camped at Mrs. Ellison's house, on the middle Raymond Road. Upon this same road the Yankees were camped in large force within a few miles of Loring's camp. Loring informed Pemberton of the enemy to their front. The next day would be fateful for Loring's Division and for General Tilghman.

By 9 A.M. Crocker of McPherson's corps came upon the Confederate's pickets and drove them in upon the main body. They were outside of the entrenchments in a strong position, and proved to be the troops that had been driven out of Raymond. Johnston had been reinforced during night by Georgia and South Carolina regiments, so that his force amounted to eleven thousand men.

Sherman also came upon the Rebel pickets some distance out from the town, but drove them in. He was on the south and southwest of Jackson confronting the Confederates behind their breastworks, while McPherson's right was two miles north, occupying a line running north and south across the Vicksburg railroad. Artillery was brought up and reconnaissances made for an assault. McPherson brought up Logan's division while he deployed Crocker's for the assault. Sherman made similar dispositions on the right. By 11 A.M. both were ready to attack. Crocker moved his division forward, preceded by a strong skirmish line who at once encountered the Confederate advance and drove it back on the main body. When they returned to their regiment, the whole division charged, routing the Confederates completely and driving them into their main line. This stand was made more than two miles from their main fortifications. McPherson followed up with his command until within range of the guns of the Confederates from their entrenchments, when he halted to bring his troops into line and reconnoiter to determine the next move. It was noon. [366]

Sherman was confronting a Confederate battery which covered the road and commanded a bridge spanning a stream over which he had to pass. By detaching right and left the stream was forded and the Confederates flanked and driven within the main line. This brought Grant's whole line in front of the Confederate line of works, which was continuous on the north, west and south sides from the Pearl River north of the city to the same river south. Sherman was confronted with a force sufficient to hold his line back. Grant ordered him to send a force to the right, and to reconnoiter as far as to the Pearl River. Tuttle's division was sent and did not return. Grant rode out with his staff and found the Confederates had left that part of the line. Tuttle's movement or McPherson's pressure led Johnston to order a retreat, leaving only the men at the guns to stop Grant while the Confederates were getting away. [367]

Tuttle had seen this and came up in the rear of the artillery confronting Sherman and captured them with ten pieces of artillery. Grant rode immediately to the State House, where he was soon followed by Sherman. About the same time McPherson discovered the Confederates were leaving his front, and advanced Crocker. He captured seven Confederate artillery pieces and hoisted the American flag over the Confederate capitol of Mississippi at Jackson. Stevenson's brigade was sent to cut off the Rebel retreat, but was too late. McPherson had lost 37 killed, 228 wounded during the Battle of Jackson. Sherman had lost 4 killed, 21 wounded and missing. The Confederates lost 845 killed, wounded and captured. Seventeen cannons fell into Union hands. [368]

On the same day, Blair reached New Auburn and joined McClernand's 4th division. He had two hundred wagons loaded with rations. [369] That night, Grant slept in the same hotel that Johnston had used just the night before in Jackson.

The next day Grant ordered Sherman to remain in Jackson until he destroyed Jackson's railroads, and manufacturing. Grant had received the message sent from sent from Johnston to Pemberton on the 13th. A spy had delivered the message to Grant. Grant had received the message on the 14th and he immediately ordered McPherson to move back to Bolton. Bolton was twenty miles from Jackson. He also told McClernand of the capture of Jackson and sent him the following message: "It is evidently the design of the enemy to get north of us and cross the Big Black, and beat us into Vicksburg. We must not allow them to do this. Turn all your forces toward Bolton station and make all dispatch in getting there. Move troops by the most direct road from wherever they may be on the receipt of this order." Grant also sent General Blair a message ordering him to Bolton.[370]

Johnston stopped his army on the Canton road only six miles north of Jackson on the 14th. Johnston asked Pemberton to unite the rest of the army. Johnston wanted Pemberton to cut off Grant from his supplies from the Mississippi and force him to fall back. Both Pemberton and Johnston were to link up at Clinton.[371]

McPherson moved along the road parallel with and near the railroad. McClernand's command, with Hovey's division, was on the road McPherson had to take, but with a start of four miles. Osterhaus was at Raymond, on a converging road that intersected the other near Champion's Hill: Carr's had to pass over the same road with Osterhaus, but being back at Mississippi Springs, would not be detained by it; Smith's with Blair's division, was near Auburn with a different road to pass over. McClernand faced about and moved promptly. His cavalry from Raymond seized Bolton by 9:30 A.M., driving the Confederate pickets and capturing several men. [372]

On the 15th Hovey was at Bolton; Carr and Osterhaus were about three miles south, but abreast, facing west. Smith was north of Raymond with Blair in his rear. McPherson's command, with Logan in front, had marched at 7 A.M. and by four reached Hovey and went into camp. Crocker camped just in Hovey's rear on the Clinton road. Sherman with two divisions, was in Jackson completing the destruction of roads, bridges, and factories. Grant rode out to Clinton. When he arrived, he ordered McClernand to move early the next day on Edward's Station, and to watch for the Rebels and not bring on an engagement unless he felt certain of success. [373]

Grant expected Pemberton to obey Johnston's orders and attack the Union forces at Clinton, but he had decided to move south from Edward's Station and get between Grant and his base of supplies. Grant had no base of supplies, having abandoned it more than a week before. On the 15th Pemberton had actually marched south from Edward's Station, but the rains had swollen Baker's Creek, so much that he could not cross it, and the bridges had washed away. This brought him back to the Jackson road, on which there was a good bridge over Baker's Creek. Some of his troops were marching until midnight to get there. Receiving a message from Johnston, Pemberton was again ordered to join him at Clinton. Pemberton decided to obey the order. He ordered the troops that were already marching south to turn north and rendezvous with Johnston's force at the town of Clinton. They were about halfway there when the Federals intercepted them, at a hill on the farm of a man named Sid Champion. [374]

At 5 A.M. on the 16th two men, who had been employed on the Jackson and Vicksburg railroad, were brought to Grant. They reported that Pemberton was still marching east, and had eighty regiments of infantry, and ten batteries, in all about twenty-five thousand men. [375]

Grant immediately ordered Sherman out of Jackson and to join his command at Bolton. He ordered Blair, who was at Auburn, to move to Edward's Station. McClernand was ordered to join Blair. Blair's division was a part of Sherman's 15th Corps, but since the 15th Corps was on its way to join McClernand's Corps, it struck the Union left first, now that the Union forces were turned around and were moving west. The 15th Corps would be on the extreme Union right. McPherson was ordered to get his trains out of the way of the troops, and to follow Hovey's division. McClernand had two roads about three miles apart, converging at Edward's Station, over which to march his troops. Hovey's division of his corps had the advance on the Clinton road still farther north. McClernand was directed to move Blair's and A. J. Smith's divisions by the southern-most of these roads, and Osterhaus and Carr by the middle road. Orders were to move cautiously with skirmishers to the front to feel for the Confederates.[376]

Union Major General Andrew Jackson Smith's division on the most southern road was the first to encounter the Confederate pickets, who were driven in. He quickly came under the fire of Confederate General W. W. Loring's artillery. The most important battle of the Vicksburg Campaign was about to begin. Grant's 32,000 Federals would face 23,000 Confederates under Pemberton. The oncoming battle at Sid Champion's farm would be the most important battle of the Vicksburg Campaign.[377]

CHAPTER EIGHT

"A Hill of Death"

Champion's Hill was an excellent position. As Grant said: "It is one of the highest points in that section, and commanded all the ground in range."[378] On the east side of the ridge is a ravine running from north, then west, terminating at Baker's Creek. It was covered with large trees and undergrowth, making it extremely difficult for troops to penetrate. The ridge occupied by the Confederates ended abruptly where the ravine turns west. The left of the Rebel line occupied the north end of the ridge. The Bolton and Edward's Station wagon road turns almost due south at this point and ascends a ridge, which it follows for about a mile, then turning west, descends by a gentle decline to Baker's Creek, nearly a mile away. On the west side, the ridge had a slope that was gradual and devoid of trees and ran from near the summit to the creek. There was a narrow belt of timber near the summit west of the road. From Raymond there was a direct road to Edward's Station, which was located three miles west of Champion's Hill. There was also a road to Bolton. [379]

At 8 A.M. Pemberton informed W. W. Loring that Johnston wanted Pemberton to link up with him at Brownsville, since Johnston was falling back from Jackson, Mississippi. Loring now must move towards Edwards Depot. The Yankees had already formed into line of battle preparing to attack Loring. Union General A. J. Smith soon came upon Loring's pickets, and a cannonade opened up on the morning air. Loring suggested that Pemberton must form a line of battle as quickly as possible. Pemberton at first ordered Tilghman's brigade in a line of battle upon the ground it was occupying, but then changed his mind and ordered Featherstone's and Buford's brigades along with Tilghman, which was Loring's entire division, into line of battle on a ridge about three quarters of mile west of Mrs. Ellison's plantation and across Jackson Creek. This line was again changed for one still farther back, where Loring's artillery was posted on both sides of the road, the field to the front being entirely open as far as Mrs. Ellison's house. At 9 o'clock in the morning, Brig. General Tilghman, commanding the brigade, received orders to move his brigade from just beyond the Ellison's house, where it had camped Friday night, to a ridge about half a mile in their rear. The order was followed and the brigade formed into line of battle to the right of the division. From 9 till 12 p.m. nothing of importance happened, but at that time the whole division changed its position by the left flank, Brig. General Abe Buford moving to the support of Brig. General Bowen, on his left; Brig. General Featherstone closing up, so as to be in supporting distance, and Brig. General Tilghman, with his brigade and two batteries-the Cowan battery, with six guns, and Wither's regiment of artillery, and the McLendon battery with it's four guns, of Ward's battalion, by direction of the Loring, taking position on the Raymond road and Edward's Depot road, to prevent a flank movement of the Yankees down it on their right. At the same time, he was told to hold himself in readiness to move up the support of other brigades of the division should it become necessary.[380]

As mentioned earlier Union General A. J. Smith's division was the first to encounter the Confederates pickets, who were driven in. Osterhaus rode forward with his force of 2,386 men. He had to cross a chaos of ravines and narrow hills, sloping very abruptly into sink hole like valleys, which ran in all directions. All the area was covered with trees and brush, except the road, which winds its track in bizarre curves, and followed the hills and valleys, without permitting at any point an open view of more than fifty or one hundred yards. Osterhaus ordered General Garrard to advance. Only one section of Lamphere's battery was taken with Garrard. Osterhaus also deployed the Second Brigade under Col. Lindsey, with two sections of the 7th Michigan Battery and the First Wisconsin Battery, on an open and commanding ridge in the field which the advancing First Brigade, under Garrard, was left behind.

The 3rd Illinois Cavalry, commanded by Capt. Campbell, led the way carefully, and supported by the skirmishers[381] of the 7th Kentucky, they advanced into the timber and against the Confederates, who was in brush. The ground was so rough that Osterhaus had to recall the 3rd Illinois Cavalry, and sent the Cavalry to connect with General Smith on his left.

The 7th Kentucky, with the 49th Indiana Infantry and one section of Lanphere's Battery, formed the advance, and drove the Confederate skirmishers from one ravine to another, and pushed to within one mile beyond the Second Brigade in the field. Osterhaus found a good position for his artillery and placed it there supported by two companies of infantry. The cannons were loaded with canister. The 7th Kentucky on the right and the 49th Indiana on the left of the road advanced about one mile beyond the section of artillery, when the fire and resistance of the Confederates became fierce. Osterhaus called up the 69th Indiana and the 118th Illinois to deploy on the left of the road to reenforce the already engaged regiments of his command. They forced the Confederates to form several positions by charging up and down the hills.

By this time General Hovey was also engaged. Hovey had arrived on the field at 10:00 A.M. and found the Confederates posted on the crest of the hill, with a battery of four guns in the woods near the road, and on the highest

Battle of Champion's Hill, General Logan leads a Union Assault on Champion's Hill. (Currier & Ives print)

point for many miles around. Hovey ordered General McGinnis to form his brigade into two lines, three regiments being the advance and two in reserve. The Second Brigade, under Col. James Slack, was formed on the left of the First Brigade, two regiments in advance and two in reserve. They came to within sight of the Confederates battery. Grant and McPherson, with his command arrived. As soon as McPherson's line was ready to take part in the battle, which was about 10:30 A.M., Hovey ordered General McGinnis and Col. Slack to press their skirmishers forward up the hill, and follow them. In a few minutes the fire opened upon the whole line, from Hovey's extreme left to the right of the forces engaged by McPherson and at 11 A.M. the battle opened all along the line. For over six hundred yards up the hill Hovey's division drove the Confederates before them, capturing eleven cannons and over three hundred prisoners. The 11th Indiana, under Col. Macauley, and the 29th Wisconsin, under Col. Gill, captured the four guns under Captain Samuel J. Ridley's Mississippi Battery, which was positioned on the brow of the hill, at the point of bayonet. Ridley fell with six wounds, and later died. Col. Bringhurst, of the 46th Indiana, drove the Confederates from two guns on the right of the road, and Col. Bryan, with his 24th Iowa, charged a battery of five guns on the left of the road, driving the Confederates away, killing the gunners and horses.

At this time General McGinnis took one section of the 16th Ohio Battery, under Captain Mitchell, up the hill. The cannons under Captain Mitchell fired sixteen rounds and was withdrawn, for the fear of being captured. Captain Mitchell was killed while taking his guns back down the hill.

The Confederate forces were now concentrated against Hovey and Osterhaus. The Confederate artillery rained down shell and shot. Hovey and Osterhaus now advanced until they came to a clearing in the timber. The Confederates tried to prevent Hovey and Osterhaus from joining. Heavy columns of Confederates were advancing. Osterhaus added the 42nd Ohio Infantry to his First Brigade, and the 114th Ohio Infantry to support one section of artillery in lieu of two companies of the 49th Indiana, which Osterhaus ordered to join their regiment in the front.

Osterhaus ordered Col. Lindsey, with his two remaining regiments, which was the 16th Ohio and the 22nd Kentucky Infantry, to take a position in the edge of the timber and open fire against the Confederates position. These two regiments were not able to repel or resist the large numbers of Confederates, so Major General McClernand was asked to send reenforcements from Carr's Division, which was to Osterhaus rear. A regiment was ordered to the support of Col. Lindsey, who proceeded to attack the Confederate forces. Leaving the timber, he charged the retreating infantry to the very muzzle of the battery covering them. The promised support had not arrived to follow up the attack, so Col. Lindsey fell back into the timber and awaited the reenforcements. Col. Lawler's brigade of General Carr's division was ordered to support Lindsey. The Confederates opened with the artillery. A few rounds from General Lawler's artillery were enough to silence the Rebel guns and compel him to remove them to a safer distance.

During this time Hovey asked for reenforcements. Grant sent Col. George Boomer, commanding the Third Brigade, of Quinby's division, and came up the hill. Col. Samuel Holmes, with two small regiments, the 10th Missouri and the 17th Iowa also came to his assistance. Hovey's entire force was being forced to fall back by the counterattack under General Bowen. Col. Francis Cockrell's Missouri brigade on the left and Brig. General Martin Green's

Arkansas brigade on the right hit the Federals under Hovey. When the 24th Indiana began to break under the assault, Lt. Col. R. F. Barter seized the regimental colors to rally his terrified men, but he too was shot down by a volley. In minutes, two hundred and one men of the five hundred of the 24th Indiana fell. With the 24th Indiana and other units being pushed back under Bowen's assault, Col. Boomer and Col. Holmes rushed in with their commands, but the Confederates had massed their forces, and slowly pressed his whole line with reenforcements backward to a point near the brow of a hill. Here a stubborn stand was made. By 2:30 P.M. Hovey had driven Pemberton's left back until the Confederate line faced almost due north; and Osterhaus advanced from the east and now threatened Bowen's right flank. At the same time Hovey ordered the First Missouri Battery, commanded by Captain Schofield and the 16th Ohio Battery, under 1st Lieutenant Murdock, to take a position in an open field, beyond a slight mound on his right, in advance of, and with parallel ranges of their guns with Hovey's line. About the same time Captain Dillon's Wisconsin battery was put in position two sections of the 16th Ohio Battery on the left, the Wisconsin battery in the center, and Captain Schofield's battery on the right. Through the Rebel ranks these batteries fired a shower of shot and shell, entirely enfilading the Rebel columns.

The fire was terrific for several minutes, then Hovey's men began to cheer from the brow of the hill, foretelling the victory. The Confederates fell back, and the Union forces, under General McGinnis, Col. Slack, and Col. Boomer, and Col. Holmes, drove them again over the ground which had been contested for the third time during the day, five more of the eleven guns not taken down the hill falling a second time into the Union hands.

At 3:00 P.M. the battle of Champion's Hill ended. Loring was ordered to support the crumbling Confederate line, but by the time he got moving it was too late. The Confederate soldiers were now running in every direction. Pemberton issued a retreat. But General Logan's men had cut off the Jackson Road, and the only means of escape across Baker's Creek was the Raymond Road bridge on Pemberton's southern flank. They were heading in Tilghman's direction.[382]

About 1 o'clock General Tilghman countermarched the brigade and moved down the Raymond and Edward's Depot road about a quarter of a mile. He took a new right hand road, which communicated with the Confederate left wing. Tilghman intended to join Major General Loring by this route. After proceeding only a few hundred yards, Lt. General Pemberton met Tilghman's brigade and ordered it back to a position on the main road they had just left. General Tilghman received an order that countermanded the one he had just received, which ordered him to move and hold his position, but this order had been sent to him nearly an hour before. [383]

At the time of the movement from their first position, on the Raymond and Edwards Depot road, and before the rear of the brigade had crossed that road, a heavy column of the Yankees, under Major General Stephen Burbridge's brigade were seen advancing in line of battle out of the woods, immediately around the Ellison's House. Col. R. Lowry, of the Sixth Mississippi Regiment, who was in the rear, was at once directed to throw out a heavy line of skirmishers, composing nearly one half the regiment, moving

Battle of Champion's Hill. Union General Ulysses S. Grant's troops attack Confederate General John Pemberton's line on Champion's Hill. (Library of Congress)

too far to the left, became separated from the brigade and, placed itself with the left wing of the army, fell back with it, first to Big Black Bridge, and then finally to Vicksburg.

Soon after the formation of the second line of battle at 1:30 P.M., Major General Loring came up with the other two brigades of the division, and formed them immediately on the left of the First Brigade. He informed General Tilghman that the left wing of the army was retreating to the Big Black River, and that, in order to cover the movement, General Pemberton had directed him" to maintain his position at all hazards" until sundown. Tilghman made a strong battery on a hill near old man Champion's gin house. From this point he gave orders to distant parts of the field by signal and was "fighting like a tiger." The Yankees, under Union General Stephen Burbridge's brigade, had taken possession of the hill abandoned by the First Brigade, a continuous fire from both artillery and skirmishers was kept up. Burbridge's men were protected under the crest of a hill and his sharpshooters were picking off so many of Tilghman's gunners they had to abandon some of their guns. Burbridge asked for reenforcements from General Smith. Smith sent the 19th Kentucky and the 77th Illinois, of Col. Landram's brigade. Four guns of the 17th Ohio Battery, which were part of the Chicago Mercantile Battery, were also sent and began to fire. General Smith ordered Burbridge's brigade to halt. Burbridge in his official report wrote that if he had been supported by Blair's division, he could have captured the whole Rebel force, and reached Edward's Station before sunset.[384]

At 5:20 P.M., Brig. General Lloyd Tilghman, who up to that time had commanded the First Brigade with "marked ability", dismounted and took command of a section of field artillery, under the 1st Mississippi Light Artillery, and was in the act of sighting a six pound howitzer when he was struck in the hip by a cannonball, from the Chicago Mercantile Battery's Number two gun. As he fell he said to his son who caught him: "Tell your mother; God bless her." He lived about three hours, after he was wounded and carried to a peach tree where he died while in the arms of Captain Powhattan Ellis, Jr., Tilghman's Assistant Adjutant General. The command devolved upon Col. A. E. Reynolds. During the battle, Tilghman displayed great courage towards the Union forces, but Tilghman forgot that he was a Brigadier General who was ultimately responsible for the command of his troops. By dismounting his horse and manning a cannon, he had reduced himself to a regular soldier, but the Southern notion of honor and courage guided Tilghman's actions. When Tilghman was killed in battle, he was automatically assured a place in the annals of Southern martyrdom, where courage and bravery were more important than wise and sound leadership.

Reynold wrote an after battle report on the Battle of Champion;s Hill and had this to say of Tilghman:

As a man, a soldier, and a general, he had few if any superiors. Always at his post, he devoted himself day and night to the interests of his command. Upon the battlefield cool, collected, and observant, he commanded the entire respect and confidence of every officer and soldier under him, and the only censure ever cast upon him was that he always exposed himself too recklessly. At the time he was struck down he was standing in the rear of a battery, directing a change in the elevation of one of the guns. The tears shed by his men on the occasion, and the grief felt by his entire brigade, are the proudest tribute that can be given the gallant dead.[385]

E. T. Eggleston, was also a eye witness to General Tilghman's death. He was an Orderly Sergeant of Capt. James Cowan's Battery, Company G, Col. W. T. Wither's Regiment of Artillery. He said that General Tilghman:

...came to our position, in an open field, on foot. He was in particular good humor. He wore a new fatigue uniform. When he arrived near our guns our officers were mounted, and were in position prescribed for dress parade, each Lieutenant, George H. Tompkins and Thomas J. Hanes, in their positions, and Captain Cowan mounted on a large grey horse, making a conspicuous target for the Federal sharpshooters. We were all tyros in war at that time. The General in a pleasant manner said to our Captain, "I think you and your Lieutenants had better dismount. They are shooting pretty close to us, and I do not know whether they are shooting at your fine grey horse or my new uniform." They very promptly obeyed the suggestion. Having to go to his headquarters daily with reports, I had become personally acquainted with the affable, gallant, and genial officer. Only a few minutes before his death we were sitting on a log near a strip of woodland discussing the line of battle we then held, comparing it with the one we had shortly before occupied. He got up from the log and went to one of our guns, a 12 pound Napoleon, Corporal "Tommie" Johnson, gunner, and remarked to him "I think you are shooting rather to high," and sighted the gun himself. He returned to a little knoll within a few feet of the log on which I was still sitting and was standing erect, his field glasses to his eyes, watching for the effect of the shot from our gun when he received the fatal wound not from a "splinter from a shell", however, but from a solid shot. It is true that a horse was killed by the same missile and I noticed that the horse was dead some time before the General ceased to breathe, though he was unconscious.[386]

Eggleston went on to say: "It was some little time after the General fell before his son, a youth, could be found, and I shall never forget the touching scene when the grief and lamentations he cast himself on his dying and unconscious father. Those of us who witnessed this distressing scene shed tears of sympathy, for the bereaved son and of sorrow for our fallen hero, the chivalrous and beloved Tilghman." [387]

Private James Spencer, 1st Mississippi Light Artillery, Moore's Brigade, was also a witness to Tilghman's death, and wrote of his account, saying:

About 3:00 P.M. the Federal force appeared in our front and General Loring withdrawing his division rode up to our Battery and said to Capt. Cowan, "I intend to save my Division as I have been cut off by the defeat of Gen. Stevenson. I want your Battery to hold this position until sundown, or captured. If you succeed in holding until sundown, fall back, following my line of retreat." The Chicago Mercantile Battery had gone into position 400 yards in our front, with 6, 10lb. Parrott guns. We had 4, 6lb. Guns & 2, 10lb Howitzers. The Federal battery opened on us, firing accurately. General Tilghman & his staff rode up to Capt. Cowan & ordered him to open fire. The General dismounted & said to Capt. Cowan, "I will take a shot at those fellows myself," & walked up to field piece No. 2 & sighted & ordered it fired & shell from the Federal Battery passed close to him while our gun was being reloaded. Tilghman remarked, "They are trying to spoil my new uniform." He then sighted the gun again & as he stepped back to order fire, a Parrott shell struck him in the side, nearly cutting him in twain. Just before he dismounted, he ordered his son, a boy of about 17 yrs. to go with a squad & drive some sharpshooters from a gin house on our left, who were annoying our cannoneers. The son had been gone 10 or 15 minutes on this mission before his father was killed.[388]

F. W. M. also wrote an account of Tilghman's death. He wrote the article from Plant City, Florida on July 13th 1893. He said that General Tilghman was killed between 4 and 5 P.M.

General Loring's Division occupied the right of Pemberton's line: Tilghman's brigade, composed of two Mississippi regiments (15th and 22nd), 1st Louisiana, Rayburn's Mississippi battalion and McLendon's battery, occupied the extreme right...For hours the enemy seemed to be in full force, and ready to advance upon us. Bowen's division having been driven from it's position, our division dropped back to keep in alignment with Bowen's and soon after this, which was then sometime after midday, the enemy advanced in force and was there held in check by Loring's Division until night came on. After repulsing the enemy's first assault they threw forward their line of sharpshooters, and with their artillery on the main line, kept up the fight until dark. About two hundred yards, to the front, and a little to the left of our battery, there was a large farm house and a row of plantation cabins. These cabins were taken possession of by the enemy's sharpshooters and they were picking our men off rapidly. General Tilghman directed the gun sergeant to train his gun, a 12 pound howitzer, and dislodge the enemy from the cabins. He dismounted from his horse and gave some directions about sighting the gun. While this was being done a shell from one of the enemy's guns on the line exploded about fifty feet to the front. A ragged fragment of this shell struck the General in the breast, passing through him and killing the horse of his Adjutant a little farther to the rear. His death occurred, of course, very soon, and his remains were carried to the rear. That night they were started to Vicksburg, accompanied by his personal staff and his son, Lloyd Tilghman, Jr. and the next evening they were buried in the city cemetery in Vicksburg." "The last act of a brave man was to sight a field gun and direct the cutting of a shell fuse, so as to do the best execution upon the invaders of our country.[389]

General Loring was also a witness of the battle at Champion's Hill. He reported:

During this time Tiglhman, who had been left with his brigade upon the road, almost immediately after our parting, met a terrible assault of the enemy, and when we rejoined him was carrying on a deadly and most gallant fight. With less than 1,500 effective men he was attacked by from 6,000 to 8,000 of the enemy with a fine park of artillery, but being advantageously posted, he not only held him in check, but repulsed him on several occasions, and this kept open the only line of retreat left to the army. The bold stand of his brigade under the lamented hero saved a large portion of the army."[390]

Loring said of Tilghman's death: "Quick and bold in the execution of his plans, he fell in the midst of a brigade that loved him well, after repulsing a powerful enemy in deadly fight, struck by a cannon-shot. A brigade wept over the dying hero; alike beautiful as it was touching.[391]

After Reynolds took command of the First Brigade, he was ordered off the field, the fire of the Yankees was fierce. Cowan's battery had several men wounded, and nearly used up all its ammunition, and yet from orders received by Reynolds had to be kept in position. The McLendon Battery lost several men and horses, and were exposed to heavy fire rendering the use of their guns hazardous. Reynolds learned that General's Buford and Featherstone's brigades were moving off to the rear, and that Reynolds was directed to bring off his brigade in the rear of General Featherstone. The Yankees were pressing them closely at the same time, so that Reynolds deemed it best to move off by the left flank through the fields rather than by the right down the road, and by doing so the Yankees were to believe that Reynolds was moving to the left. He deceived the Yankees and avoided any serious pursuit. After moving a little more than a mile, Reynolds received orders from the Major General to have his artillery move out of regular line and set up in front of General Featherstone's brigade. The march was continued for twenty four hours, in which they had traveled forty miles.[392]

Grant lost 410 killed, 1,844 wounded, and 187 missing. Hovey alone lost 1,200 killed wounded and missing, more than one third of his division. Pemberton lost 3,839. After the six hour battle, General W. W. Loring and his 6,500 men were cut off from the retreating army and never got back into Vicksburg. Pemberton that night crossed the Raymond road bridge to the Big Black River. Union General Logan captured 1,300 prisoners and eleven cannons. Union General Hovey captured three hundred under fire and about seven hundred in all. After the attack Champion's Hill according to Hovey was *"literally the hills of death; men, horses, cannon, and the debris of an army lay scattered in wild confusion. Hundreds of the 12th Division were cold in death or writhing in pain, and with large numbers of Quinby's gallant boys, lay dead, dying, or wounded, intermixed with our fallen foe."*

On May 16th McPherson's command camped from two to six miles west of the battlefield, along the line of the road to Vicksburg. Union Generals Carr and Osterhaus were at Edward's Station and General Blair was about three miles southeast. Union General Hovey remained on the field. The Confederates started to abandon equipment. Thirty three pieces of artillery were picked up off the battlefield.

On the 19th, the Loring's entire division reached Jackson, Mississippi and rejoined Johnston's troops.

CHAPTER NINE

"All Was Now Ready For the Pick and Spade." -Ulysses S. Grant

After the battle of Champion's Hill, Grant was assured of his position between Johnston and Pemberton, without a possibility of a joining of their forces. Sherman left Jackson with the last of his troops on the 16th and reached Bolton, twenty miles west, before halting. His rear guard didn't get in until 2 A.M. the 17th, but renewed their march by daylight. He paroled his prisoners at Jackson. At Bolton he was informed of Grant's victory at Champion's Hill. He was ordered to begin the march and diverge from the road he was on to Bridgeport on the Big Black River, eleven miles above the point where Grant expected to find the Confederates. Blair was ordered to join him there with the pontoon train as soon as possible.

At 3 A.M. on the 17th Carr resumed the march, followed by Osterhaus, McPherson bringing up the rear with his corps. The Confederates were found in position on the Big Black. The Rebels under Pemberton had constructed a parapet along the inner bank of the bayou by using cotton bales from the plantation close by and throwing dirt over them. Carr's division was deployed on the Union right, Lawler's brigade forming his extreme right and reaching through these woods to the river above. Osterhaus' division was deployed to the left of Carr and covered the Confederate's entire front. McPherson was in column on the road, the head close by, ready to come in wherever he could be of assistance.

Lawler led a successful charge on the Confederates. The Confederates fled from the west bank of the river, burning the bridge behind them and leaving the men and guns on the east side to fall into Grant's hands. Many tried to escape by swimming the river. Some succeeded and some drowned in the attempt. Eighteen cannons were captured and 1,751 men were taken prisoner. Grant lost thirty-nine killed and two hundred and thirty-seven wounded and three missing. The bridge was totally destroyed, and a new bridge had to built. Three bridges were ordered to be built. By 8 A.M. on May 18 all three bridges were complete and the troops began to cross.

Sherman reached Bridgeport about noon on the 17th and found Blair with the pontoon train already there. Two divisions were crossed that night and the third the following morning.

On the 18th Grant moved along the Vicksburg road in advance of the troops and joined Sherman as soon as possible. Grant and Sherman moved in advance of the column and well up with the advance skirmishers. Some detached works along the crest of the hill were still occupied by the Rebels. Bullets began to fly. McPherson, after crossing the Big Black, came into the Jackson and Vicksburg road which Sherman was on, but to his rear. He arrived at night near the lines of the enemy, and went into camp. McClernand moved by the direct road near the railroad to Mount Albans, and then turned to the left and put his troops on the road from Baldwin's Ferry to Vicksburg. This brought him south of McPherson. Grant had his three corps arriving before the Vicksburg defenses.

By the 19th Grant had totally surrounded the city from the north, east, and south-east. Sherman was on the right, and covered by high ground from where it overlooked the Yazoo. McPherson joined on his left, and occupied ground on both sides of the Jackson road. McClernand took the high ground to his left and extended as far toward Warrenton as he could, keeping a continuous line. There was constant skirmishing with the Confederates while Grant's men were getting into position. At 2 P.M. Grant ordered an assault. It resulted in securing a better advanced position.

The 20th and 21st were spent in strengthening Grant's position and making roads in the rear of the army, from Yazoo River or Chickasaw Bayou. Grant devised a plan for a second assault. Johnston was in Grant's rear, only fifty miles away and being reinforced. Grant must attack before Johnston moved out to assist Pemberton. At 10 A.M. on the 22nd Grant attacked along the whole line. All three corps of Grant's army succeeded in getting up to parapets of the Confederate works, but at no place were his men to enter the works. General McClernand reported that he had gained the Confederate entrenchments at several points, and wanted reinforcements. Grant occupied a position from which he could see what took place in his front, and he did not see the success McClernand reported. But his request for reinforcements being repeated, Grant could not ignore it, and sent McClernand Quinby's division of the 17th Corps. Sherman and McPherson were both ordered to renew their assaults as a diversion in favor of McClernand. This last attack only served to increase Grant's casualties without giving any benefits whatsoever. As soon as it was dark Grant's men who had reached the Confederate lines and had been obliged to remain there for security all day, were withdrawn, and thus ended the last assault upon Vicksburg.

Next, Grant would lay siege to the city. The navy held the river, and the troops held the outer city. No food, men or ammunition was allowed to enter Vicksburg. Grant's line was fifteen miles long, extending from Haines Bluff to Vicksburg, then to Warrenton. The Confederate line was about seven miles long. Grant also built a defensive line to his rear facing the other way. Halleck sent reinforcements to man the second defensive line.

The ground around Vicksburg was excellent for defense. On the north it was two hundred feet above the Mississippi River at the highest point and very much cut up by the washing rains; the ravines were grown up with cane and underbrush, while the sides and tops were covered with a dense forest. Farther south the ground flattened out and was in cultivation. But there too it was cut up by ravines and small streams. The Confederate lines of defense followed the crest of a ridge from the river north of the city east, then south around to the Jackson road, a full three miles back of the city, then in a southwest direction to the river. Deep ravines lay in front of the defenses. The Confederate line would run from near the head of one gully nearly straight to the head of another, and an outer work triangular in shape, generally open in the rear, was thrown up on the point; with a few men in this outer work they commanded the approaches to the main line completely.

Grant had no siege guns except six thirty-two pounders. Admiral Porter supplied Grant with a battery of navy guns of large caliber and with these and the field artillery the city was laid to siege. The first thing for Grant was to place the artillery where they would occupy commanding positions, then establish camps, under cover from the fire of the Confederates but as near up as possible, and then construct rifle pits and covered ways, to connect the entire command by the shortest route. The Rebels didn't harass Grant as much while he was constructing his batteries.

In no place was Grant's artillery more than six hundred yards from the Rebels. It was necessary to cover Grant's men with more than a parapet. Sand bags, bullet proof, were placed along the tops of the parapets far enough apart to make loop holes for the rifles. On top of those, logs were placed. The men were able to walk about erect when off duty, without fear of being taken out by the Rebel sharpshooters. The Confederates used explosive musket balls, hoping that the rounds would burst above the heads of Grant's troops. No one was injured by the explosive musket balls.

Grant had no mortars, but he improvised by taking logs of the toughest wood, boring them out for six or twelve-pound shells and binding them with strong iron bands. These answered as coehorn mortars, and shells were successfully thrown from them into the Confederate trenches.

By June 30th two hundred and twenty guns were in position, mostly light field pieces, besides a battery of heavy guns from the navy.

On June 22nd Grant received information that Johnston had crossed the Big

Black River for the purpose of attacking Grant's rear, to raise the siege and to release Pemberton. Grant ordered Sherman to command forces from Haines Bluff to the Big Black River. This force amounted to half the troops around Vicksburg. Besides these, Herron and A. J. Smith's divisions were ordered to hold themselves in readiness to reinforce Sherman. Haines Bluff had been strongly fortified on the land side, and on all commanding points from there to the Big Black. At the railroad crossing, batteries had been constructed.

At three points on the Jackson road, in front of Leggett's brigade, a sap was run up to the Rebels parapet, and by June 25th Grant had it undermined and the mine charged. The Confederates had countermined, but did not succeed in reaching Grant's mine. At that particular point, the hill on which the Rebel work stands rises abruptly. Grant's sap ran close up to the outside of the Confederate parapet. This parapet was Grant's protection.

Grant's mine had been started some distance back down the hill, and was many feet below the parapet. The Confederates couldn't find and destroy it. On June 25th at 3 o'clock the mine was exploded. A heavy artillery fire all along the line had been ordered to open with the explosion. The effect was to blow the top of the hill off and make a crater. The breach was not sufficient to let Grant's men pass a column of attack through it. The Confederates had thrown a line farther back, where most of the men guarding that point were placed. A few men were left at the advance line, and others working in the countermine, which was still being pushed to find Grant's mine. All that were there were thrown into the air.

As soon as the explosion took place, the crater was seized by two of Grant's regiments who were nearby, under cover, where they had been placed for the event. The Confederates tried to expel them, but failed, and soon retired behind the new line. From there they threw hand grenades. The Rebels could roll down hand grenades upon Grant's assaulting force, while from the Union side they had to be thrown over the parapet, which was at considerable height. During the night Grant's men made efforts to secure their position in the crater against the Rebel missiles, so as to run trenches along the outer base of their parapet, right and left; but the Confederates continued throwing their grenades, and brought boxes of shells, the fuses of which they would light with port fires and throw them by hand into the Union lines. The Union soldiers found it impossible to continue this work. Another mine was started which exploded on July 1st, destroying an entire Rebel redan, killing and wounding a large number of Rebels and leaving an immense crater. No attempt was made to charge the crater.

From that time forward the work of mining and pushing the Union position nearer to the Confederates was done with vigor, and Grant determined to explode no more mines until they were ready to explode a number at different points and assault immediately after. The Union soldiers were at three different points, one in front of each corps, to where only the parapet of the Confederates divided them.

At that time an intercepted dispatch from Johnston to Pemberton informed Grant that Johnston intended to make a determined attack upon his lines to relieve the garrison at Vicksburg. On June 21st, Grant was told that Pemberton was planning to escape, by crossing the Louisiana side under cover of night. Pemberton ordered boats to be constructed.

Grant set about to make sure that the Confederates would not escape. Pickets were doubled; Porter was notified, so that the river might be more closely watched; material was collected on the west bank of the river to be set on fire and light up the river if the attempt was made; and batteries were placed along the levee crossing the peninsula on the Louisiana side.

By July 1st Grant's approaches had reached the Confederate's ditch at a number of places. At ten points the Union soldiers could move under cover to within five to one hundred yards of the Rebels. Orders were given to make ready for an assault on July 6th. The debouches were ordered widened to afford easy egress, while the approaches were also to be widened to admit troops to pass through four abreast. Plank, and bags filled with cotton packed tightly, were ordered prepared, to enable the troops to cross the ditches.

On July 1st, Johnston was between Brownville and the Big Black and wrote Pemberton from there that about the 7th an attempt would be made to create a diversion to enable him to cut his way out.

On July 1st, Pemberton, seeing no hope of relief, asked his generals whether they should retreat or surrender. Two of his generals suggested surrender, and two others practically did the same. Pemberton wrote Johnston asking if he should discuss peace terms and the release of the garrison. Johnston forbade it.

On July 3rd at 10 A.M. white flags appeared on a portion of the Rebel works. Hostilities ceased along that part of the line. General Bowen and Colonel Montgomery were seen coming toward the Union lines bearing a white flag. A letter was addressed to Grant. Bowen was taken to A. J. Smith. The letter was to discuss capitulation terms of Vicksburg. Grant would met Pemberton in front of McPherson's corps at 3 P.M. Grant also wrote Pemberton a letter saying that he would only discuss the complete unconditional surrender of the city and garrison.

At 3 P.M. Pemberton appeared in front of McPherson's corps. The meeting was on a hillside within a few hundred feet of the Rebel lines. Nearby stood a stunted oak tree. Grant knew Pemberton from the Mexican War, and greeted him as an old friend. He soon asked what terms Grant proposed to give his army if it surrendered. Grant replied that he only wanted unconditional surrender. Pemberton then said snappishly "The conference might as well end" and turned abruptly as to leave. Grant said, "Very well." General Bowen was very anxious that the surrender should consummated. He proposed that he and one of Grant's generals should have a conference. Grant had no objection. Smith and Bowen had a conference, during which Pemberton and Grant, moving a short distance away toward the Confederate lines were in conversation. After a while Bowen suggested that the Confederate army should be allowed to march out with the honors of war, carrying their small arms and field artillery. The interview ended. Grant would send his final terms by 10 P.M.

When Grant returned to his headquarters, he sent for all his corps and division commanders at Vicksburg. He asked for their opinions and then wrote Pemberton his letter. He asked for the surrender of the city of Vicksburg with all its public stores. He would march one division as a guard, and take possession at 8 A.M. As soon as rolls could be made out, and paroles be signed by officers and men, Pemberton would be allowed to march out of the Union lines, the officers taking with them their side arms and clothing, and the field and staff and cavalry officers one horse each. The rank and file would be allowed their clothing. Thirty wagons would also be allowed to transport cooking utensils and rations. Grant changed his mind on the unconditional surrender because thirty thousand prisoners would have to be sent to Cairo, which would have burdened the army on the Mississippi.

Late at night Pemberton sent a reply agreeing to the surrender. The next morning the garrison of Vicksburg marched out of their works and formed a line in front, stacked arms and marched back in good order. Logan's division was the first to march in, and the flag of one of the regiments of his division was soon flying over the courthouse.

On July 4th, 1863, Pemberton surrendered to Grant. The Confederacy was spilt in two. Grant had control of the Mississippi River from the North all the way down to Gulf exposing the heart of the Confederacy. In the Eastern Theater, another blow to the Confederates was inflicted when Confederate General Robert E. Lee lost at Gettysburg with appalling losses; 51,000 men were lost at Gettysburg.

The capture of Vicksburg helped lighten the morale of the North. Hopes for the final success of the Union cause were inspired. The victory at Gettysburg, Pennsylvania, added to their hopes. At Vicksburg 31,600 prisoners were surrendered, together with 172 cannon, and 60,000 muskets and a large amount of ammunition. Up to that time Grant's men were equipped with flint lock muskets changed into percussion, or the Belgian musket imported early in the war and a few new improved arms. They were of many different caliber which made it an ordnance disaster. The Confederates at Vicksburg were equipped with new arms which had run the blockade and were of the same caliber. After the surrender Grant ordered the inferior muskets in his command to be replaced with the stack of captured arms. With the close of Vicksburg, Grant's army was unsurpassed, in proportion to its numbers.

CHAPTER TEN

Tilghman's Legacy

After the death of Tilghman, disaster would strike the Tilghman family once again. On August 6, 1863, near Selma, Alabama, young Lieutenant Lloyd Tilghman, Jr. was thrown from his horse and killed instantly when his head came in contact with a bar of railroad iron. Like his father, he gave up his life for the cause they both held so dear.

Lloyd Tilghman was survived by his wife Augusta Murray Boyd, and his two sons, Frederick and Sidell.

Tilghman was buried in Vicksburg, Mississippi, close to where he was mortally wounded.

In 1878 President Jefferson Davis said of Tilghman:

Martyrdom has generally been considered, and with reason, a fruit of the sanctity of the cause in which the martyr died. You know how many examples your army furnished of men who piously served and piously died from wounds received in battle. The proofs of martyrdom if I were to attempt to enumerate, would exceed your time and my strength on this occasion. Yet I am not willing to pass by as silent memory some of those examples of heroism, of patriotism, of devotion to country which the Army of Tennessee furnished. The Greek who held the pass, the Roman who for a time held the bridge have been immortalized in rhyme and story. But neither of those more heroically, more patriotically, more singly served his country than did Tilghman at Fort Henry, when approached by a large army, an army which rendered the permanent defense of the fort impossible, with a handful of devoted followers went into the fort and continued the defense until his brigade could retire in safety to Fort Donelson; then when that work was finished, when it was impossible any longer to make a defense, when the wounded and dying lay all around him, he, with the surviving remnant of his little band, terminated the struggle and suffered in a manner thousands of you who have been prisoners of war know how to estimate. All peace and honor to his ashes, for he was among those, not the most unhappy, who went hence before our bitterest trials came upon us. [393]

After the Civil War, General Tilghman's widow brought their children to New York. In 1901, Tilghman was removed from his grave site in Mississippi and moved to Woodlawn Cemetery in New York City. The General's sons wanted their father to be buried next to their mother, who died in New York in 1898 and who was also buried in Woodlawn Cemetery.[394] After the war, Fred Tilghman became Vice President of the National Humane Alliance of New York. He helped raise funding for a monument to his father General Tilghman in Paducah. The Paducah Chapter United Daughters of the Confederacy paid $5,000 dollars and the sons of General Tilghman paid about $10,000 dollars for the statue. On May 16th, 1909 General Tilghman's monument was unveiled in Paducah, Kentucky. The monument was inscribed with "Brig. Gen. Lloyd Tilghman, C.S.A. Killed in the Battle of Champion's Hill, Miss. May 16, 1863." "To the faithful sons of the Confederate States of America who gave all to uphold the constitutional liberty and States rights."[395] The monument was made by H. H. Kitson, of New York and Boston. The monument is a life size statue of General Tilghman. The monument is six feet tall and stands on a mount. General Tilghman is in full uniform.

On May 19, 1926 Frederick and Sidell Tilghman donated to the Vicksburg National Battlefield Park another monument to their father. The monument shows Tilghman grasping the reins of his horse with one hand while the other clutches his sword. The sculptor was F. William Sievers.[396]

In 1921 the Tilghman family donated the funds to buy land for the Tilghman High School in Paducah. The school was actually named after Augusta Tilghman, but when it was rebuilt in the 1950's it became Paducah Tilghman High School in honor of the entire family. The school exists to this present day.[397]

In 1992 the *Tilghman Heritage Center and Civil War Interpretive Center* began with the acquisition of the Tilghman home in Paducah, Kentucky, with the sole purpose of restoring the building and creating a cultural asset to the community. From 1992 to 1996 Federal and State grants were pursued with no success. The building was condemned by the City of Paducah and in 1997 the board of Directors started Phase I with a private capital investment of $150,000 dollars to prevent it from being torn down. The Tilghman House has luckily been restored by the Tilghman Heritage Foundation. Phil and Rose Phillips, who run Dixie Leather Works in Paducah, and Howard Randle have made Phase I a reality. The home has been beautifully restored to its former beauty. The next phase of the project is to open a Tilghman House museum. The Tilghman home was built in 1852 and is a six thousand foot antebellum, Federal style house.

Tilghman's presentation sword was recently published for the first time in *The Civil War Battles of the Western Theater* by the author. There is also his line sword at the Civil War Battles of the Western Theater Museum in Bardstown, Kentucky. No letters have appeared to date that Tilghman may have written to his wife during the war. Hopefully one day these letters may appear to help explain the whole story of Tilghman's life, but the *Official Records of the War of the Rebellion*, and many other sources have helped the author to explain the amazingly brave war career, and public career of one of the most misunderstood and mysterious generals of the Civil War. Tilghman must be commended for his bravery, his unwavering sense of loyalty and duty to his country and to the Confederate cause he believed was right, but he must also be faulted for his leadership. At Fort Henry, Tilghman chose not to stay in command at Fort Donelson and decided to fight with the artillerists at Fort Henry. By fighting at Fort Henry with his artillerists, he had reduced himself to a subordinate officer. Tilghman exposed himself to the shots and shells of cannons. The South needed experienced officers. If Tilghman had been killed at Fort Henry, his loss would have cost the Confederacy an able bodied officer. By staying at Fort Henry, Tilghman opened a command structure gap at Fort Donelson. General Albert Sidney Johnston had to appoint some of the more incompetent generals to command Fort Donelson, which led to the eventual surrender of the fort. If Tilghman had stayed at Fort Donelson instead of Fort Henry, there would have been no vacuum in the command structure at Fort Donelson. Events might have developed differently if Tilghman had stayed in control at Fort Donelson. Tilghman knew his men and the terrain at Fort Donelson better than Generals Buckner, Pillow, and Floyd.

At the Battle of Champion's Hill, Tilghman should have continued to order his command as a general should, but by dismounting his horse and manning a cannon, Tilghman again exposed his life, when the South desperately needed to keep every officer they had. By manning a cannon, Tilghman reduced himself to common soldier, not a general officer.

But one should not fault Tilghman too critically for his actions at Fort Henry and Fort Donelson. Tilghman was a courageous and brave man. Tilghman was a product of his age. He truly believed that courage, bravery, and the unerring devotion to the Southern cause were the most important traits for a Southern commander. The notions of Southern honor and courage guided Tilghman's actions. When Tilghman died in battle, he fulfilled the Southern notion of bravery and courage.

APPENDICES

Resources

The War of the Rebellion: A Compilation of the Official Records of the Union and Confederate Armies, 128 Vols., Washington, D. C.: Government Printing Office, 1880-1901.

Beach, Damian, *Civil War Battles, Skirmishes, and Events in Kentucky*, Louisville, Kentucky: Different Drummer Books, 1995

Underwoord, Robert & Buel, Clarence, *Battles & Leaders of the Civil War*, Volumes 1-4, (digital version, H-Bar Enterprises, 1997.

William Davis, *The Orphan Brigade*: *The Kentucky Confederates Who Couldn't Go Home*, Baton Rouge & London: Louisiana University Press,1980.

Bush, Bryan, *The Civil War Battles of the Western Theater*, Paducah, Turner Publishing Co., 2000.

20th Century Biographical Dictionary of Notable Americans, (Gale Group, 1968)

Ambrose, Stephen, *Duty, Honor, Country: A History of West Point*, John Hopkins Press, 1999.

Fleming, Thomas, *West Point: The Men and Times of the U.S. Military Academy*, William Morrow Publishing, 1969.

Raab, James, *A Dual Biography: Lloyd Tilghman and Francis Asbury Shoup: Two Forgotten Confederate Generals*, Murfreesboro: Southern Heritage Press, 2001.

Smith, Jean, *Grant*, New York, Simon & Schuster, 2001.

Phillips, David, *Civil War Chronicles: Crucial Land Battles*, New York, Michael Friedman Publishing Group, Inc., 1996.

Foote, Shelby, *The Civil War: A Narrative*, Richmond, Virginia, Time Life Books, Inc., 1963, reprint 1999.

Faust, Patricia, ed., *The Historical Times Illustrated Encyclopedia of the Civil War*, New York: Harper & Row, 1986.

Moore, Frank, ed., *Record of the Rebellion: A Diary of American Events, with Documents, Narratives, Illustrative Incidents, Poetry, Etc.*, New York: G. P. Putnam Publisher, 1862-1868.

Grant, Ulysses S., *Memoirs and Selected Letters: Personal Memoirs of U. S. Grant: Selected Letters 1839-1865*, New York: The Library of America, 1990.

Connelley, William Elsey & Coulter, E.M., *History of Kentucky*, Five Volumes, Volume II, Chicago & New York, The American Historical Society, 1922.

Evans, Clement, *Confederate Military History Extended Edition: A Library of Confederate States History Written by Distinguished Men of the South*, Wilmington, NC: Broadfoot Publishing Company, 1988.

Edwin Bearss, *The Vicksburg Campaign-Volume I and II*, Ohio: Morningside House Publishing, 1985.

Korn, Jerry, *War on the Mississippi: Grant's Vicksburg Campaign*, Alexandria, Virginia: Time Life Books, 1985.

Chidsey, Barr, Donald, *The War with Mexico*, New York: Crown Publishing Inc., 1968.

Nevin, David, *War with Mexico*, Alexandria, Virginia: Time Life Books, Inc. 1978.

Weems, John Edwards, *To Conquer a Peace: The War Between the U.S. and Mexico*, Garden City, New York: Doubleday and Co. Inc., 1974.

Losson, Christopher, Tennessee's Forgotten Warriors: Frank Cheatham and his Confederate Division, 1989, University of Tennessee Press, Knoxville.

Cooling, Benjamin Franklin, *Forts Henry and Donelson: The Key to the Confederate Heartland*, Knoxville: University of Tennessee Press, 1987.

Foster, Stephen, Civil War Cards, Atlas Editions

Page, Dave, *Ships Vs. Shore*, Rutledge Hill Press 1994.

Horn, Stanley, *Army of the Tennessee*, Indianapolis & New Yorkk: Bobbs-Merrill Co. Publishing, 1941.

Hughes, Nathaniel, Jr., *The Battle of Belmont: Grant Strikes South*, Chapel Hill & London: University of North Carolina Press, London, 1991.

Mathless, Paul, ed., Vicksburg, Voices of the Civil War, Richmond, Virginia: Time Life, Inc., 1997.

Woodworth, Steven, *Jefferson Davis and His Generals: The Failure of Confederate Command in the West*, Lawrence: University of Kansas, 1998.
Gott, Kendall

Magazines:
Southern Bivouac
Blue & Gray
Confederate Veteran
The Courier-Journal Louisville, Kentucky

Letters
The Tilghman Letters, The United States Military Academy, West Point, New York.

The Cyrus B. Love Letters, Mary Counts Burnett Library, Texas Christian University.

The Brown Water Navy

During the Battle of Fort Henry and Donelson, Island No. 10, Fort Pillow, Memphis and the Vicksburg Campaign, the Union naval gunboats played an important role. As early as August of 1861, the United States Congress allotted $1,500,000 for the construction of iron clad warships and authorized the creation of a board of naval officers to examine proposals and make recommendations for what type of iron clads to build. In September of 1861 the board recommended contracts for the building of three vessels. The first contract was for the building of the Galena and the Monitor and the New Ironsides, which was a lightly armored wooden vessel. The army had already contracted for seven ironclads for service on the Mississippi River and its tributaries. The seven new ironclads would be called "Pook's Turtles". Samuel M. Pook designed the seven ironclads and on August 7, 1861, James Eads was given the contract to build the vessels and have them ready for their crews in sixty-five days. Eads employed Thomas Merritt as engine designer. Within two weeks, more than four thousand people in seven states were employed in the construction of the boats, cutting trees for lumber, building twenty-one steam engines and thirty-five boiler, and rolling iron for the iron armor. Four were built at Carondelet, near St. Louis, Missouri, and three were built in Mound City, Illinois. The workers built the ironclads during the day and night to fulfill the contract and on October 12, 1861, the first of the gunboats, the St. Louis, was launched. By January 15, 1862, all seven were accepted by the War Department and would begin their careers on the Cumberland and Tennessee Rivers. [6]

The gunboats cost the army $100,000 each, and were called "city class", since the ships were named after cities located on the western rivers. Besides the St. Louis there was the Carondelet, Cincinnati, Louisville, Mound City, Cairo and Pittsburgh. Each round-nosed, flat bottomed vessel weighed 512 tons, was 175 feet long and 51.5 feet wide and drew only six feet of water. Plated with two and one half inch thick iron, the gunboats had flat sides, with front and rear casemates sloping at a 25 degree angle, and carried 13 heavy guns each, both rifled and smooth bore. Propelled by a stern paddle wheel that was completely covered by the rear casemate, the coal powered Pook Turtles proved to be underpowered and cumbersome, but they were deadly. [7]

The turtles were manned by sailors of the regular navy, volunteers, but were detailed with army personnel and contracted civilians. These seven gunboats became the backbone of the Union river fleet. [8]

But the city class ironclads were not the only type of iron clad ships floating on the Western Rivers. The Union Navy Department also converted four large vessels into casemated ironclads. The Benton was a converted snag, the Essex was a rebuilt center wheeled ferryboat. The Benton carried sixteen heavy guns, but the Essex carried six. The Lafayette and the Choctaw were side wheelers, which were converted into ironclads. The Lafayette would have a sloping casemate, the Choctaw would have a stationary turret with inclined sides and a curved top and held four guns. Just forward and aft of the wheels were two small casemates. On top of the forward casemate was two howitzers which were to sweep the decks if the Confederates boarded the ship during battle. The howitzers were located in the conical pilothouse. The pilothouse had two inches of iron plating. The Choctaw had two one inch layers of iron and a one inch layer of vulcanized India rubber cushions, and the Lafayette's sloping casemate was covered with one inch iron over inch India rubber. [9]

The navy quickly picked up from the army the need for ironclads and built the Chillicothe, Tuscumbia, and Indianola, which were built by Joseph Brown in Cincinnati. All three of these ironclads were failures.

The Union navy also included converted vessels which had a draft less than three feet into "tinclads". The ships were covered with iron plating that was less than an inch thick. The armor was thick enough to stop musket fire and light artillery fire, but was no match for heavy artillery fire from large caliber cannons. As stern wheel and side wheel steamers with shallow drafts, these converted gunboats could go anywhere on the western rivers. Sixty ironclads were built during the Civil War. The first "tinclad" was the USS Rattler. The "tinclads" were armed with eight howitzers and Parrott guns, in calibers ranging from twelve pounders to thirty pounders. The thirty-pound Parrot rifle from the USS Rattler was recently on display in Cincinnati for their special exhibit called "Liberty on the Border". "Tinclads" participated in the Vicksburg Campaign and the Red River Campaign. Some of the other "TinClads" that won fame during the Civil War were the Forest Rose, Juliet, Marmora, Romeo, and Signal. [0]

Monitors were also built for the Western river, and again James Eads was contracted to build three single turreted monitors. The three monitors were named the Osage, Neosho, and Ozark. They were propelled by stern wheels. Eads received a second contract to built four double turreted ironclads. The guns were mounted on a steam operated elevator which dropped them to a lower deck where they were loaded and then hoisted and run out through the ports opened by automatic steam operated shutters. These vessels carried four guns, two to each turret, and were the only ironclads to be built with triple screws and rudders. These ironclads used in the Mobile Bay area were the most serviceable of all the river monitors. [1]

Although warships played an important role in the Western River, steamboats must not be forgotten. Both the North and South used steamboats to transport men, supplies, animals, and ammunition. During the Battle of Colubus_Belmont, the seizure of Paducah, the landing at Bruinsburg during the Vicksburg Campaign, steamboats were used to transport soldiers. Steamboats were also used to transport Union soldiers at Pittsburg Landing. Western steamboats were built so they could pull alongside a riverbank almost anywhere and unload their men and cargo without wharves. Many of the steamboats came under the fire of the enemy, and many of these captains won respect from the navy and army. Most of the captains of these ships were not in the military and had no military experience. Most of the steamships were either chartered or contracted by the Union government for their services. Over six hundred and forty steamships were contracted or chartered by the Union army on the Western Rivers alone. [2]

Brigadier General John Cook

John Cook was born on June 12, 1825 in Belleville, Illinois. After college he was a merchant in St. Louis and Springfield. He served as the sheriff of Sacramento County, and later as State Quartermaster General.

John Cook was the grandson of Governor Ninian Edwards, who was Lincoln's brother_in_ law and the son of the man whom Cook county was named. On July 25, 1861 John Cook, who had settled in St. Clair, Illinois, enlisted in the Union army for three years. He was officially mustered in at Mound City, Illinois. He was the commander of the 7th Illinois Infantry. Soon after his enlistment into the Union army he was relieved command of the 7th Illinois and given command of the 4th Brigade and sent to command Fort Holt, Kentucky. The regiments under his command were the 7th Illinois, under Colonel John Cook, the 28th Illinois, under Colonel A. K. Johnson, the 2nd Illinois Cavalry (two companies), and the 1st Illinois Light Artillery, Battery D under Capt. E. McAllister.

Since Kentucky was a neutral state and the Emancipation Proclamation had not been passed, Cook had to assist with the Fugitive Slave Act, which basically said that if a slave ran away from the South and went to the North, he would have to be returned to his master. General Order No. 22 was issued, which stated commanding officers of regiments and detachments at Fort Holt Kentucky are required to search or cause to be searched the quarters of their respective command the fugitive slaves and have all such fugitives forthwith expelled the lines of the camp. General Order No. 17 was issued On November 23, 1861 which stated that An officer or soldier shall be allowed to arrest, secrete or harbor or in any way interfere with persons held to service (Negroes), property of citizens of slaveholding States." Fugitive Slaves were running away from their masters, and it was rumored that many of them were being harbored in the barracks at Fort Holt. Slave Masters were wanting to enter the fort to reclaim their slaves. Cook had no other choice but to allow the masters to reclaim their property.

These matters would be set aside for more pressing matters. The war was soon approaching the borders of Kentucky. On December 1, 1861, at 3:15 P.M. three Confederate gunboats were less than forty-four miles from Fort Holt. Fort Holt's batteries opened up on the three gunboats when they came into view. Fort Holt fired the first shots from its extreme right fortifications then the sixty-four pounder, named "Lady Grant", fired on the extreme left. The first shot came to within two hundred yards of the advance gunboat. The second gunboat returned fire, but the rounds were short. The sixty-four pounders under McAllister fired at the oncoming gunboats with great effect considering the guns were only equipped with thirty-two pounder shells. The shells overshot the gunboats several times because the angle was hard to establish with the shells. The shot from the gunboats always fell short of the fort.

After the gunboats had retreated, Cook sent out Captain Delano's cavalry, together with one company from the 28th Illinois, to reconnoiter the area for Confederates. The parties returned reporting that no Rebels were near or around the fort.

Cook had gotten his first taste of battle, and it would not be his last. On February 3, the 7th Illinois left Fort Holt, and boarded the steamer City of St. Louis, to join forces now assembling around Fort Henry, Tennessee. His men landed at Paducah, Kentucky. When Cook arrived in the city, he was given orders saying that he would command the Third Brigade, which consisted of the 7th Illinois, 7th Iowa, 12th Iowa, 13th Missouri, and the 15th Illinois , with Captain Richardson's battery of twenty pounder rifled guns of the 1st Missouri Light Artillery. On March 4, 1862, Cook, with his command, were transported by boat down the river until they arrived at Camp Halleck, which was four miles below Fort Henry. His brigade was placed under the command of General McClernand. On March 6, Cook left Camp Halleck by land for Fort Henry. A severe rainstorm the previous night, together with swollen streams made it very difficult for the men to cross the streams by foot. But the firing of gunboats were heard by the men, and they quickly tried to rush to the scene. Captain Richardson's artillery became bogged down in the mud, and the infantry had to be used to try and dislodge the guns. At 2:00 P.M. orders arrived from General Grant, saying that they should leave the artillery behind and advance the infantry. The troops reached the outer works of Fort Henry, but the Fort had already surrendered to the gunboats under Andrew Foote. Cook's men had to camp on the soggy ground with no blankets, or knapsacks. Captain Richardson's artillery was stuck in the mud and would not be able to reach Fort Henry. The men were exhausted, wet, and hungry from their long march.

On February 7, Cook's men were quartered in Fort Henry in tents and barracks, which were built by the Confederates.

On March 8, the baggage was brought up and Captain Richardson's artillery arrived the next day. On the same day, the 13th Missouri arrived from Smithland to join the brigade. On March 11, the 7th Iowa was transferred from the brigade and the 52nd Indiana added, and Major Cavende's entire battalion of First Missouri Light Artillery was temporarily assigned to the brigade.

On March 12, the brigade left Fort Henry and headed for Fort Donelson. They marched for twelve miles and arrived to within a mile and a half of Fort Donelson at 3:00 P.M. the brigade took a position on a high ridge one mile in length, and overlooking the Confederates works on their right.

On March 13, the brigade was moved up the Dover Road to a point within one half mile from Fort Donelson's outer work's. He deployed the 7th Illinois on the right and the 52nd Indiana on the left as skirmishers. The brigade moved steadily forward through the dense timber, cross-ing the deep ravine without resistance until the 7th Illinois found itself facing a battery, which immediately began to fire when the flag was seen. The cannon fire took its toll immediately, Captain N. E. Mendell, Company I, was killed instantly, and several others were wounded. The regiment fell back beyond the range of the Rebel guns and to support Captain Richardson's bat-tery, which was unlimbering and getting into position. With the four remaining regiments, Cook proceeded to the summit of a ridge overlooking the fort. When he arrived he saw the immense abatis covering the whole area for nearly 600 yards. The Confederates rifle pits and palisades were hidden from view. It was decided that he would not storm the fort and hold his position.

During the night, the men rested on their arms without fires and without blankets.

On Saturday February 15, it began to snow and it became severely cold. The four regiments were allowed to fall back to their original position to stay out of the range of the guns in order to cook their breakfasts and thaw out their frozen clothes. The 13th Missouri was sent to the right to support a battery which was left unprotected when Colonel McArthur's brigade, and the 52nd Indiana, Colonel Smith was ordered to the extreme left to repel any sally which the Confederates might make from that area of the battlefield. A gap in his breastworks, which left the 12th Iowa and 15th Illinois, with one battalion of Birge's Sharpshooters to engage the Confederates along a line a half mile ling. At 2:00 P.M., General Smith ordered the number of skirmishers from his command to engage the Confederates attention, while he and Colonel Lauman's brigade, and the 52nd Indiana, stormed the entrance to the gap in the breastworks.

General Smith stormed the earthworks and took them, pushing the Confederates back. Cook sent a message to Grant, asking him permission to move his brigade up to support Colonel Lauman, and if possible to take the Confederates batteries, which were raking his men with murderous fire of grape, canister, and shell. Cook was awaiting orders when it was learned theat the Union flag was waving over the main battery of the Confederates. Orders were given to cease fire. The skirmishers were withdrawn and fell back to rejoin their commands.

The Union flag was raised by the Rebels so that Cook's men might come into range of their guns. Cook abandoned his position, and proceeded over the abatis, under a heavy fire of grape and canister. The Confederate guns over shot their targets and shredded the flag of the 7th Illinois, which had been ordered by General Grant to join Cook. Two pieces of the Union artillery had been already placed in position within the entrenchments, and succeeded with the infantry in silencing the Confederate battery, giving Cook full position of the Confederates outer works on his right, and the Confederates had to take cover under his entrenchments. The 52nd Indiana was ordered back by General Smith and were instructed to hold the position obtained during the night and prepare for a combined assault the following morning, with the simple command from General Smith "Take it, Sir!"

On March 16, Cook was ordered to take two regiments to help Colonel Lauman. The 7th Illinois was to act as reserve since they were low on ammunition, having only nine rounds left per man. The Ammunition wagons soon arrived and the men began to fill their cartridge boxes. Great cheers were soon heard all around the woods. It was soon discovered that Fort Donelson had surrendered. Cook lost 121 men killed, wounded, or missing.

On March 21, 1862, Cook was appointed Brigadier General.

On September 30, 1864, Brigadier General John Cook was sent by the War Department to command the District of Illinois. He would be kept very busy trying to control the spies and conspirators that was roaming the streets of Illinois. One of the largest camps in Illinois was Camp Douglas, in Chicago. Many Confederates prisoners were sent there. Col. Sweet, who commanded Camp Douglas, became nervous and reported to John Cook about the suspicious characters who had arrived in the city. Some were escaped prisoners of war, others were from Canada. During the Chicago Convention, Confederate spies were plotting to release the prisoners of war at Camp Douglas. Colonel Marmaduke and Captain Thomas Henry Hines, of Confederate General John Hunt Morgan's command, along with others of Morgan's command were hiding in the city. Sweet only had eight hundred men to guard eight thousand to nine thousand prisoners. Sweet was going to arrest these Confederate officers and several leading men in the community who might have been behind the plot. Sweet surmised that arresting the prominent citizens would cause uprisings. He asked for troops from Brigadier General Cook.

Captain Thomas Henry Hines was known as the "Grey Fox". He originally started out under Morgan's command but in March of 1864, he was ordered by President Jefferson Davis to assist in starting uprisings in the Northwest territory. He was to work with the Copperhead organizations, such as the Sons of Liberty, the Knights of the Golden Circle, and the Order of the American Knights. In early June 1864, Hines planned an uprising in the Northwest which was timed with a raid by General Morgan in the Ohio_Kentucky area. Morgan started his raid on June 11, 1864. Morgan seized Cynthiana, Kentucky, and this was the signal for the Copperheads to rise up in Kentucky. Morgan waited for the message that the uprising had begun. No message ever arrived. The Copperheads were being arrested all over the state for treason. The Sons of Liberty had been infiltrated by a spy named Felix Stidger. Felix had turned all his information to Col. Carrington. Morgan was driven by Union Brig. General Burbridge into Virginia.

On August 25, 1864, Hines organized an uprising which was set for the National Democratic Convention that was being held in Chicago on August 29, 1864. His force was armed with pistols at Toronto. For his planned uprising, Hines was given the best of Morgan's command. He had one hundred men at his command. The Confederate soldiers were to sneak into Chicago in civilian dress. It would be hard to recognize the Confederate faces in the thousands of other faces that were attending the Convention. The Confederate officers were to be assisted by the Sons of Liberty and other guerillas, who came armed to the convention from Kentucky, Missouri, Indiana, and Illinois and were to be under the immediate command of Brig. General Charles Walsh, of the Sons of Liberty. The men were to revolt on the morning of the Convention. Colonel Sweet, who commanded Camp Douglas, heard from a detective that Hines was behind the Confederate plot. Colonel Vincent Marmaduke knew the detective. Marmaduke told the ex_Confederate, turned Union detective, the whole plot. The information was also turned over to General Cook. Sweet immediately issued arrest warrants. Three thousand Union troops arrived. Hines escaped Chicago and entered Indiana, then Ohio. The danger passed and the reenforcements around the garrison were sent elsewhere.

On November 1, another expedition was planned by Hines. The attempt was to burn New York, Buffalo, Chicago and other Northern cities, which would coincide with the uprising of the Copperheads during the convention of the Copperheads on Election Day. The plan for Chicago was for Hines and others to storm the small force of 796 guarding the 8,352 prisoners at Camp Douglas and release and arm the prisoners of war, cut the telegraph wires, burn the railroad depots, seize the banks and stores containing arms and ammunition, take possession of the city, and start a campaign for the release of other prisoners in the states of Illinois and Indiana. Godfrey Hyams was in Toronto and learned of the plot and gave all information and list of names of the raiders in New York, and Chicago, including the whereabouts of Hines to the Federals for the price of $70,000 in gold. Sweet learned through the arrests of members of the Sons of Liberty that the Sons of Liberty were going to interfere with the election and release the prisoners at Camp Douglas. Sweet wrote to John Cook, commander of the District of Illinois, and Col. William Hoffman, who was commissary General of prisoners, for instructions. Cook gave the permission for the arrests. On November 7, 106 bushwackers, guerillas, and rebel soldiers had been arrested. On November 11, forty-seven double barrel shot guns, thirty Allen breech loaders, and one Enfield rifle were seized at Walsh's barn, in Chicago. On November 13, Patrick Dooley, secretary of the Sons of Liberty in Chicago, was arrested and on him were papers showing the intentions and purposes of the organization. On November 14, many members of the Sons of Liberty were arrested. The plot was foiled.

The Confederates had spent one million dollars to get the Copperheads to rise up, but to no avail. The President was elected, and the prison in Chicago was not overthrown. There was over $422,000 dollars worth of damage in New York, but General Butler imposed martial law, and the uprising did not occur in New York. Hines managed to escape into Toronto, and remained there until the war was over.

On August 23, 1865, John Cook was breveted Major General for his war service and was mustered out the same day. After the war, John Cook entered politics and was an Indian agent. John Cook died on October 13, 1910 in Ransom, Michigan.

General John Cook's wine goblet and dice are pictured on page 159.

ENDNOTES

[1]The 20th Century Biographical Dictionary of Notable Americans, Vol. 10 (Gale Group, 1968)

[2]Ibid.

[3]Fleming, Thomas, *West Point: The Men and Times of the U.S. Military Academy* (William Morrow Publishing, 1969): Ambrose, Stephen, *Duty, Honor, Country-A History of West Point* (John Hopkins University Press, 1999).

[4]Ibid.

[5]Ibid.

[6]Ibid.

[7]Fleming, Thomas, *West Point: The Men and Times of the U.S. Military Academy*; (William Morrow Publishing, 1969); Stephen Ambrose, *Duty, Honor, Country-A History of West Point* (John Hopkins University Press, 1999)

[8]Ibid.

[9]Ibid.

[10]Ibid.

[11]Ibid.

[12]United States Military Academy Register of Graduates and Former Cadets

[13]Tilghman Papers, Manuscripts and Special Collections and Archives Division, United States Military Academy, West Point, New York.

[14]The 20th Century Biographical Dictionary of Notable Americans: Vol. 10

[15]Donald Barr Chidsey, *The War with Mexico*, (Crown Publishing Inc: N.Y. 1968);

David Nevin, *War with Mexico*, (Time Life Books, Inc.: New York, 1978); John Edwards Weems, *To Conquer a Peace: The War Between the U.S. and Mexico* (Doubleday and Co. Inc.: Garden City, New York, 1974).

[16]Ibid.

[17]Ibid.

[18]David Nevin, *The Mexican War*, Time Life Books; To Conquer a Peace: The War between the U.S. and Mexico; The War with Mexico

[19]Ibid.

[20]Ibid.

[21]Ibid.

[22]Ibid.

[23]David Nevin, *The Mexican War*, Time Life Books; *To Conquer a Peace*: *The War between the U.S. and Mexico*; *The War with Mexico*

[24]Ibid.

[25]Tilghman Papers, U.S. Military Academy, Special Collections and Manuscripts

[26-55]Ibid.

[56]Tilghman Papers, U.S. Military Academy, Special Collections and Archives

[57] Nevin, *The Mexican War*, Weems, To Conquer a Peace: The War between the U.S. and Mexico; Chidesy, *The War with Mexico*

[58]Tilghman Papers, U.S. Military Academy, Special Collections and Archives

[59]Nevin, *The Mexican War*, Weems, *To Conquer a Peace: The War between the U.S. and Mexico*; Chidesy, *The War with Mexico*

[60-77]Ibid.

[78]Tilghman Papers, U.S. Military Academy, Special Collections and Archives

[79]Nevin, *The Mexican War*, Weems, *To Conquer a Peace: The War between the U.S. and Mexico;* Chidesy, *The War with Mexico*

[80-94]Ibid.

[95]Tilghman Papers, U.S. Military Academy, Special Collections and Archives

[96]Nevin, *The Mexican War*, Weems, *To Conquer a Peace: The War between the U.S. and Mexico*; Chidesy, *The War with Mexico*; Tilghman Papers, U.S. Military Academy, Special Collections and Archives

[97]Nevin, *The Mexican War*, Weems, *To Conquer a Peace: The War between the U.S. and Mexico*; Chidsey, *The War with Mexico*

[98]Stephen Foster, Civil War Cards; *The Mexican War*, (Atlas Editions, 1997) ; Nevin, *The Mexican War*, Weems, *To Conquer a Peace: The War between the U.S. and Mexico*; Chidsey, *The War with Mexico*

[99]Tilghman Papers, U.S. Military Academy, Special Collections and Archives

[100]Ibid.

[101]William Davis, *The Orphan Brigade*: The Kentucky Confederates Who Couldn't Go Home (Baton Rouge & London: Louisiana University Press,1980), 7-9; Ellis Merton Coulter, *The Civil War and Readjustment in Kentucky*, (Chapel Hill: North Carolina Press, 1926), Chapter 1.

[102]Evans, Clement, *Confederate Military History Extended Edition: A Library of Confederate States History Written by Distinguished Men of the South*, (Wilmington, NC: Broadfoot Publishing Company, 1988), 17

[103]Coulter, *The Civil War and Readjustment in Kentucky*, Chapter 1.

[104]Ibid.

[105]Evans, *Confederate Military History Extended Edition*, 18

[106]Evans, *Confederate Military History*, 19

[107]Ibid.. 19

[108]*Military History of Kentucky*, 153; Coulter, *The Civil War and Readjustment in Kentucky*, Chapter 1

[109]Military History of Kentucky, 153

[110]Military History of Kentucky, 154-155

[111]Ibid. 155

[112]Ibid. 155-156

[113]Moore, Frank, ed., *Record of the Rebellion: A Diary of American Events, with Documents, Narratives, Illustrative Incidents, Poetry, Etc.*, (New York: G. P. Putnam Publisher, 1862-1868) Interview between Colonel Tilghman and Col. Prentisss, May 11, 1861.

[114-121]Ibid.

[122]Moore, *Rebellion Records*, 194-195, Doc. 139

[123]Coulter, *The Civil War and Readjustment in Kentucky*, Chapter III

[124]Ibid. Chapter III

[125]Coulter, *The Civil War and Readjustment in Kentucky*, Chapter III

[126]Coulter, *The Civil War and Readjustment in Kentucky*, Chapter III

[127]Coulter, *The Civil War and Readjustment in Kentucky*, Chapter III

[128]Confederate Military History, 22

[129]Military History of Kentucky, 157

[130]Moore, *Rebellion Record*, 1860-1861, 164

[131]Stanley Horn, *The Army of Tennessee*,

[132]Military History of Kentucky, 159

[133]*Confederate Military History*, 25-27

[134]*Confederate Military History*, 29-30.

[135]Ibid.

[136]Ibid, 29-30.

[137]Confederate Military History, 29-30

[138]Stanley Horn, *The Army of Tennessee*

[139]O.R. Chapter XII Operations in Kentucky and Tennessee: Advance of Confederates into Kentucky, Etc., 181-185

[140]Steven Woodworth, *No Band of Brothers: Problems of the Rebel High Command* (University of Missouri Press, Columbia and London, 1999), 14-17

[141]Ibid., 17

[142]Military History of Kentucky, 163

[143]Steven Woodworth, *Jefferson Davis and His Generals: The Failure of Confederate Command in the West*, (Lawrence: University of Kansas, 1990), 45

[144]O.R. I, Series IV-Sept. 6th, Occupation of Paducah by U.S. troops. Report No. 2 Brig. Gen. Grant U. S. Army, commanding District of Southeast Missouri, with instructions relative to occupation of town.

[145]Grant, Ulysses, *Memoirs of Union General Grant*, 1015

[146]O.R. Series I,

[147]O.R. Series I,

[148]O.R. Series I.

[149]Beach, Damian, *Civil War Battles, Skirmishes, and Events in Kentucky*, (Louisville, Kentucky:

Different Drummer Books, 1995)
[150] O.R. I-Series III-Correspondence May 10-Nov. 18, 1861.
[151] Confederate Military History, 36-38
[152] O.R. Series 1-Vol. IV Chapter XII
[153] O.R. Series I-Vol. IV Chapter XII
[154] O.R. Series I-Vol. IV
[155] Confederate Military History, 38
[156] Military History of Kentucky, 168-169
[157] Ibid. 169
[158] Stanley Horn, *The Army of Tennessee*,
[159] Stephen Foster, Civil War Cards, (Atlas Editions, 1997)
[160] O.R. Series I-Vol. IV Chapter XII
[161] Steven Woodworth, *Jefferson Davis and His Generals: The Failure of Confederate Command in the West*, (Lawrence: University of Kansas), 54
[162] Confederate Military History, p. 41
[163] Filson Club Manuscripts and Archives. Letter dated Oct. 16, 1861 from Col. Tilghman to Gen. A. J. Johnston. (Louisville, Kentucky).
[164] Benjamin Cooling, *The Battle of Forts Henry and Donelson: The Key to the Confederate Heartland*, (Knoxville: The University of Tennessee Press, 1987)
[165] Confederate Military History, 44
[166] O.R. Series I-Vol. IV Chapter XII
[167] O.R. Series I, Vol. Chapter XII.
[168] O.R. Series I-Vol. IV Chapter XII
[169] O.R. Series I-Vol. IV Chapter XII
[170] O.R. Series I-Vol. IV Chapter XII
[171] O.R. Series I-Vol. IV Chapter XII
[172] O.R. Series I-Vol. IV Chapter XII
[173] O.R. Series I-Vol. IV Chapter XII
[174] O.R. Series I-Vol. IV Chapter XII
[175] Military History of Kentucky, 170-171
[176] O.R. Series I-Vol. IV Chapter XII
[177] O.R. Series I-Vol. IV Chapter XII
[178] O.R. Series I-Vol. IV Chapter XII
[179] The Cyrus B. Love Letters, Mary Counts Burnett Library, Special Collections.
[180] O.R. Series I-Vol. IV Chapter XII
[181] Ibid.
[182] Bryan Bush, *The Civil War Battles of the Western Theater*, 17
[183] Ibid.
[184] Ibid.
[185] Bryan Bush, *The Civil War Battles of the Western Theater*, (Paducah: Turner Publishing, Inc., 1999), 18.
[186] Bryan Bush, *The Civil War Battles of the Western Theater*. 18
[187] Confederate Military History,. 52
[188] Cyrus Love Letters, Mary Counts Burnett Library, Special Collections
[189] O.R. Series I-Vol. IV Chapter XII
[190] O.R. Series I-Vol. IV Chapter XII
[191] O.R. Series I-Vol. IV Chapter XII
[192] O.R. Series I-Vol. IV Chapter XII
[193] O.R. Series I-Vol. IV Chapter XII
[194] Confederate Military History, p. 53
[195] Stanley Horn, *The Army of Tennessee*,
[196] O.R. Series I-Vol. IV Chapter XII
[197] O.R. Series I-Vol. XII
[198] O.R. Series I-Vol. XII Correspondence, Orders and Returns relating to Operations in Ky, Tenn., Northern Ala., and Southwest Va., from Nov. 19, 1861 to March 4, 1862. Conf. Correspondence, Etc., 1
[199] O.R. Series I-Vol. XII Corr., Orders, and Returns relating to operations in Ky, Tenn., Northern Ala., and Southwest Va., from Nov. 19, 1861 to March 4, 1862 Conf. Corr., #1
[200] Ibid.
[201] O.R. Series I-Vol. XII Corr., Orders, and Returns relating to operations in Ky, Tenn., Northern Ala., and Southwest Va., from Nov. 19, 1861 to March 4, 1862 Conf. Corr., #3

[202]Ibid.

[203]O.R. Series I Vol. 7 Jan. 15-25, 1862. Reconnaissance from Paducah to Fort Henry. No. 2 Reports of Brig. Gen. Lloyd Tilghman, C.S. Army.

[204]Ibid.

[205]Bryan Bush, *Civil War Battles of the Western Theater*, 20.: Blue & Gray Magazine, *The Battle of Mill Springs.*

[206]Ibid.

[207]Ibid.

[208]Bryan Bush, *Civil War Battles of the Western Theater*, 41; Blue & Gray Magazine: *The Battle of Mill Springs.*

[209]Ibid.

[210]Ibid.

[211]Bryan Bush, *Civil War Battle of the Western Theater,* 41: Blue & Gray Magazine: The Battle of Mill Springs.

[212]O.R. I-Vol. 7 Feb. 6, 1862-Capture of Fort Henry. No. 8 Reports of Brig. Gen. Lloyd Tilghman, C. S. , Commanding Ft. Henry

[213]O.R. Series I Vol. 7 Conf. Correspondence. Letter from A. S. Johnston to General S. Cooper, Jan. 22, 1862.

[214]O.R. Series I Vol. 7 Jan. 15-25 Reconnaissance from Paducah to Ft. Henry. Report No. 2 Reports of Brig. Gen. Lloyd Tilghman.

[215]O.R. I-Vol. 7 Capture of Fort Henry. No. 6 Report of J. H. Gilmer, Lt. Co. Of Engineers, and Chief Engineer Western Department.

[216]Ulysses S. Grant, *Memoirs and Selected Letters*, 190-191

[217]O.R. I-Vol. 7 Feb. 6, 1862 Capture of Fort Henry. No. 8 Reports of Brig. Gen. Tilghman, C. S. Commanding Ft. Henry

[218]O.R. I-Vol. 7 Feb. 6, 1862 Capture of Fort Henry. No. 8 Reports of Brig. Gen. Tilghman, C. S. Commanding Ft. Henry.

[219]Ibid.

[220]Ibid.

[221]Ibid.

[222]O.R. Series I-Vol. 7 Feb. 6, 1862. Capture of Fort Henry. No. 8 Reports of Brig. Gen. Tilghman, C. S., Commanding Ft. Henry.

[223]*Battles and Leaders of the Civil War*, Recollections of Captain Walke; O.R. I-7 Feb. 6, 1862 Capture of Fort Henry. No. 8 Reports of Brig. Gen. Lloyd Tilghman, C. S. Commanding Ft. Henry; I-7 No. 2 Flag Officer A. H. Foote, U.S. Navy, commanding naval force on Western rivers.

[224]Ibid.

[225]O.R. I-7 Feb. 6, 1862 Capture of Fort Henry. No. 8 Reports of Brig. Gen. Lloyd Tilghman, C. S. Commanding Ft. Henry; No. 2 Report of Flag Officer A. H. Foote, U.S. Navy, commanding naval force on Western rivers.

[226]*Battles and Leaders of the Civil War*, Recollections of Captain Walke; O.R. I-7 Feb. 6, 1862 Capture of Fort Henry. No. 8 Reports of Brig. Gen. Lloyd Tilghman, C. S. Commanding Ft. Henry; I-7 No. 2 Flag Officer A. H. Foote, U.S. Navy, commanding naval force on Western rivers.

[227]*Battles and Leaders of the Civil War*, Recollections of Captain Walke; O.R. I-7 Feb. 6, 1862 Capture of Fort Henry. No. 8 Reports of Brig. Gen. Lloyd Tilghman, C. S. Commanding Ft. Henry; I-7 No. 2 Flag Officer A. H. Foote, U.S. Navy, commanding naval force on Western rivers.

[228]*Battles and Leaders of the Civil War*, Recollections of Captain Walke.

[229]Ibid.

[230]Ibid.

[231]Ibid.

[232]Ibid.

[233]O.R. I-7 Feb. 6, 1862. Capture of Fort Henry No. 8 Report of Brig. Gen. Tilghman, C. S., Commanding Ft. Henry; No. 2 Report of Flag Officer A. H. Foote, U.S. Navy, commanding naval force on the Western Rivers.

[234]O.R. I-7 Feb. 6, 1862. Capture of Fort Henry No. 8 Report of Brig. Gen. Tilghman, C. S., Commanding Ft. Henry; No. 2 Report of Flag Officer A. H. Foote, U.S. Navy, commanding naval force on the Western Rivers.

[235]O.R. I-7 Feb. 6, 1862. Capture of Fort Henry No. 8 Report of Brig. Gen. Tilghman, C. S., Commanding Ft. Henry; No. 2 Report of Flag Officer A. H. Foote, U.S. Navy, commanding naval force on the Western Rivers.

[236]O.R. I-7 Feb. 6, 1862 Capture of Fort Henry No. 10 Report of Col. A. Heiman, 10th Tenn. Inf..

[237]O.R. I-7 Feb. 6, 1862 Capture of Ft. Henry No. 7 Report of Maj. Gen. Polk, commanding at Columbus, Ky.

214

[238]O.R. I-7 Feb. 6, 1862 Capture of Ft. Henry. No. 5 Report of Gen. A. S. Johnston, commanding Western Department.
[239]Ibid.
[240]O.R. LII/2 Conf. Correspondence, Orders, & Returns. Operations in Southwest Va., Ky., Tenn., Miss., Ala., West Fla., & N. Ga. #11
[241]O.R. Series II, Vol. III
[242]O.R. Series II, Vol. III
[243]Stephen Foster, Civil War Cards, *Fort Warren*; Faust, Patricia, *Historical Times Illustrated Encyclopedia of the Civil War* .
[244]O.R. Series II, Vol. III
[245]Ibid.
[246]Rebellion Records
[247]O.R. II, Vol. III
[248]Rebellion Records
[249]Rebellion Records
[250]O.R. Series II, Vol. III
[251]O.R. Series II, Vol. III
[252]Bryan Bush, *The Civil War Battles of the Western Theater*, 29.
[253]Bryan Bush, *The Civil War Battles of the Western Theater*, 29-30.
[254]Ibid.
[255]Bryan Bush, *The Civil War Battles of the Western Theater*, 30.
[256]Ibid.
[257]Ibid.
[258]Ibid.
[259]Bryan Bush, *The Civil War Battles of the Western Theater*, 30.
[260]*Battles & Leaders of the Civil War*; Faust, Patricia, *Historical Times Illustrated Encyclopedia of the Civil War*, 386
[261]Ibid.
[262]O.R.
[263]Patricia Faust, *Historical Times Illustrated Encyclopedia of the Civil War*,. 587; O.R. Series I, Vol. X, Naval Engagement at Plum Point, near Fort Pillow, Tenn.
[264]Ibid.
[265]Ibid.
[266]O.R. Series I, Vol. X, Naval Engagement at Plum Point, near Fort Pillow, Tenn.
[267]Ibid.
[268]Ibid.
[269]O.R. Series II, Vol. IV.
[270] O.R. Series II, Vol IV
[271]O.R. Series I, Vol. XV
[272]O.R. Series I, Vol. XV
[273]O.R. Series I, Vol. IV
[274]O.R. Series I, Vol. IV
[275]Patricia Faust, *Historical Times Illustrated Encyclopedia of the Civil War*, 387.
[276]Ibid., p. 387
[277]O.R. Series I, Vol. IV
[278]O.R. XVII
[279]Bryan Bush, *The Civil War Battles of the Western Theater*, 32
[280]Ibid. 33
[281]Ibid. 33
[282]Ibid. 33
[283]Ibid.. 33
[284]Ibid. P. 33
[285]O.R. Series I, Vol. XVII
[286]Grant: Memoirs and Selected Letters, P. P. 283
[287]Edwin Bearss, *The Vicksburg Campaign*, Vol. I, Bearss, 1985; *Grant: Memoirs and Selected Letters*, 283
[288]The Vicksburg Campaign, Vol. I, Bearss, 1985.
[289]O.R. Series I, vol. 24
[290]O.R. Series I, vol. 24
[291]O.R. Series I, vol. 24
[292]O.R. Series I, vol. 24

[293]O.R. Series I, Vol. XVII/2 General Order No. 33

[294]Edwin Bearss, *The Vicksburg Campaign*, Vol. I

[295]O.R. I, Vol. XVII/1 Oct. 31, 1862-Jan 10, 1863. Report No. 8 Reports of Col. Theophilus Lyle Dickey, 4th Illinois cavalry

[296]Ibid.

[297]ibid.

[298]O.R. I, Vol. XVII/1 Oct. 31, 1862-Jan 10, 1863. Report No. 8 Reports of Col. Theophilus Lyle Dickey, 4th Illinois cavalry

[299] O.R, Vol. XVII/1 Report 11.Tilghman's Report, O.R. I, Vol. XVII/1 Oct. 31, 1862-Jan 10, 1863. Report No. 8 Reports of Col. Theophilus Lyle Dickey, 4th Illinois cavalry,;Vicksburg campaign, Edwin Bearss, 1985

[300]O.R, Vol. XVII/1 Report 11.Tilghman's Report, O.R. I, Vol. XVII/1 Oct. 31, 1862-Jan 10, 1863. Report No. 8 Reports of Col. Theophilus Lyle Dickey, 4th Illinois cavalry,;Edwin Bearss, The Vicksburg Campaign, 1985.

[301]Ibid.

[302]Grant: Memoirs and Selected Letters, 288

[303]Ibid. 288-289

[304]Ibid. 289

[305]Grant: Memoirs and Selected Letters, 289-290

[306]Ibid. 291

[307]Civil War Cards: the Battle of Chickasaw Bluffs; Patricia Faust, *Civil War Times Illustrated Encyclopedia of the Civil War*, O.R. I, vol. XVII Report No. 1 Report of Major General William T. Sherman.

[308]Ibid.

[309]Civil War Cards: the Battle of Chickasaw Bluffs, Civil War Times Illustrated Encyclopedia of the Civil War; O.R. I, vol. XVII Report No. 1 Report of Major General William T. Sherman.

[310]Ibid.

[311]Ibid.

[312]Civil War Cards: the Battle of Chickasaw Bluffs, Patricia Faust, *Civil War Times Illustrated Encyclopedia of the Civil War*, O.R. I, vol. XVII Report No. 1 Report of Major General William T. Sherman.

[313]Ibid.

[314]ibid.

[315]ibid.

[316]Civil War Cards: the Battle of Chickasaw Bluffs, Patricia Faust, *Civil War Times Illustrated Encyclopedia of the Civil War*, O.R. I, vol. XVII Report No. 1 Report of Major General William T. Sherman.

[317]Ibid.

[318]ibid.

[319]Civil War Cards: the Battle of Arkansas Post, Patricia Faust, *Civil War Times Illustrated Encyclopedia of the Civil War*, O.R. I, Vol. XVII Report No. 1 Report of Major General William T. Sherman.; O.R. I, Vol. XVII No. 4 Report of Brig. Gen. George Morgan, commanding 13th Army Corps.

[320]Civil War Cards: the Battle of Arkansas Post, Civil War Times Illustrated Encyclopedia of the Civil War; O.R. I, vol. XVII Report No. 1 Report of Major General William T. Sherman.; O.R. I, Vol. XVII No. 4 Report of Brig. Gen. George Morgan, commanding 13th Army Corps

[321]Ibid.

[322]ibid.

[323]Civil War Cards: the Battle of Arkansas Post, Patricia Faust, *Civil War Times Illustrated Encyclopedia of the Civil War*, O.R. I, Vol. XVII Report No. 1 Report of Major General William T. Sherman.; O.R. I, Vol. XVII No. 4 Report of Brig. Gen. George Morgan, commanding 13th Army Corps

[324]ibid

[325]Ibid

[326]ibid.

[327]O.R. I, Vol. XVII Report of Brig. Gen. Churchill

[328]Civil War Cards: The Battle of Arkansas Post, Patricia Faust, *Civil War Times Illustrated Encyclopedia of the Civil War*,

[329]Grant: Memoirs and Selected Letters, 295

[330]Grant: Memoirs and Selected Letters, 295

[331]Grant: Memoirs, Chapt. XXXI, 299

[332]Ibid. 299

[333]O.R. Series I, Vol. XXIV Report of Col. Albert L. Lee commanding cavalry.

[334]Ibid.

335Grant: Memoirs and Selected Letters, 300
336O.R. I, Vol. XXIV/1 Confederate Correspondence
337Grant: Memoirs and Selected Letters, p. 300
338O.R. I, Vol. XXIV/1 No. 9 Report of Major General W. W. Loring
339Ibid.
340O.R. I, Vol. XXIV/1 No. 9 Report of Major General W. W. Loring
341Ibid.
342Grant: Memoirs and Selected Letters, 302
343Grant: Memoirs and Selected Letters, 302
344Ibid. p. 306
345Ibid. 307
346O.R. I, Series XXIV/1 No. 24 Report of Brig. Gen. Lloyd Tilghman, C. S. Army
347Grant: Memoirs and Selected Letters, 315
348O.R. Series I, XXIV No. 24 Report of Brig. Gen. Lloyd Tilghman, C. S. Army
349Ibid.
350Grant: Memoirs and Selected Letters, 318
351O.R. Series I, XXIV/3
352Grant: Memoirs and Selected Letters, 321
353*War on the Mississippi*, 102-104; Grant Memoirs, 322.
354O. R. Series I, Vol. XXIV No. 24 Report of Brig. Gen. Lloyd Tilghman, C. S. Army
355O.R. Series I, Vol. XXIV No. 24 Report of Brig. Gen. Lloyd Tilghman, C. S. Army
356Grant's Memoirs, 327
357Grant's Memoirs, 328
358Edwin Bearss, The Vicksburg Campaign, Vol. I
359Grant's Memoirs, 329
360Grant's Memoirs, 330
361Ibid., 330
362Ibid. 331
363Grant's Memoirs, 331
364Ibid. 333
365Grant's Memoirs, 334
366Grant's Memoirs, 337
367Grant's Memoirs, 337
368Grant's Memoirs, p. 337
369Ibid. 338
370Ibid. 338-339
371Ibid. 339; *War on the Mississippi*, p. 116
372Ibid. 339-340
373Grant's Memoirs, p. 340
374Ibid. p. 340
375O.R. Series I, vol. XXIV, Report No. 7, Grant
376Grant's Memoirs, 341
377Ibid., 341
378Grant's Memoirs, p. 342
379Grant's Memoirs, p. 342
380O.R. Series I, Vol XXIV/2 S #37, Report No. 24, Battle of Champion's Hill, Col. A. E. Ryenolds, 26th Miss. Inf., Commanding First Brigade, First Division.
381**Skirmish line**: "A Civil War army on the march protected itself with lines of skirmishers, which were troops deployed in loose formation in advance and/or on the flanks of the main body. These troops drew the enemy's fire, developed his position, and warned the main body of infantry of an imminent clash- Patricia Faust, *Historical Times Illustrated Encyclopedia of the Civil War*, 691.
382War on the Mississippi, 121
383O.R. XXIV/2 S#37, No. 24 Report of Col. A E. Reynolds, 26th Miss. Inf., Commanding First Brigade.
384O.R. Series I, Vol. XXIV Report No. 8 Battle of Champion's Hill, Brig. Gen. S. G. Burbridge, commanding 1st Brigade, 10th Division, 13th A.C.
385O.R. Series I, Vol. XXIV/2, S #37 Report No. 24 Col. A. E. Reynolds, 26th Miss. Inf., commanding the First Brigade.
386Confederate Veteran P. 296 Scenes Where General Tilghman was killed.
387Ibid.

[388]Vicksburg, Voices of the Civil War, Time Life, p. 70
[389]Confederate Veteran, p. 274 Career and Fate of Gen. Lloyd Tilghman, p. 274
[390]O.R. Series I, Vol. XXIV/2 S#37, Report No. 23, Maj. Gen. W. W. Loring, Commanding.
[391]Ibid.
[392]O.R. Series I, Vol. XXIV/2, S #37 Report No. 24 Col. A. E. Reynolds, 26th Miss. Inf., commanding the First Brigade.
[393]Confederate Veteran
[394]The Courier-Journal-Kentucky-December 16, 1997 "Rebel General from Paducah rests in Yankee soil."
[395]Confederate Veteran
[396]4. Vicksburg National Military Park
[397]The Courier-Journal, B7, Dec. 16, 1997
[398]Bryan Bush, The Civil War Battles of The Western Theater, 189
[399]Ibid.
[400]Ibid.
[401]William Davis & Bell Wiley, The Civil War Times Illustrated Photographic History of the Civil War, Fort Sumter to Gettysburg, (New York: Black Dog & Leventhal Publishing, 1981 reprint, 1994), 501-503.
[402]Stephen Foster, Tinclads, (Atlas Editions, 1997).
[403]Stephen Foster, Steamboats, (Atlas Editions, 1997)
[404]Ibid.

INDEX

ABOUT THE AUTHOR

Bryan Bush was born in 1966 in Louisville, Kentucky and has been a native of that city ever since. He graduated with honors from Murray State University with a degree in history and psychology. Bryan has always had a passion for history, especially the Civil War. He has been a member of many different Civil War historical preservation societies, has consulted for movie companies and other authors, coordinated with other museums on displays of various museum articles and artifacts, has written for magazines, such as *Kentucky Civil War Magazine, North/South Trader*, and *Back Home in Kentucky*. He has worked for many different historical sites, and has always fought hard to maintain and preserve Civil War history in the Western Theater. In 1999, Bryan published his first work: *The Civil War Battles of the Western Theater* to much acclaim. *Kentucky Monthly* said Bryan Bush's *The Civil War Battles of the Western Theater* "has with his first book created a needed addition to any serious Civil War library." Since then, Mr. Bush has had published *Terry's Texas Rangers: The 8th Texas Cavalry, My Dearest Mollie: The Civil War Letters of Brig. Gen. Daniel F. Griffin, 38th Indiana Volunteer Infantry,* and was contributor to *Kentucky's Civil War Battles.* Bush has been a Civil War reenactor for twelve years, portraying an artillerist. For five years Bryan was on the Board of Directors and curator for the Old Bardstown Civil War Museum and Village: The Battles of the Western Theater Museum in Bardstown, Kentucky. For the last two years, Bryan has been co-chairman for the Battle of Corydon. On December 15, 2005, Mr. Bush completed his master's thesis at the University of Louisville.

OLD BARDSTOWN VILLAGE

Special thanks must be given to the Old Bardstown Village, Civil War Museum of the Western Theater, the War Memorial of Mid America Museum, and the Women's Role of the Civil War Museum. Many of the artifacts in *Confederate General Lloyd Tilghman and the Western Theater* are currently located in the Civil War Museum of the Western Theater.

War Memorial of Mid-America

Old Bardstown Village

The Civil War Museum of the Western Theater Museum is located in Bardstown, Kentucky. *North South* magazine voted the Civil War Museum of the Western Theater Museum the fourth finest Civil War Museum in the United States. The museum is also part of the General John Hunt Morgan Trail. The museum is dedicated to the War in the West. Some of the artifacts in the museum are original photographs, uniforms, cannons, rifles, handguns, flags, medical equipment, band instruments, drums, rare saddles, wagons, and some of the finest presentation swords. Collectively, the artifacts and display panels tells the story of the battles fought in the Western theater, such as the battle of Shiloh, Perryville, Stone's River, Vicksburg, Chickamauga, Chattanooga, Atlanta, and the March of the Sea campaign.

The War Memorial of Mid America museum features artifacts from the Revolutionary War though Desert Storm. The museum contains artifacts from General Hal Moore, Vietnam Hero and author of "We Were Soldiers Once." The museum also contains rare Civil War artifacts, such as items from Union General James Shackelford, Confederate General John Hunt Morgan, Confederate General Bushrod Johnston, and Union General George H. Thomas.

Both museums are open year round- Hours are 10:00 A.M. to 5:00 P.M. March 1 through December 15, January and February Saturday and Sunday only. The museum is located on 310 East Broadway, Bardstown, Kentucky. For more information or reservations: (502) 349-0291 or visit www.bardstown.com/~civilwar